A Translation of the Epistles of Clement of Rome, Polycarp and Ignatius, and of the First Apology of Justin Martyr

You are holding a reproduction of an original work that is in the public domain in the United States of America, and possibly other countries.You may freely copy and distribute this work as no entity (individual or corporate) has a copyright on the body of the work.This book may contain prior copyright references, and library stamps (as most of these works were scanned from library copies).These have been scanned and retained as part of the historical artifact.

This book may have occasional imperfections such as missing or blurred pages, poor pictures, errant marks, etc. that were either part of the original artifact, or were introduced by the scanning process. We believe this work is culturally important, and despite the imperfections, have elected to bring it back into print as part of our continuing commitment to the preservation of printed works worldwide. We appreciate your understanding of the imperfections in the preservation process, and hope you enjoy this valuable book.

A

TRANSLATION

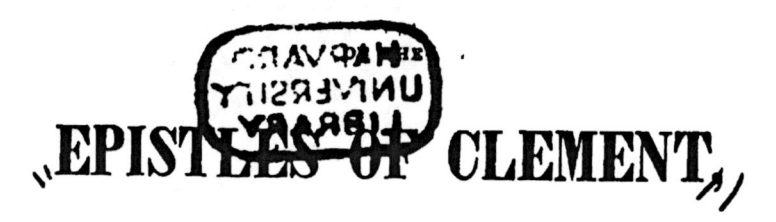

OF THE

EPISTLES OF CLEMENT,

OF ROME,

POLYCARP, AND IGNATIUS,

AND OF THE

FIRST APOLOGY OF JUSTIN MARTYR,

WITH

AN INTRODUCTION AND BRIEF NOTES ILLUSTRA-
TIVE OF THE ECCLESIASTICAL HISTORY
OF THE FIRST TWO CENTURIES.

BY THE REV. TEMPLE CHEVALLIER, B. D.,
Late Fellow and Tutor of Catharine Hall, Cambridge,
England.

EDITED

BY WM. R. WHITTINGHAM, D. D.,

[NOW BISHOP OF MARYLAND.]

NEW-YORK:
HENRY M. ONDERDONK & CO., 25 JOHN-ST.

1846.

C 568.67.19

ADVERTISEMENT.

On the publication of the THIRD Volume of the Standard Works, in the year 1831, it was distinctly stated, that the FOURTH would "not immediately succeed," on account of the "deliberation, care, and accuracy," which were required by the importance of its proposed contents. It was also stated, that "the FOURTH, FIFTH, AND SIXTH VOLUMES would go to press almost simultaneously," and might be expected "within four or five months." But the illness of the editor, (which led to a delay even of the FIRST Volume, and rendered it necessary that "the writings of the Apostolical Fathers," instead of forming the SECOND Volume, as originally proposed, should be made to constitute the FOURTH,) has continued to be the painful cause of retarding his exertions, and disappointing the fond hopes which he indulged.

He commenced an *original translation* of the Treatises which constitute this Fourth Volume; but his loss of health, and the perplexing variety of his employments, led him to discontinue it, and to adopt and reprint the following excellent translation, recently published in England by the Rev. Mr. Chevallier. Having seen the present volume just about to issue from the press, he was at last compelled, a few days since, to repair to the south of Europe; leaving, to be delegated to another, little more than to furnish a title page, and say a few words by way of advertisement.

It will be found, that the same care which has been bestowed on the other volumes of the series, has been

ADVERTISEMENT.

here employed in minutely examining all references, correcting some of them, and giving others more in detail.

In the APOLOGY OF JUSTIN MARTYR, sections 34 and 35, it will be discovered, that parts of a few notes in the English edition, containing statements of the opinions of certain sects of Gnostics, and not suited to the purposes of general readers, have been omitted.

Some of the quotations in the notes have been translated; only one original note has been added by the American editor; but, beside the great care which he has expended in securing accuracy, he has furnished an ample index to the work.

Any further explanations that may be thought requisite, will be given in due time, should the editor, by GOD's answer to the many fervent prayers offered for him, be restored to his wide field of usefulness, and resume his valuable labors in the cause of JESUS and the Church. J. F. S.

NEW-YORK, June, 1834.

CONTENTS.

INTRODUCTION.

GENERAL observations,	page ix
Epistle of Clement,	xiv
Polycarp,	xxv
Epistle of the Church of Smyrna,	xxvii
Epistle of Polycarp,	xxviii
Ignatius,	xxxiii
Epistle of Ignatius,	xxxviii
Justin Martyr,	xliii

THE EPISTLE OF CLEMENT TO THE CORINTHIANS.

§		
I. II.	CLEMENT commends the Corinthians for their order and piety before their schism began,	1
III.	The origin of their strife,	2
IV.–VI.	He shows, by numerous examples, that envy and strife have been the fruitful cause of many evils,	3, 4
VII. VIII.	He exhorts them to look up to the rule of their high calling, and displays the promises of mercy made to the penitent,	4, 5
IX.–XII.	He refers them to the instances of	
	Noah,	6
	Abraham,	ib.
	Lot,	7
	Rahab,	ib.
XIII.–XV.	And exhorts the Corinthians to follow these examples in humility, meekness, and godliness, according to the precepts of Scripture,	8, 9
XVI.	He refers to the example of JESUS CHRIST, who came in great humility,	10
XVII. XVIII.	And to Elijah, Elisha, Ezekiel, Job, Daniel and David,	11
XIX.	And thence exhorts them to orderly obedience,	12
XX.	He shows that order is the principle of the universe,	13
XXI.	He exhorts them to obedience, in compliance with the will of GOD; who is ever present,	14
XXII.	And enforces his advice by an appeal to the Scriptures,	ib.
XXIII.	The promises and threatenings of GOD will surely and speedily come to pass,	15
XXIV.–XXVI.	The resurrection is certain. It is illustrated by natural changes, as those of day and night: and by the example of the Phœnix,	15, 16
XXVII.	Hence GOD is faithful, and will perform his promises,	17
XXVIII.–XXX.	A further exhortation to obedience, purity, humility, and moderation,	17, 18
XXXI. XXXII.	The blessedness of those who have been obedient,	18, 19
XXXIII. XXXIV.	And an exhortation not to be weary in well-doing; and to live in concord,	19, 20
XXXV.	For this purpose GOD hath made to us many glorious promises,	20
XXXVI.	And given us our great High Priest, JESUS CHRIST,	21

CONTENTS.

§ XXXVII.–XXXIX.	The natural constitution of human society teaches us the necessity of different orders of men, page	22, 23
XL.	And GOD hath accordingly appointed every thing to be done decently and in order in the Church,	24
XLI.	Hence he exhorts them to the observance of order,	25
XLII.	The orders of ministers were established in the Church of CHRIST, by the Apostles, according to Divine command,	ib.
XLIII.	Even as the priesthood was especially appointed by GOD, under the Jewish law,	26
XLIV.	The Apostles foretold that contentions should arise respecting the ministry,	27
XLV.	He again refers them to the examples of obedience in the Scriptures,	28
XLVI.	And to the precepts therein contained,	ib.
XLVII.	Especially to the Epistle of St. Paul to them,	29
XLVIII.	The higher gifts a man may have, the more humble-minded he ought to be,	30
XLIX.	Christian charity is shown by obedience and Christian meekness,	ib.
L.	It is the gift of GOD, and must be sought for by prayer,	31
LI.	He exhorts those who had caused these divisions to repent,	32
LII.–LIV.	And again refers to the precepts and examples of Scripture,	32, 33
LV.	And to other examples among the Heathen,	34
LVI.	He recommends mutual prayer,	35
LVII.	And humiliation,	36
LVIII.–LX.	He concludes with a commendation of the Corinthians to GOD; and with a blessing upon them,	ib.

Note (A)	On the preaching of St. Paul in the West,	38
—	The probable duration of St. Paul's preaching after his first imprisonment,	39
—	Evidence to prove that St. Paul visited Spain,	ib.
—	Evidence in favor of his preaching in Britain,	40
Note (B)	On the Epistle of Clement, c. xvi. p. 16,	42
—	Passages in which Clement speaks of the Divine nature of CHRIST,	ib.
—	Extract from the Epistle to Diognetus,	43

THE EPISTLE OF POLYCARP TO THE PHILIPPIANS.

§ I.	POLYCARP congratulates the Philippians, on the reception which they gave the confessors of the faith of CHRIST,	46
II.	Exhorts them to perseverance from the consideration of the resurrection: and reminds them of the precepts of CHRIST,	47
III.	Polycarp assumes not the authority or wisdom of St. Paul, to whose Epistle to them he refers,	48
IV.–VI.	But exhorts them to the practice of various Christian duties, according to their several stations; as husbands, deacons, young men, and elders,	49, 50

CONTENTS.   iii

§ VII.	Whosoever confesses not that CHRIST is come in the flesh, is antichrist,	page 50
VIII. IX.	He exhorts them to patience by the imitation of CHRIST, and of the Apostles and others,	51
X.	And to be steadfast in the faith,	ib.
XI.	Polycarp expresses his regret for the misconduct of Valens and his wife,	52
XII.	Recommends the study of the Scriptures, and sends them his blessing,	ib.
XIII. XIV.	He refers to the Epistles of Ignatius, and desires to know if they have received any certain intelligence respecting him,	53

THE EPISTLE OF IGNATIUS TO THE EPHESIANS.

I.	IGNATIUS thanks the Ephesians for sending their Bishop Onesimus to meet him, as he was passing bound from Syria to Rome,	56
II.	He congratulates them on the possession of other faithful servants, and exhorts them to obedience,	ib.
III. IV.	He disclaims all personal superiority, but in charity recommends them to obey their Bishop and the Presbytery,	57
V. VI.	He expatiates upon the character of Onesimus, and the Episcopal authority generally,	58
VII.	He warns them of false teachers,	ib.
VIII.	Commends the integrity of their faith,	59
IX.	And their refusal to listen to error,	ib.
X. XI.	He exhorts to prayer and holiness, since the last times are at hand,	60, 61
XII.	And contrasts his own condition with theirs,	61
XIII.	He recommends their frequent assembling,	ib.
XIV.	And exhorts to faith and charity,	62
XV.	Unostentatious faith is better than unreal profession,	ib.
XVI. XVII.	He warns them against false doctrine,	62, 63
XVIII.	Expresses his willingness to die for the cross of CHRIST,	63
XIX.	The Prince of this world knew not the virginity of Mary, nor the birth of CHRIST, nor his death,	ib.
XX.	He purposes sending to them a second Epistle, declaring the faith more fully,	64
XXI.	Beseeches their prayers for the Church which is in Syria, and bids them farewell,	65

EPISTLE OF IGNATIUS TO THE MAGNESIANS.

I.	IGNATIUS salutes the Church at Magnesia,	66
II.	Whose Bishop, Damas, he had seen,	ib.
III. IV.	He exhorts them to reverence their Bishop, in obedience to the ordinance of GOD,	66, 67
V.	The difference of the faithful and the unfaithful,	67
VI. VII.	He exhorts them to be obedient to the Bishops, Presbyters, and Deacons, and to preserve the unity of the Church,	67, 68

CONTENTS.

§		
VIII.-X.	Warns them not to live according to the Jewish law; but after Christ, who is our life,	page 68, 69
XI.	Ignatius disclaims any personal authority,	70
XII.	Commends their faith,	ib.
XIII.	Exhorts them to be established in the doctrines of Christ and the Apostles, in all obedience,	ib.
XIV. XV.	And concludes with entreating their prayers, and with a salutation,	ib.

The Epistle of Ignatius to the Trallians.

I.	Ignatius commends the purity and godliness of the Trallians, of which he has been assured by their Bishop, Polybius,	72
II. III.	Their obedience to their Bishops, the Presbytery, and the Deacons, without whom there is no Church,	72, 73
IV. V.	He refrains from boasting, and from speaking of heavenly things,	73
VI.-VIII.	Exhorts them to avoid unsound doctrine; and to continue in the unity of the Church,	74, 75
IX.-XI.	To stop their ears if any spake to them against Jesus Christ, or declared that he existed and suffered in appearance only,	75
XII. XIII.	He salutes them in his own name and that of the faithful who are at Smyrna and Ephesus,	76

The Epistle of Ignatius to the Romans.

I.	After a salutation to the Church at Rome, he recommends them not to interfere to hinder his martyrdom,	77
II.-IV.	But to permit him to be offered up, as he was ready to be, for the sake of Christ; and to strengthen him with their prayers,	78
V.	He mentions the evil treatment which he endured from the soldiers, on his passage from Syria to Rome,	79
VI.	But expresses his full determination to die for Christ,	80
VII.	And declares that the love of Christ in him had conquered all his earthly desires,	ib.
VIII.	He again urges them not to prevent the accomplishment of his wishes,	81
IX.	Entreats their prayers for the Church of Syria,	ib.
X.	And mentions with honor those who were with him,	82

The Epistle of Ignatius to the Philadelphians.

I.	Ignatius recommends Church unity, praises their Bishop,	83
II.-IV.	And exhorts them to flee divisions and false doctrines, and to partake of one Eucharist,	83, 84
V.	He entreats their prayers,	84
VI.	Warns them against Judaizing teachers,	85
VII.	Reminds them of his previous exhortations to obedience to the Bishop, Presbytery, and Deacons,	ib.
VIII.	He warns them against those who preferred the writings of the Old Testament to the Gospel,	ib.

§ IX.	And shows the excellence of the Gospel above the law,	page 86
X.	He advises the Philadelphians to send a Deacon to congratulate the Church of Antioch, on the peace which they enjoyed,	ib.
XI.	And concludes with a salutation,	87

The Epistle of Ignatius to the Smyrneans.

I.	IGNATIUS praises their immoveable faith in CHRIST who *truly* lived and suffered for us,	88
II. III.	As He also *truly* raised himself from the dead, and appeared to Peter and to many,	88, 89
IV.	He warns them against heretics, and commands them to pray for them; although their conversion rests with CHRIST,	90
V.	Ignatius will not mention the names of those who hold erroneous opinions,	ib.
VI. VII.	But refers to their conduct, and refusal to partake of the Eucharist; and exhorts the Smyrneans to abstain from such men,	91, 92
VIII. IX.	And to follow their Bishop, Presbytery, and Deacons, according to GOD's ordinance,	92, 93
X.	He commends them for receiving Philo and Rheus,	93
XI.	Glories in that he is counted worthy to suffer; recommends them to send to congratulate the Syrian Church, for the peace which it enjoyed,	ib.
XII. XIII.	And concludes with a salutation,	94

The Epistle of Ignatius to Polycarp.

I.	HE exhorts Polycarp to persevere in the diligent discharge of his Episcopal office,	96
II.	To be wise as a serpent and harmless as a dove,	ib.
III.	To endure all things,	97
IV.	To care for all,	ib.
V.	He exhorts the married and single,	97, 98
VI.	And adds advice to the whole Church,	98
VII.	Recommends messengers to be sent to Antioch,	ib.
VIII.	Directs Polycarp to write to the Churches near him; and concludes with a salutation,	99

THE MARTYRDOM OF IGNATIUS,	101–106
THE CIRCULAR EPISTLE OF THE CHURCH OF SMYRNA, CONCERNING THE MARTYRDOM OF POLYCARP,	107–121

The Apology of Justin Martyr.

I.	JUSTIN addresses the Emperor Antoninus Pius, Marcus Aurelius, and Lucius Verus,	125
II.	And represents that their names and station required them to regard truth alone,	126
III.	He demands that the charges against the Christians should be examined: that the Christians should be	

CONTENTS.

	impartially treated, according as they deserved, and not be punished for a mere name,	page 127
§ IV.	Christianity ought not to be judged of, from the misconduct of some who only profess the name,	128
V.	Justin attributes the injustice of the Heathens toward the Christians, to the instigation of demons,	129
VI.	And declares that the Christians worshipped only GOD, the FATHER, SON, and HOLY SPIRIT,	ib.
VII.	He requires that the actions of all those accused should be examined,	131
VIII.	The Christians suffer only because they dare not deny the truth,	132
IX.	And will not pay honor to false gods and senseless idols,	133
X.	Knowing that GOD requires not material offerings, but purity and holiness of life; and will admit those who obey his will, to immortality and glory,	ib.
XI.	The kingdom which Christians expect, is not of this world,	134
XII.	Their religion is the best means of preserving peace,	135
XIII.	And enables them to defy their persecutors,	ib.
XIV.	JESUS CHRIST foretold their persecutions,	136
XV.	Justin proceeds to show what Christianity is,	ib.
XVI.	The worship of the Christians consists in prayer and praise to GOD, the Creator, to his Son, JESUS CHRIST, and to the HOLY SPIRIT,	ib.
XVII.	A most beneficial change had taken place in the lives of those who had become Christians,	137
XVIII.	Many precepts of CHRIST teach chastity,	138
XIX.	—the love of all men,	139
XX.	—the patient endurance of evil,	140
XXI.	—and that men should not swear,	ib.
XXII.	CHRIST declared that they who live not as he taught, are not Christians indeed,	141
XXIII.	And commanded his followers to pay tribute, and honor those in authority,	ib.
XXIV.	The superstitions of the Heathens themselves might make them believe that the soul survives death,	142
XXV.	The resurrection of the body is not so incredible as its first formation would be, to one who had no experience of it,	144
XXVI.	CHRIST taught that things impossible with man are possible with GOD,	145
XXVII.	The punishment of hell reserved for the unrighteous, is hinted at by some Heathens,	ib.
XXVIII.	It is, therefore, unreasonable that Christians alone should be hated, while poets and philosophers, who entertain less just and sublime notions, are honored,	146
XXIX.	Justin compares the opinions which the Heathen falsely maintained respecting Jupiter and others, with the more reasonable tenets of the Christians,	ib.
XXX.	And shows that their opinions respecting CHRIST might well obtain credence from those who held notions of a similar nature respecting their own deities,	147

CONTENTS. vii

§ XXXI. The truths of Christianity are more ancient than the fables of heathenism, - - - page 148
XXXII. Yet Christians alone are punished, while the most absurd idolatries are permitted, - - - 149
XXXIII. They have reformed their lives in embracing a purer faith, - - - ib.
XXXIV. Even after the ascension of CHRIST the evil spirits have instigated men to call themselves gods: as in the instance of SIMON MAGUS and Menander, - - 150
XXXV. The heresy of Marcion, - - - - 151
XXXVI. Justin refutes the calumnies brought against the Christians, of devouring children, and incest: and retorts the charges upon the Heathen, - - - 152
XXXVII. The purity and continence of the Christians, - - 154
— Lest the miracles of CHRIST should be ascribed to magic, Justin appeals to prophecy, - - 155
XXXVIII. And relates the history of the translation of the Hebrew Scriptures into Greek by the order of Ptolemy, - ib.
XXXIX. In those prophecies, the miraculous birth of JESUS, his being made man, his miracles, sufferings, death, resurrection and ascension, his Divine nature, and the extension of his religion over the whole world are expressly predicted, - - - - - 156
XL.–LII. This is shown by various quotations, - - - 156–165
LIII. Justin explains why the Holy prophetic Spirit speaks of future events as already past, - - - 166
LIV. Christians consider not that events happen by fatal necessity; which would be inconsistent with the free-will of man, - - - - - ib.
LV. But believe this only to be irreversibly determined, that they who choose the good shall be rewarded, and they who choose the evil shall be punished, - - 167
LVI. This is proved by quotations from Scripture, - ib.
LVII. And shown to agree with the opinion of Plato, - 168
LVIII. Prophecy, therefore, implies not a fatal necessity, but shows the foreknowledge of GOD, - - ib.
LIX. The evil spirits endeavored to prevent the knowledge of prophecy, but in vain, - - - ib.
LX. David predicted that GOD the Father should receive CHRIST into heaven, - - - - 169
LXI. Justin asserts that all men, in all ages, who lived agreeably to right reason, were Christians in spirit, - 170
LXII. Various prophecies, showing that Jerusalem should be destroyed, - - - - - 171
LXIII. That CHRIST should heal the sick and raise the dead, - - - - - - ib.
LXIV. That He should be made man, and suffer many things, and come again in glory, - - - 172
LXV. That He hath an origin which cannot be expressed, - 173
LXVI. The fulfilment of these prophecies is an earnest that those yet unaccomplished will be fulfilled, - - 174
LXVII. And, therefore, that CHRIST will come the second time to judgment, - - - - - 175

CONTENTS.

§ LXVIII. These prophecies had fully persuaded the Christians to believe CHRIST, who was crucified, to be the first-born of the unbegotten GOD, - - - - page 175

LXIX. The conversion of the Gentiles was foretold, - - 176

LXX. The evil demons, knowing the prophecies respecting CHRIST, invented fables of a similar nature, to deceive men, - - - - - - - 177

LXXI. As in the fables of Bacchus, Bellerophon, Perseus, and Hercules, - - - - - - ib.

LXXII. But in no fable was the crucifixion of CHRIST imitated, 178

LXXII. The figure of the Cross is almost universally employed. ib.

LXXIII. The demons also, after the ascension of CHRIST, raised up men, such as Simon and Menander, before mentioned, in § 34, - - - - - - - 179

LXXIV. The malice of these evil spirits can, however, only instigate the enemies of the Christians to destroy them, 180

LXXV. They raised up Marcion to deceive men, - - ib.

LXXVI. LXXVII. Plato obtained his notions respecting the creation of the world, and other opinions, from the writings of Moses, - - - - - - - 181

LXXVIII. It is not, then, that the Christians adopt the opinions of others, but others, theirs, - - - - 182

LXXIX. Justin explains the manner in which believers are baptized, - - - - - - - 183

LXXX. Shows that this new birth is necessary; and that baptism is performed in the name of GOD the Father, and of JESUS CHRIST, and of the HOLY SPIRIT, - 184

LXXXI. Justin then digresses to show that the evil spirits imitated the practice of baptism; as they caused the action of Moses, who put off his shoes at the burning bush, to be imitated, - - - - ib.

LXXXII. He declares that it was the Son of GOD, who appeared to Moses in the bush, - - - - 185

LXXXIII. And to the prophets in various forms, - - - 186

LXXXIV. And asserts that the demons imitated what they learned from the writings of Moses, in several instances, - 187

LXXXV. Justin then returns to describe the administration of the Eucharist to those who had been baptized, - ib.

LXXXVI. He explains the nature of that sacrament; that the elements are not common bread, nor common drink; and relates the manner of its institution, - - 189

LXXXVII. The Christians assemble on Sunday. An account of the manner of public worship in the primitive Church, 190

LXXXVIII. The collection of alms, - - - - - ib.

LXXXIX. The reason of assembling on Sunday, - - 191

XC. Justin concludes with desiring that the Christians may not be condemned unheard; but expresses their resignation to the will of GOD, and subjoins the Epistle of Adrian in their favor, - - - - ib.

— The Epistle of Antoninus Pius to the Common Assembly of Asia, - - - - 192

Note (C) On Ignatius's Epistle to the Magnesians, § viii. - 194

INTRODUCTION.

In the history of the Christian Church, there are few periods of greater interest and importance than that which succeeded the death of the Apostles. As long as any of those holy men survived, who had personally received instruction from our LORD, they connected the Church on earth with its spiritual head. The miraculous powers with which the Apostles were endowed, and the undisputed authority with which their high office invested them, placed them in a position, which none of their successors could ever occupy. In cases of difficulty and doubt, an appeal to their more than human wisdom was the last resource: in times of peril, their example and their prayers strengthened the wavering, and confirmed the faithful: and at all periods they were justly regarded as the pillars, on which the Christian Church securely rested.

But when the Apostles were removed from the scene of their earthly labors, the condition of the Church was changed. The efforts of its enemies were exerted with greater energy to suppress Christianity, as the numbers of those who professed the faith increased; while the apparent means of defence were materially impaired. Our attention is therefore roused to inquire what men they were, who, on this trying occasion, stood forth in defence of Christianity; with what weapons they combated their enemies; with what zeal they laid down their lives for the sake of the Gospel.

These early ages of the Church claim our attention for another reason. In contemplating the history of that period, we view Christianity, as a system of

Vol. IV.—b

ecclesiastical polity in its nascent state. It was then that the Canon of Scripture was formed; that church government took a consistent form. The oral teaching of the Apostles and their immediate successors was still vividly impressed upon the minds of those who had heard them: and many passages of Scripture, which to us appear ambiguous, might by such means be then clearly understood.

Hence the conclusions, which the primitive Christian Church formed, respecting questions, which in after ages have been fruitful subjects of controversy, are entitled to the highest regard: not, indeed, as infallible; but as representing the doctrines maintained by sincere and earnest inquirers after the truth, by men who were best able to form a sound determination, before their judgment was warped by prejudice or modified by system.

The writings of the early Christian Fathers will therefore be carefully consulted by all who would trace the Scriptures up to the period in which they were written, and learn the doctrines which were taught as essential, in the times nearest to the apostolic age.

These early ages of the Church possess also a charm peculiar to themselves. The records of ecclesiastical history in subsequent years too often display a melancholy picture. The turbulent passions of the worldly minded, the fiery zeal of the intemperate, the arts of the designing, the follies of the weak, all present themselves in dazzling colors and in prominent positions: while it requires a practised eye and a patient investigation to discover the milder and retiring forms of unobtrusive Christian piety. The earlier Christians were not, as individuals, free from the infirmities and sins of human nature. But the primitive Christian Church did certainly stand forth in a purity and simplicity which it has never since enjoyed. And the contemplation of the age in which this goodly spectacle was presented to the world, has ever been a delightful employment to minds endowed with a kindred feeling.

Of late years a considerable impulse has been given, among ourselves, to the study of the early Christian writers. The labors of the learned Bishop of Lincoln, [Dr. KAYE,] in elucidating the works of Justin Martyr and Tertullian, and those of Dr. BURTON, are specimens of the valuable matter which is yet to be extracted from the stores of Christian antiquity.

The present work lays claim to no such pretensions. Its object is to put the English reader in possession of some of the genuine remains of Christian writers of the first and second centuries, and to furnish occasional information upon such points as seem to require explanation. For this purpose it appeared more advisable to give the whole of such pieces as should be selected, than to select certain parts only. Extracts must always fail to give a faithful representation of the whole manner of reasoning and train of thought which characterized the first advocates of Christianity; and may unintentionally give erroneous notions of their opinions. It is well known that detached passages are quoted from these writings, in favor of very different notions. To judge therefore of the real sentiments of the writers, the general tendency of their argument is to be regarded, more than the mere verbal expression of particular parts. If we would know how these fathers of the Church thought and wrote, we are not at liberty to omit what may appear to us superfluous and fanciful in illustration, or diffuse and inconclusive in reasoning; or simply uninteresting, because it refers to errors which have long since passed away. The very manner of treating a subject is an indication of the habits of thought and of the moral condition of the age in which it was discussed. A more striking and graphic representation is often given of the state of society, and of the condition of the Christian world in general, by an application of a passage of Scripture, by a slight allusion to an objection against the religion of the Gospel, by a casual reference to some difficulty which its professors encountered, or by some elaborate refutation of an absurd calumny, than we should have received from a detailed description of the circumstances.

Besides, those very parts of the writings of the early Fathers, which seem least valuable both for style and matter, have this incidental advantage, that they set in a clear point of view the immeasurable superiority of the Scriptures of the New Testament. The inspired books were written principally by men who had not the same advantages of education and literary training, as some of the Ecclesiastical writers enjoyed: yet they are totally free from the blemishes which disfigure the most elaborate productions of later ages of the Church.

Had not the pens of the Evangelists and Apostles been guided by a wisdom superior to any which those writers possessed by ordinary means, they never could have produced a work, which, even as a specimen of plain yet majestic narration, and of consistent, sober, rational discussion of the most abstruse questions, is entirely unrivalled. We should have found—as we do find in the writings even of those who had been thoroughly instructed in scriptural truth, and had deeply imbibed the spirit of Christianity—some error mixed with truth; some inconclusive reasoning; some vague declamation; some incautious over-statement of doctrine or fact; some merely mystical application of the Scriptures of the Old Testament; some exaggerated sentiment.

In uninspired writers we should have detected the prejudices of their education and of the age in which they lived. We should have found some extravagant eulogies of martyrdom; some fanciful notions respecting spiritual beings; some captious and scrupulous objection to practices in themselves indifferent. And, in their public defences of the faith before their adversaries, we should have perceived them, not only speaking boldly, as they ought to speak, but sometimes displaying a subtilty too nearly allied to the craftiness of the disputer of this world; and on other occasions indulging in sarcasm or invective against the various errors of Heathen worship.

In the Scriptures of the New Testament, we find none of these faults: they are uniformly dignified, simple, reasonable. But a very limited acquaintance with the writings of those who endeavored to follow their steps will show that, if the Apostles and Evangelists were preserved from such extravagance and error, they owed it to a wisdom which was not of this world.

The works, which have been chosen for the present purpose, are the *Epistle of* CLEMENT OF ROME *to the Corinthians;* that of POLYCARP; the genuine *Epistles of* IGNATIUS, with the *Accounts of the Martyrdom of Ignatius and Polycarp:* the *first Apology of* JUSTIN MARTYR; and the *Apology* of TERTULLIAN.*

These Epistles, and the short histories of the Martyrdoms, have been long known to the English reader, in Archbishop WAKE's very valuable translation. It may appear presumptuous to have changed, in any degree, language which is at once so faithful and so scriptural as that which he has employed. And no

---

* [The two last named works are not included in the present edition; being reserved for a subsequent volume of the series.]

alteration has been made, except after due deliberation. In Archbishop WAKE's translation, however, the quotations from the Scriptures are given in the words of the authorized English version. Now the original quotations from the Old Testament are often taken from the Septuagint or some other version, so as to differ considerably from the Hebrew text, and consequently from the English version: and in other instances, references are made to the Old and New Testaments in such a manner as to express the general sense of passages, rather than the words. As the intention of this work is to give as accurate a representation of these writings of the Fathers as the difference of idiom will admit, it seemed advisable to translate these quotations also as faithfully as possible, even in the instances in which they deviate from the literal sense of the original Scriptures. It is not always easy to determine how closely a writer intended to quote a passage; and in many cases, such references may be regarded as a kind of comment upon the text to which allusion is made.

EPISTLE OF CLEMENT.

IT is a happy circumstance, that of the very few remains [a] of the writings of the first century, except the books of the New Testament, we should possess the truly Apostolical Epistle of CLEMENT OF ROME.

CLEMENT is believed, upon the general testimony of Ecclesiastical historians,[b] to have been the same whom St. Paul mentions among "his fellow-laborers, whose names are written in the book of life."[c] Of his early

---

[a] It is perhaps the *only* remaining writing of the first century. The *Epistle*, ascribed to BARNABAS, and the *Shepherd* of HERMAS, existed in the second century: but probably were written after the apostolic age.

[b] EUSEBIUS *Hist. Eccles.* iii. 12. [c] Phil. iv. 3.

years little is certainly known. It is believed, however, that he was born of a noble family at Rome, and sent to Athens for the purpose of education: that his conversion to Christianity arose from unsuccessful inquiries into which he had been led respecting the immortality of the soul; that he was instructed and baptized by St. Peter, and for some time continued to be his disciple.

That Clement was bishop of Rome is a fact which is not disputed: but the time of his accession to that see is variously computed. IRENÆUS [d] and EUSEBIUS mention Clement to have been the third in succession from the Apostles: and EUSEBIUS [e] expressly states the twelfth year of Domitian's reign, A. D. 92, as the year in which Clement succeeded Anencletus. TERTULLIAN[f] says that he was ordained bishop by St. Peter; whence it has been supposed that Linus was ordained bishop of the Gentile Church of Rome by St. Paul, and Clement, bishop of the Church of Jewish converts by St. Peter; that Linus was succeeded by Anencletus or Anacletus, and at his death, about A. D. 91, the two Churches were united, and the episcopacy of Clement over them both began. This is by many considered the most probable way of reconciling the difficulties which exist in determining the succession of the first bishops of Rome;[g] and was the opinion of CAVE, when he wrote the Life of Clement.[h] But at a subsequent period,[i] he adopted the conclusion of DODWELL,[k] that Linus and Anencletus lived as bishops of Rome but a very short time, and that

---

[d] IRENÆUS *adv. Hæres.* iii. 3.   EUSEB. *Hist. Eccles.* v. 6.

[e] EUSEBIUS *Hist. Eccles.* iii. 13–15. See LARDNER, *Credibility of the Gospels*, Part ii. c. 2.

[f] TERTULLIAN, *De Prescriptione Hæreticorum*, c. 32.

[g] See note (a) on his *Epistle*, Sect. 54. p. 33.

[h] CAVE's *Lives of the Fathers.*   [i] *Historia Literaria*, 65.

[k] DODWELL, *Disputatio Singularis de Romanorum Pontificum Successione.*

Clement succeeded them about A. D. 64 or 65, and continued to the year 81. Bishop PEARSON[1] concludes that Clement was bishop of Rome from A. D. 69 to 83.

The date of the Epistle of Clement to the Corinthians is involved in equal uncertainty. Archbishop WAKE[m] supposes it to have been written soon after the termination of the persecution under Nero, between the years 64 and 70. LARDNER[a] refers it to the year 96. There are but few internal marks of time in the Epistle itself, and none which can be regarded as decisive. It is plain that it was written at the close of some persecution; for, at the beginning of it, the Church of Rome refers to "the sudden and repeated dangers and calamities which had befallen them." Persecution however, for the sake of the Christian faith, was already so common, that it cannot be certainly said whether these words are an allusion to some local distress, or to a general persecution. But they might refer either to A. D. 64, at the end of the persecution under Nero, or to A. D. 94, after that under Domitian.

In favor of the earlier of these dates, Clement in Sect. 5. seems to speak of the Apostles, Peter and Paul, as having been recently put to death. The expressions in Sect. 41. respecting the Temple at Jerusalem, seem to countenance the opinion, that the Temple was still standing, and that the Jewish war, which began A.D. 67, had not yet broken out. The Fortunatus also, whose name is found in Sect. 59. is conceived to have come from Corinth, and to have been the same, who is mentioned by St. Paul[•] together with Stephanus, whose

---

[1] *Disputatio de Successione primâ Romanorum Pontificum.*
[m] See also DODWELL, *Addit. ad* PEARSON, *Dissert:* ii. c. 24. CAVE *Hist. Literar.* 65.
[a] *Credibility,* Part ii. c. 2.   [•] 1 Cor. xvi. 15–17.

DATE OF THE EPISTLE OF CLEMENT. xvii

house was the first fruits of Achaia. If this supposition be correct, it is a presumption in favor of the earlier date: since at the later date, Fortunatus, if alive, could hardly have been capable of undergoing so long a journey.

On the other hand, in Sect. 44. Clement seems to speak as if there had been a succession of intermediate persons in the Church, between himself and the Apostles.

The phrase "in the beginning of the Gospel," and the appellation of "ancient Church," applied to the Corinthians,[p] have also been adduced as favoring a later date.

The high value which the ancient Christian Church set upon this Epistle of Clement is ascertained by the commendations which they bestow upon it. IRENÆUS[q] describes this Epistle as having been written by the Church of Rome under Clement, to the Corinthians, and speaks of it as a most powerful Epistle. EUSEBIUS[r] denominates it "a great and admirable Epistle." Dionysius, bishop of Corinth, about the year 170 testifies to the fact that this Epistle was read in the Church of Corinth from ancient times:[s] and other writers[t] show that it was publicly read in other Christian Churches. Eusebius observes also that there is a great similarity in the style of this Epistle and that of the Epistle to the Hebrews: and that Clement on several occasions quotes that book of the New Testament.

Notwithstanding the great esteem in which the primitive Church held this Epistle of Clement, and the

---

[p] Sect. 47.   [q] *Adv. Hæres.* iii. 3. EUSEB. *Hist. Eccles.* v. 6.
[r] *Hist. Eccles.* iii. 16.   [s] EUSEBIUS *Hist. Eccles.* iv. 23.
[t] EUSEBIUS *Hist. Eccles.* iii. 16. JEROME *de Viris Illustribus,* c. 15. EPIPHANIUS *Hæres.* xxx. Num. 15. PHOTIUS, *Biblioth.* Cod. 123.

numerous quotations from it, scattered over the pages of ecclesiastical writers, the Epistle itself was for many centuries considered to be lost. At length it was discovered, at the end of a manuscript containing the Septuagint version of the Old Testament, and the New Testament. This manuscript had been presented to King Charles the First, by Cyril, Patriarch of Alexandria, and afterward of Constantinople. The valuable treasure was discovered by Mr. YOUNG, the keeper of the Royal Library: and was first published at Oxford, in 1633. The original manuscript is now in the British Museum.

The Epistle thus happily and unexpectedly recovered, agrees in all respects with the accounts given of the Epistle of Clement, and with the quotations from that Epistle found in ecclesiastical writers.[a] The absence of one or two quotations or allusions[x] is sufficiently accounted for by the fact that a fragment is still wanting at the end of Sect. 57.

We recognise in this Epistle the dignified simplicity of style, which is mentioned[y] as one of its remarkable features, and is most characteristic of the apostolic age.

The Church of Corinth, having been distracted with seditions, appears to have made application to Clement and the Church of Rome, which was itself then exposed to persecution. After some delay, arising from this cause, Clement addresses[z] the Corinthians, in the name of the Church of GOD which is at Rome, and reminds

---

[a] CLEM. ALEXAND. *Stromat.* I. p. 289. IV. p. 516. V. p. 586. VI. p. 647. ORIGEN, *de Principiis*, ii. c. 3. *Ad Johan.* i. 29. CYRIL. HIEROSOL. *Catechea.* xviii. p. 213. EPIPHANIUS, *Hæres.* xxvii. Num. 6. xxx. Num. 15. JEROME, *In Esaiam* lii. 13. Lib. xiv. *Ad Ephes*, ii. 2. iv. 1. PHOTIUS, Cod. 126.

[x] BASIL. *De Spiritu Sancto.* c. 29.

[y] PHOTIUS, *Biblioth.* Cod. 126.   [z] Sect. 1–7.

them of the firmness of their faith, their fruitfulness in all good works, and the order and obedience which once prevailed among them. He contrasts their previous Christian discipline with their present disorder and schism: and proceeds to show by numerous examples, what evils have been produced by envy and hatred. He incidentally alludes to the recent martyrdoms of St. Peter and St. Paul, and of many others, who had suffered in times of persecution.

After this introduction, Clement[a] assures the Corinthians how sensible he is, that he himself requires to be reminded of these truths: he exhorts them to look steadfastly to the blood of CHRIST, which has obtained the grace of repentance to all the world; and refers to numerous passages of Scripture, which teach the doctrine of repentance, and give examples of faithful obedience. He expatiates upon the duty of humility and peace, after the example of CHRIST, who came in all humility, although he was "the Sceptre of the Majesty of GOD:" and in imitation of those, who went about in sheep skins and goat skins, and of other holy men.

Clement then shows,[b] in a passage of great beauty and sublimity, that GOD has impressed upon the whole creation the visible marks of order, and arranged the several parts in concord and peace; and thence exhorts the Corinthians to return to their former purity and meekness, confirmed by faith in CHRIST, not doubting the excellent gifts of his grace.

Clement proceeds[c] to remind the Corinthians that many objects of the natural world remind us of the resurrection from the dead, of which our Lord JESUS CHRIST was the first-fruits. He exemplifies this in the succession of day and night, and in the growth of seed,

---

[a] Sect. 8–19.   [b] Sect. 20–22.   [c] Sect. 24.

which first dies in the ground. He adopts the story of the Phœnix,[d] which was believed by his contemporaries, and regards it as an emblem of the resurrection; and exhorts the Corinthians to hold fast the faith, to repent, and return to God in holiness. He then again refers to examples of those who have obtained blessing from God, and to the works of God himself, as an encouragement to fulfil his will.

He teaches submission,[e] and dwells upon the magnitude and importance of the eternal gifts of God, and exhorts them to fix their minds through faith toward God in Jesus Christ our High Priest, by whom God would have us taste of the knowledge of immortality. He then notices[f] the gradations of rank in an army, and the members of the body, which all conspire to promote the general good, as examples of the order which ought to prevail in the Church. After a quotation from the Book of Job,[g] Clement shows that the order of times and seasons in religious offices, as well as various gradations of the priesthood, are appointed by God, and that the successors of the Apostles in the ministry were ordained by them, after they had been proved by the Spirit;[h] and refers to the instance of Aaron having been miraculously called to the priesthood. He explains more at large the care which the Apostles took, that chosen and approved men should constantly succeed in the ministry:[i] contrasts the divisions among the Corinthians with the examples of holy men of old; and shows the sin of schism.

Clement then refers[k] to the first Epistle of St. Paul to the Corinthians:[l] exhorts them to unity; sets forth

---

[d] Sect. 25. 26. See note, p. 16.   [e] Sect. 34–36.   [f] Sect. 37.
[g] Sect. 39.   [h] Sect. 42.   [i] Sect. 44–46.   [k] Sect. 47–57.
[l] 1 Cor. i. 12.

the excellence of Christian charity; advises them to repent, and confess their sin: and to forgive one another after the example of Moses and others. He exhorts them meekly to pray for those who are in error; and calls upon the seditious to submit themselves.

At this part of the Epistle there is a passage omitted; but the conclusion, containing an affectionate and truly apostolical benediction, is preserved.[m]

This Epistle is the only genuine writing of Clement. EUSEBIUS[n] mentions indeed another Epistle of his, which was not so generally received as the first, and was not quoted by the ancients. The fragment of a second Epistle, now extant and attributed to Clement, is generally believed to be spurious. And other writings which bear his name, *The Recognitions*, and *Homilies*, as well as the *Constitutions* and *Canons of the Apostles*, which have been ascribed to him, are certainly productions of a later age.

Little is known respecting the latter days of Clement. That his mind was made up to suffer martyrdom for the faith, is manifest from the determined but quiet spirit of resignation which he expresses.[o] But there is no sufficient evidence for the story that he was banished into the Crimea by Trajan, and there suffered martyrdom by drowning.[p] He is with more reason believed to have died in possession of his Episcopal office, about the third year of Trajan, A. D. 100. He was succeeded in the see of Rome by Evarestus.

The Epistle of Clement having been written for a particular purpose, affords only occasional information respecting the state of the Church at the period when it was written. We find in it, however, proof that,

---

[m] Sect. 58. 59. 60.   [n] *Hist. Eccles.* iii. 38.   [o] Sect. 7.
[p] See CAVE's Life of Clement, c. 7. 8.

within a few years after the death of the Apostles Peter and Paul, Christian Churches were established by their order, and governed according to directions received from them.q We have an appeal made to the acknowledged purity of life and peaceableness of deportment, which characterized the primitive Christians;r although the Corinthian Church, in which divisions had taken place at a very early period,s had much degenerated. And we have testimony, direct and indirect, to the persecutions to which the infant Church of CHRIST was so soon exposed.

Only one book of the New Testament is expressly quoted by Clement;t and there is no mention of the Gospels by name, nor of their being collected into a volume. Words of our LORD, however, are quoted with respect, which are now found in the Gospels of St. Matthew, St. Mark, and St. Luke.u There are probable allusions to the Acts of the Apostles,x to the Epistle of St. Paul to the Romans,y to both his Epistles to the Corinthians,z to his Epistles to the Galatians,a Ephesians,b Philippians,c Colossians,d the first Epistle to the Thessalonians,e both the Epistles to Timothy,f

---

q Sect. 42. 44.   r Sect. 2.   s 1 Cor. xi. 18.   t 1 Cor. i. 12. Sect. 47.

u Matt. vii. 1-12.   Luke vi. 36-38. Sect. 13.—Matt. xxvi. 24. xviii. 6.   Mark ix. 42.   Luke xvii. 2. Sect. 46.—See LARDNER, *Credibility*, Part ii. c. 2.

x Acts xx. 35. Sect. 2.—Acts xiii. 22. Sect. 18.

y Rom. ix. 4. Sect. 33.—Rom. xii. 5. Sect. 46.—Rom. xiv. 1. Sect. 38.

z 1 Cor. x. 24. Sect. 48.—1 Cor. xii. 12. Sect. 37.—1 Cor. xiii. 4. Sect. 49.—1 Cor. xv. 20, 36, 38. Sect. 24.—2 Cor. iii. 18. Sect. 36. 2 Cor. viii. 5. Sect. 56.—2 Cor. x. 17. Sect. 30.—2 Cor. xi. 24. Sect. 5.

a Gal. i. 4. Sect. 49.   b Eph. iv. 4.

c Phil. i. 10. "Ye were sincere and without offence," Sect. 2.— Phil. ii. 5-7. Sect. 16.

d Col. i. 10. Sect. 21.   e 1 Thes. v. 18, 23. Sect. 38.

f 1 Tim. i. 9. v. 4. Sect. 7.—1 Tim. ii. 8. Sect. 29.—1 Tim. iii. 13. Sect. 54.

and the Epistle to Titus.ᵍ There are also, as Eusebius noticed,ʰ many coincidences of expression between the Epistle of Clement and the Epistle to the Hebrews,ⁱ and allusions to the Epistles of James,ᵏ and to the first and second Epistles of Peter.¹

LARDNER is of opinion, that the references and allusions to some of these books are manifest, and as he thinks, undeniable; as those to the Epistle to the Romans, and the first to the Corinthians. To these he would add the Epistle to the Hebrews, except that some might "think it not impossible for a man, who had been conversant with the Apostles, who was fully instructed in their doctrine and manner of reasoning, and also well acquainted with the Old Testament, to write with that great resemblance of the Epistle to the Hebrews, both in thought and expression, without borrowing from it, or imitating it;"ᵐ and also because at a later period, in the time of Eusebius and Jerome, the Church of Rome did not receive the Epistle to the Hebrews.

Others, however,ⁿ are satisfied from this Epistle that Clement possessed our three first Gospels, the Acts of the Apostles, the Epistle to the Romans, both the

---

ᵍ Tit. iii. 1. "Ye were ready to every good work," Sect. 2.
ʰ *Hist. Eccles.* iii. 34.
ⁱ Heb. i. 3–13. Sect. 36.—Heb. iii. 2, 5. Sect. 43.—Heb. iv. 14. Sect. 58.—Heb. vi. 13–15. Sect. 10.—Heb. xi. 5. Sect. 9.—Heb. xi. 8–20. Sect. 10.—Heb. xi. 31. Sect. 12.—Heb. xi. 37. Sect. 17.—Heb. xiii. 1, 2, Sect. 11.—Heb. xiii. 17. Sect. 1.
ᵏ James i. 5. Sect. 23.—James ii. 21–24. Sect. 10. 17. 30. 31.—James iii. 13. Sect. 38.—James iv. 3. Sect. 30.
¹ 1 Pet. iv. 8. Sect. 49.—1 Pet. v. 5. Sect. 2. 30. 38.—2 Pet. ii. 5, 6. Sect. 7. 11.—2 Pet. iii. 4. Sect. 23.
ᵐ *Credibility*, Vol. I. pp. 300. 302.
ⁿ MILL, *Prolegomena*, n. 140.

Epistles to the Corinthians, and the Epistle to the Hebrews.

This valuable testimony must also be taken as expressing the sentiments, not of Clement only, but of the Church of Rome, in whose name the Epistle is written, and as implying the high authority which the books had with the Corinthians themselves.

The Epistle of Clement contains, I believe, no allusion to existing miraculous powers.

The doctrines of this Epistle are worthy of its high character. It is shown elsewhere[o] that there is no foundation for the charge advanced by PHOTIUS and others, that Clement does not express himself in terms sufficiently elevated and distinct respecting the divine nature of our LORD. Clement speaks of the necessity of spiritual aid to enlighten our understanding;[p] says that we " are not justified by ourselves, neither by our own wisdom, or knowledge, or piety, in the works which we have done in holiness of heart; but by that faith, by which ALMIGHTY GOD hath justified all men from the beginning."[q] He speaks plainly of the Atonement by the blood of CHRIST, which was given for us,[r] and is " precious in the sight of GOD; which being shed for our salvation, hath obtained the grace of repentance to the whole world."[s] He is careful also to show the necessity of repentance and holiness,[t] of peace and humility,[u] after the example of our LORD;[x] and that they who have the love of CHRIST should keep his commandments,[y] and endeavor to advance in all godliness,[z] in firm hope of a resurrection[a] to immortality and glory.[b]

---

[o] Note (B) at the end of the *Epistle of* CLEMENT.
[p] Sect. 36.   [q] Sect. 32.   [r] Sect. 21. 49.   [s] Sect. 7.
[t] Sect. 8. 29.   [u] Sect. 13. 15.   [x] Sect. 16.   [y] Sect. 30. 49.
[z] Sect. 32.   [a] Sect. 24–26.   [b] Sect. 35.

It will be remembered that all these points are touched upon only incidentally; the main object of the Epistle being to correct particular disorders in the Church of Corinth.

Such is the Epistle of Clement, which, whether we regard its purely apostolic simplicity, the piety, meekness, and Christian spirit which pervade it, or the valuable testimony which it bears to the Scriptures of the New Testament, and to the condition and doctrines of the Church in the age immediately succeeding that of the Apostles, must be regarded as one of the most valuable remains of Christian antiquity.

POLYCARP.

The birth-place and early life of Polycarp are involved in obscurity. He was, however, of eastern extraction, and appears to have been brought up as a slave by a noble matron named Callisto, who made him her heir.

That Polycarp conversed familiarly with those who had been the disciples of our Lord, and particularly received instruction from the Apostle St. John, is proved by the testimony of Irenæus,[a] who heard it from Polycarp himself. "I saw you," says Irenæus, writing in his old age to Florinus,[b] "when I was yet a youth, in the lower Asia with Polycarp; when you were distinguished for your splendid talents in the royal palace, and striving diligently to deserve his favor. I can call to mind what then took place more accurately than more recent events; for impressions made upon the youthful memory grow up and identify themselves

---

[a] Irenæus *Adv. Hær.* iii. 3. Euseb. *Hist. Eccles.* iii. 36. iv. 14. See also *the Martyrdom of Ignatius*, Sect. 3. p. 140.

[b] *Epistola ad Florinum;*—Euseb. *Hist. Eccles.* v. 20.

with the very frame and texture of the mind. Well, therefore, could I describe the very place in which the blessed Polycarp sat and taught; his going out and coming in; the whole tenor of his life; his personal appearance; the discourses which he made to the people. How would he speak of the conversations which he had held with John, and with others who had seen the Lord. How did he make mention of their words, and of whatsoever he had heard from them respecting the Lord."

Polycarp was further instructed in the Christian faith by Bucolus, Bishop of Smyrna, and by him ordained Deacon and Catechist of that Church. On the death of Bucolus, Polycarp was ordained Bishop of Smyrna. Some[c] ascribe his ordination as Bishop to the Apostle John himself: others[d] to some of the Apostles, or[e] to apostolic men.

Archbishop Usher[f] conceives Polycarp to have been "the angel of the Church in Smyrna," whom St. John addresses in the Revelation.[g]

Very few particulars are known respecting the remaining part of the life of Polycarp. He enjoyed the greatest reputation for holiness; and was regarded both by the enemies and friends of the Church, as one of the principal supporters of the faith. He was appointed to go to Rome, on occasion of the controversy between the Eastern and Western Churches respecting the celebration of Easter. Irenæus[h] relates how successful Polycarp was during that visit, in bringing back to the faith those also who had erred; and relates a conversation with Marcion, who seems to have been desirous

---

[c] Tertullian, *De Præscriptione Hæreticorum*, c. 32.
[d] Irenæus *Adv. Hær.* iii. 3.   [e] Euseb. *Hist. Eccles.* iii. 36.
[f] *Prolegomena ad Ignat. Epist.* c. 3.   [g] Rev. ii. 8-10.
[h] Irenæus *Adv. Hær.* iii. 3.   Euseb. *Hist. Eccles.* iv. 14.

of obtaining, if not the approbation, at least the tacit acquiescence of the venerable Polycarp. The heretical leader accosted him in the words, "Dost thou acknowledge me?" "I do," was the reply of Polycarp; "I acknowledge thee for the first-born of Satan." The tenets of Marcion and the Gnostics were so totally subversive of the fundamental doctrines of Christianity, that it is not surprising that Polycarp should express himself in terms of strong reprobation respecting them. And the very same phrase having been used by Polycarp, in his Epistle to the Philippians,[i] adds probability to the narrative, and is an internal mark of the genuineness of the Epistle.

The life of Polycarp was prolonged to a great age.[k] CAVE, after EUSEBIUS and JEROME,[l] places his martyrdom in the year 167, and conceives him then to have been nearly a hundred years old. He considers, with TILLEMONT, that the assertion of Polycarp himself, "Fourscore and six years have I continued serving CHRIST,"[m] refers to the period which had elapsed after his conversion, and not to the length of his whole life. Bishop PEARSON,[n] however, with more probability places his martyrdom in the year 147, in the reign of Antoninus Pius, about the period in which JUSTIN MARTYR's first Apology was written. An ancient inscription is in favor of this date.[o]

The circular *Epistle of the Church of Smyrna*[p] contains a full account of the martyrdom of Polycarp, and

---

[i] Sect. 7.   [k] IRENÆUS *Adv. Hæres.* iii. 3.

[l] CAVE's Life of Polycarp. cc. 6. 15. JEROME *de Viris Illustr.* c. 13.

[m] *Martyrdom of Polycarp*, Sect. 9.

[n] *Dissert. Chron.* Part ii. cc. 14. 20.

[o] CHISHULL's *Travels*, p. 11, referred to by LARDNER, *Credibility*, Part ii. c. 6.

[p] P. 107 of this volume.

xxviii INTRODUCTION.

was so highly prized, that Eusebius has inserted almost the whole of it in his history. It is a very valuable memorial of Christian antiquity, and is remarkable for discouraging, rather than inciting persons to offer themselves voluntarily for persecution.[q] The resigned spirit of the venerable Polycarp is beautifully portrayed. His prudent retirement for a time, his calm submission to his persecutors, his dignified demeanor before the Proconsul, and the piety which he displayed in his prayers, both at the period of his apprehension and at the hour of death, complete a picture of a Christian martyr, worthy of a follower of the Apostles and of the high character which he had maintained during his life.

Polycarp is believed[r] to have written several Epistles, but of these none is extant except his Epistle to the Philippians, which was always highly esteemed,[s] and was publicly read in the Churches of Asia.[t] In style and matter it bears a great resemblance to the Epistle of Clement to the Corinthians.[u]

This Epistle forms an appropriate introduction to the Epistles of Ignatius, although, in strictly chronological

---

[q] Sect. 4.

[r] Irenæus, *Epist. ad Florin.* ap. Euseb. *Hist. Eccles.* v. 20. Hieron. *Epist. ad Levinum.* The fragments ascribed to Polycarp, by Victor of Capua in the sixth century, (see Grabe's *Irenæus*, p. 205.) are probably spurious. Lardner thinks that Irenæus and Eusebius had seen no writing of Polycarp, but his Epistle to the Philippians.

[s] Irenæus *Adv. Hær.* iii. 3.

[t] Hieron. *de Script. Eccles.* in Polycarp.

[u] Photius, in the ninth century, states that this Epistle was then read, and observes that it was contained in the same book with the Epistle of Clement to the Corinthians.

See Pearson, *Vindiciæ Ignatianæ*, Part i. c. 5. where it is fully shown, that the Epistle, which we now have, is the same to which the earliest Christian writers bear testimony.

order, it would follow them. Ignatius had recently passed through Smyrna, bound with chains, and guarded by a band of soldiers, who treated him with great cruelty, as he was being led to Rome, there to seal his testimony to the faith with his blood. As he came to the different cities, it appears from his letters that the Churches sent men chosen to meet him and attend him: and at Smyrna he conversed with Polycarp, and exhibited to the Church there a splendid example of patience and Christian fortitude. It seems probable, from the commencement of Polycarp's Epistle, that certain of the Philippians had accompanied Ignatius, on his departure from their city toward Rome. Soon after that time, and before any accurate intelligence of his death hath reached the Church of Smyrna,[x] Polycarp addressed this letter to the Church at Philippi, sending, at the same time, the Epistles which Ignatius had written to himself and to the Smyrneans,[y] and several other of his Epistles.

Polycarp begins his Epistle by commending the Philippians for their attention to those who had suffered for the faith, and for their own steadfastness; and exhorts them to continue in faith and piety. He reminds them of the doctrine which St. Paul had taught them, in his Epistle addressed to them, and proceeds to set before them the duties of faith, hope, and charity.[z] He admonishes them to beware of covetousness; rehearses the duties of husbands, wives, and widows; of deacons, young men, presbyters, and virgins: and enforces these duties by the consideration that all must give an account to GOD of their actions.[a]

He then proceeds to matters of faith: refers to the nature and sufferings of CHRIST; to his atonement, and

---

[x] Compare Sect. 9, 14.   [y] Sect. 13.   [z] Sect. 1–3.   [a] Sect. 4–6.

to the example afforded by Him, and by the Apostles and martyrs, as motives to mutual charity and good order.[b]

Having expressed his regret for the misconduct of Valens and his wife, in the true spirit of Christian charity for the offenders, while their offence is rebuked, he declares his confidence that the Philippians are exercised in the holy Scriptures; prays for them; and commands them to pray for others: and, in conclusion, gives directions respecting the letters of Ignatius.[c]

The brief Epistle of Polycarp contains numerous references to the books of the New Testament. There are expressly quoted as the writings of St. Paul, the first Epistle to the Corinthians,[d] his Epistle to the Philippians,[e] and probably that to the Thessalonians.[f] There is also a passage[g] in which the Epistle to the Ephesians seems to be quoted under the appellation of " the holy Scriptures."

With reference to this passage, LARDNER[h] observes that the words " Be ye angry and sin not," are in the Septuagint version of Ps. iv. 4. " But," he adds, " as the latter advice 'Let not the sun go down on your wrath,' is no where found in the Old Testament, and both these precepts are together in the Epistle to the Ephesians, it seems to me that Polycarp does expressly refer the Philippians to St. Paul's Epistle to the Ephesians, and calls it Scripture. If this be so, then we see, that the writings of the New Testament had now the name of ' Sacred Writings,' or ' Holy Scriptures,' and that they were much read by Christians in general."

In another place[i] Polycarp appears to refer to the Scriptures of the New Testament in general, in the

---

[b] Sect. 7–10. [c] Sect. 11–14. [d] Sect. 11. [e] Sect. 3.
[f] Sect. 11. Compare 2 Thes. i. 4. [g] Sect. 12. Eph. iv. 26.
[h] *Credibility*, Part ii. c. 6. [i] Sect. 7.

REFERENCES IN THE EPISTLE OF POLYCARP. xxxi

phrase, "Whosoever perverts *the oracles* of the LORD to his own lusts, and says there is neither resurrection nor judgment, he is the first-born of Satan:" and there are other references[k] to passages now found in the Gospels, as the words of our LORD.

In the translation of this Epistle a reference is made to many passages of the New Testament to which Polycarp alludes. Others are subjoined.[1]

---

[k] Sect. 2. 7.

[1] Matt. v. 44. Sect. 12. "Pray for those who persecute and hate you."
Rom. xiii. 9, 10. Sect. 3. "For if any one have these things, he hath fulfilled the law of righteousness."
2 Cor. vi. 7. Sect. 4. "Let us arm ourselves with the armor of righteousness."
Gal. iv. 26. Sect. 3. "Edified in the faith delivered to you, which is the mother of us all."
Phil. ii. 16. Sect. 9. "All these have not run in vain."
Col. i. 28. Sect. 12. "That ye may be perfect in CHRIST."
1 Thes. v. 22. Sect. 2. "Abstain from all unrighteousness."
2 Thes. i. 4. Sect. 11. "For he glories in you, in all the churches, which alone had known GOD."
Thessalonica being the capital city of the Province of Macedonia in which Philippi was, Polycarp might consider the Epistle to the Thessalonians as addressed also to the Philippians. See Sect. 3. note 1.
1 Tim. ii. 1, 2. Sect. 12. "Pray for all the saints. Pray also for kings," &c.
1 Tim. iii. 8. Sect. 5. "The deacons must not be double-tongued." The whole chapter resembles 1 Tim. iii.
2 Tim. ii. 11. Sect. 5. "If we walk worthy of him we shall also reign with him."
2 Tim. iv. 10. Sect. 9. "They loved not this present world."
Heb. iv. 12. Sect. 4. "He sees all blemishes, and nothing is hid from him," &c.
1 Pet. ii. 17. Sect. 10. "Lovers of the brotherhood."
1 Pet. iv. 5. Sect. 2. "Who comes to be the judge of quick and dead."
1 Pet. v. 5. Sect. 10. "Be ye subject one to another."
Jude, ver. 3. Sect. 3. "Ye may be able to be edified in the faith delivered unto you."
The words in Sect. 12. "Now the GOD and Father of our Lord

In this very short Epistle we have then references to two of the Gospels, to the Acts of the Apostles, to ten of the first thirteen Epistles of St. Paul, and probably to the Epistles to the Colossians and to the Hebrews: to the First Epistle of St. Peter,[m] and to the First Epistle of St. John.[n]

Of a writing, which is so scriptural in its language, it is needless to observe that the doctrines are pure. Faith in CHRIST, who is our hope, and the earnest of our righteousness,[o] who suffered for us, that we might live through him, "our everlasting High Priest, the Son of GOD;"[p] a faith bringing forth the fruits of holiness, purity, and meekness;[q] salvation by grace, not of works but by the will of GOD, through JESUS CHRIST;[r] watchfulness unto prayer, perseverance in fasting, and supplication to GOD not to lead us into temptation,[s] and for all conditions of men;[t] the imitation of the example of CHRIST, and of his faithful disciples;[u] the study of the Scriptures,[x]—these are the doctrines of this truly Apostolical Epistle. And these doctrines are employed to enforce the fullest discharge of all the relative duties of different stations in life.[y]

The profession of Polycarp was no vain display. Their influence upon his own life is exemplified in the calm serenity with which he met his death; and in the humble confidence which he expressed in his last prayer.[z]

JESUS CHRIST, and he himself who is our everlasting High-priest, the Son of GOD, JESUS CHRIST, build you up in faith and truth:" seem to be an allusion to Heb. iv. 14. vi. 20. vii. 3.

[m] EUSEBIUS, *Hist. Eccles.* iv. 14. says that Polycarp in his Epistle to the Philippians uses testimonies from the First Epistle of Peter.

[n] See LARDNER, *Credibility*, Part ii. c. 6. 41.

[o] Sect. 1. 8. [p] Sect. 12. [q] Sect. 2. 12. [r] Sect. 1.
[s] Sect. 7. [t] Sect. 12. [u] Sect. 8. 9. [x] Sect. 12.
[y] Sect. 4-6. [z] *Martyrdom of Polycarp*, Sect. 14.

IGNATIUS.

IGNATIUS appears to have been a man of much more ardent mind than Polycarp. The place of his birth and even his country are entirely unknown. The tradition has been preserved[a] that he was a disciple of St. John, that he conversed with the Apostles, and was instructed by them both in the familiar and more sublime doctrines of Christianity; but it appears[b] that he had never conversed with our LORD himself.[c] So highly was he esteemed that, about the year 70, on the death of Euodius, he was ordained Bishop of the important Church of Antioch, the metropolis of Syria, possibly by the imposition of the hands of the Apostles,[d] who still survived. The high character which he bore is manifest from the terms in which he is described,[e] as "a man in all things like the Apostles;" one who, "like a skilful pilot, by the helm of prayer and fasting, by the constancy of his doctrine and spiritual labor, withstood the raging floods, fearing lest he should lose any of those who wanted courage, or were not well-grounded in the faith."

SOCRATES,[f] in the fifth century, ascribes to Ignatius the introduction of the custom of singing hymns alter-

---

[a] *Martyrdom of Ignatius*, Sect. 1. 3. EUSEBIUS, *Hist. Eccles.* iii. 36. CHRYSOSTOM *Homil. in S. Ignat.* Tom. V. p. 499. 17. Savile.

[b] CHRYSOSTOM, Tom. V. p. 503. 36.

[c] See Note (a), p. 55.

[d] EUSEBIUS, *Hist. Eccles.* iii. 36. CHRYSOSTOM *Hom.* Tom. V. p. 499. 32. In the *Apostolical Constitutions*, vii. 46. Ignatius is said to have been ordained Bishop by St. Paul. Others mention St. Peter also. The improbability of this is shown in Dr. BURTON's *Lectures on the Ecclesiastical History of the First Century.* Lect. xii.

[e] *Relation of the Martyrdom of Ignatius*, Sect. I.

[f] SOCRATES, *Hist. Eccles.* vi. 8.

nately in the choir, at Antioch. And some have thought [g] that, although Flavianus and Diodorus, in the time of Constantius, were the first who introduced at Antioch the custom of thus singing the Psalms of David, yet hymns might be so used at a period as early as the time of Ignatius.

If the tradition be unfounded, the use made of the name of Ignatius shows at least that his memory was held in great respect at Antioch so long after his death.

But the best memorial of his pastoral zeal and diligence is found in the letters which he wrote to the different Churches, as he was carried prisoner from Antioch to Rome, in order to be put to death.

The date of the martyrdom of Ignatius is differently computed. According to the Acts of his martyrdom, it took place in the year 107, the ninth year of Trajan's reign. And this date is accordingly followed by many chronologists. Others,[h] however, with great probability fix upon the year 116.

Whatever was the precise date, he was called to answer before Trajan, as he passed through Antioch, elated with his late victory over the Scythians and Dacians, and about to set out on his Parthian expedition. The peculiar circumstances in which Trajan was placed may perhaps show why that prince, who was usually mild and considerate, exercised such severity toward Ignatius. In the history of the martyrdom of Ignatius the rigor of the Emperor is ascribed to his desire of reducing the Christians, as well as others, to submission to his will. It is not improbable however, that Trajan on his arrival at Antioch, found a persecution already raging there-

---

[g] See BINGHAM, *Ecc. Antiquities*, xiv. 1. 11.

[h] Bp. PEARSON, *Dissertatio de anno quo S. Ignatius ad bestias erat condemnatus*. LLOYD, apud PAGI *ad Baron.* an. 109. GRABE, ad *Acta Ignatii*.

Times of public rejoicing were usually periods of peculiar vexation to the primitive Christians, who were then especially urged to comply with some of the idolatrous customs of the Heathen. The arrival of the Emperor was calculated to call forth the most vivid feelings both of loyalty and superstition: and all his subjects were not likely to imitate the decent flattery of PLINY, who, in ascribing to his imperial patron the highest virtues of which human nature is capable, complimented him upon his refusing to receive divine honors.[i]

Ignatius might thus probably be pointed out to Trajan as a leader of a sect which refused to sacrifice to the gods for the safety of the Emperor, and the success of his arms: and the venerable Bishop was not of a disposition to shrink from the severest trial to which his profession of the faith exposed him. He voluntarily offered to be brought before Trajan, and there expressed himself in the noble manner recorded in the Acts of his martyrdom.

The result of his conference with the Emperor was such as might have been expected. He who gave Pliny directions not to seek for the Christians, in his province, but, if they were brought before him, and proved to be such, to punish them capitally,[k] acted only in consistency with his own principles, when he condemned Ignatius to suffer death.

It is not so easy to account for the reason which induced Trajan to send him from Antioch to Rome, to

---

[i] Discernatur orationibus nostris diversitas temporum, et ex ipso genere gratiarum agendarum intelligatur, cui, quando sint hactenus ut deo, nunc nusquam ut numini blandiamur. Non enim de tyranno, sed de cive: non de domino, sed de parente loquimur. PLINII *Panegyricus*, sub init. Compare TERTULLIAN *Apol.* c. 34.

[k] PLIN. *Epist.* Lib. x. Epist. 98.

be exposed to the wild beasts. If the advisers of the Emperor intended, by such a cruel delay, either to break the spirit of the martyr, or to give him an opportunity of recanting, their object was far from being attained. Ignatius rejoiced that he was counted worthy to suffer for the faith of CHRIST. Although deeply conscious of his own infirmity as a man, and sensible of his inferiority to the Apostles, in whose steps he trod, his only fear was lest the love of the brethren at Rome or elsewhere should prevent him from attaining the crown of martyrdom.

In reading his passionate appeals, especially in his Epistle to the Romans,[1] we cannot but feel that the ardent and almost impatient spirit, by which he was animated, is strongly contrasted with the dignified calmness of St. Paul, when he was "in a strait betwixt two, having a desire to depart, and to be with CHRIST, which is far better," but was yet contented to "abide in the flesh," which was more needful for his converts.[m] It must be remembered however that Ignatius lived at a period when the blood of the martyrs was appointed to be the seed of the Church: that if his notions of martyrdom appear to have been exaggerated, he expresses the most perfect resignation, the deepest humility and self abasement, in speaking of himself. And we cannot but admire the high courage of this worthy successor of the Apostles, which, as he passed from Antioch to Rome, as a condemned and degraded criminal, converted his tedious journey into a triumphal procession.

His progress is accurately described in the *Acts of his Martyrdom.* He set sail from Seleucia, and landed for a short time at Smyrna. At this place he was gratified with an interview with Polycarp, the Bishop of

---

[1] Sect. 4. 5.   [m] Phil. i. 23, 24.

that see, who had been with him a fellow disciple of St. John. And, as soon as his arrival was known, the neighboring churches of Asia sent their Bishops, and other messengers to visit the venerable martyr. The Church of Ephesus was represented by Onesimus;[a] that of Magnesia, by Damas,[o] that of Tralles, by Polybius,[p] their respective Bishops, and by others of their body. During his hurried stay at Smyrna, he found leisure to write his Epistles, to the Ephesians, Magnesians, and Trallians; and to send also his Epistle to the Romans, by some Ephesians, who were likely to reach the imperial city sooner than himself.

Ignatius had intended to write a second Epistle to the Ephesians;[q] but either he was prevented by want of time, or the Epistle has been lost.

During his abode at Smyrna he was in great anxiety for the Church of Syria which he had left under persecution; and in all the letters[r] which he wrote from that city, he entreats their prayers for his own suffering Church, which was deprived of its Bishop.[s] But when he had advanced as far as Troas, he learned that the persecution at Antioch had ceased; not improbably from some decree of Trajan himself. It should be observed, that in the three remaining Epistles, which Ignatius wrote from Troas, to the Churches of Philadelphia and Smyrna, and individually to Polycarp,[t] he incidentally expresses his heartfelt satisfaction that their prayers had been heard, and that the Church of

---

[a] IGNATIUS' *Epist. to the Ephes.* Sect. 1.

[o] *Magnesians,* Sect. 2.   [p] *Trallians,* Sect. 1.

[q] *Ephesians,* Sect. 20.

[r] *Ephesians,* Sect. 21.   *Magnesians,* Sect. 14.   *Trallians,* Sect. 13.   *Romans,* Sect. 9.

[s] *Romans,* Sect. 9.

[t] *Philadelphians,* Sect. 10.   *Smyrneans,* Sect. 11.   *Epistle to Polycarp,* Sect. 7.

Syria was at peace, and had received its "proper body;" probably by the appointment of Heros, as his successor in the episcopal office.

Ignatius would have written to other churches;[a] but was hurried away from Troas to Neapolis by those who guarded him. He thence proceeded by land through Macedonia and Epirus, to Epidamnus; embarked again for Italy; and, on his arrival at Rome, on the last day of the public spectacles, was immediately thrown to the wild beasts in the Amphitheatre; displaying in his last moments the same constancy and piety as had marked his previous life.

THE EPISTLES OF IGNATIUS.

The Epistles of Ignatius are most interesting and valuable documents of the early Christian Church. They are the unstudied effusions of an ardent and deeply religious mind; and bespeak a man who was superior to this world, and anxious to finish his course with joy. It is an internal mark of their genuineness that their style is harsh and unpolished; and occasionally not untinctured with some degree of oriental exaggeration.

Eusebius,[b] in mentioning these seven Epistles, observes that Ignatius was peculiarly desirous to repress the heretical opinions which were then first beginning to spring up in the Church, and to confirm those whom he addressed, in the faith delivered by the Apostles. The heretical tenets were those of the Gnostics; and it is evident from Ignatius' Epistles to the Asiatic Churches that the evil was very prevalent and injurious. In his Epistle to Polycarp there are only two general

---

[a] *Epist. to Polycarp*, Sect. 8.   [b] *Hist. Eccles.* iii. 36.

cautions[b] against false doctrine; and in his Epistle to the Romans, there are no allusions to the subject. That Epistle, however, was written principally to prepare the Church of Rome for his approach; and Ignatius was so far from possessing the same acquaintance with it as with the Churches of Asia, that he does not even mention the name of its Bishop. No conclusion, therefore, can be drawn from this circumstance, as to the prevalence of Gnosticism at Rome.

The evils of schism, and the great disorders arising from the disobedience of individuals, especially in the infant state of the Church, will account for the very forcible language in which Ignatius urges obedience to the Bishops, Presbyters, and Deacons, as the successors of the Apostles, according to Divine appointment.

The doctrines contained in the Epistles of Ignatius are purely scriptural. The hasty manner in which they were written, prevents them from containing any thing like a formal declaration of any doctrinal points: but constant incidental references are made to the absolute divinity of our LORD,[c] to his pre-existence,[d] and eternity,[e] and the union of the divine and human nature in his person;[f] to the influence of the Holy Spirit,[g] salvation by means of CHRIST's death alone,[h] and the necessity of personal holiness.[i]

The testimony which Ignatius bears to the writings of the New Testament is very valuable. He quotes,

---

[b] Sect. 3. 5.

[c] *Ephesians*, Introduction, Sect. 1. 7. 18. 19. 20. *Magnesians*, Sect. 7. *Epist. to Polycarp*, Sect. 8. *Martyrdom*, Sect. 2. 8.

[d] *Magnesians*, Sect. 6. 8.   [e] *Magnesians*, Sect. 6.

[f] *Smyrneans*, Sect. 4.   [g] *Ephesians*, Sect. 8. 15.

[h] *Trallians*, Sect. 2.   *Philippians*, Sect. 8. 9.   *Smyrneans*, Sect. 1. 2. 6.   *Martyrdom*, Sect. 2.

[i] *Ephesians*, Sect. 12.   *Romans*, Sect. 7.   *Epist. to Polycarp*, Sect. 1.

indeed, only one book by name, the Epistle of St. Paul to the Ephesians;[k] but LARDNER shows at length that he alludes plainly to the Gospels of St. Matthew and St. John, and probably to that of St. Luke: that he has allusions to the Acts of the Apostles, to eleven of the first thirteen Epistles of St. Paul, to the Epistle to the Hebrews, to the first Epistle of St. Peter, and to the first and third Epistles of St. John. He uses terms also which imply a collection of the Gospels, and of the Epistles of the Apostles, and of the books of the New Testament generally.[l]

These allusions, it will be seen, are usually made in an incidental, unstudied manner, without express marks of reference; precisely, indeed, in the manner in which we might expect Ignatius, under the circumstances in which he wrote, to have referred to Scriptures, with the general meaning of which both he and those whom he addressed were well acquainted; but without the formality of express verbal quotation.

It would be foreign to the present purpose to enter at any length into the well-known controversy respecting the genuineness of these Epistles of Ignatius. All that can be here attempted is to give a general view of the evidence in their favor, as it has been most laboriously collected by Bp. PEARSON[m] and others who have exhausted the subject.

The question resolves itself into two parts, whether Ignatius left behind him written Epistles; and whether they are the same with those which we now possess. Now, Polycarp, in his Epistle to the Philippians, ex-

---

[k] IGNAT. *Epist. to Ephesians*, Sect. 12.

[l] LARDNER, *Credibility*, Part ii. c. 5.

[m] *Vindiciæ Epistolarum S. Ignatii.* See also HAMMOND, *Dissertationes adversus Blondellum.* USHER, *Prolegom. ad Epist. Ignat.* BULL *Defensio Fid. Nicænæ*, ii. 2. 8.

pressly mentions Epistles written by Ignatius. Irenæus,[n] in the second century, refers also to Ignatius, and alludes[o] to a passage now found in his Epistle to the Romans. Origen,[p] in the early part of the third century, quotes two passages from the Epistles of Ignatius, now extant in the Epistles to the Romans and Ephesians.

Eusebius,[q] in the beginning of the fourth century, states that Ignatius wrote seven Epistles, four from Smyrna, and three from Troas, agreeing in their inscriptions and general character with the Epistles now extant. He quotes remarkable passages from the Epistles to the Romans, and Smyrneans; describes particularly the Epistle to Polycarp, by saying that in it Ignatius commends to Polycarp the care of the Church of Antioch; and with respect to the Epistles to the Ephesians, Magnesians, and Trallians, he says that in them Ignatius makes particular mention of the bishops of those Churches, Onesimus, Damas, and Polybius.

Such an accurate description of the Epistles of Ignatius could have been given only by one well acquainted with the Epistles themselves.

Bp. Pearson[r] shows, at length, that the chain of reference to the Epistles of Ignatius extends without interruption through Christian writers from the second century to the fifteenth.

This evidence is abundantly sufficient to prove that Ignatius wrote certain Epistles; that seven of these

---

[n] Eusebius, *Hist. Eccles.* v. 28.
[o] Irenæus, *Adv. Hæres.* v. 28.   Eusebius, *Hist. Eccles.* iii. 36.
[p] Origen: *Prolegom. in Cant. Canticor. Hom.* vi. *in Luc.* Ignat. *Epist. to the Romans,* Sect. 7. *Ephesians,* Sect. 19.
[q] Eusebius, *Hist. Eccles.* iii. 36.
[r] *Vindiciæ Ignat.* Par. i. c. 2.

existed at the beginning of the fourth century; and that they were never altogether lost sight of.

The first printed edition of any Epistles ascribed to Ignatius appeared in 1557, although an old Latin version of three Epistles had been published sixty years earlier. This edition, with two others which appeared about the same time, contained twelve Epistles; and it was soon suspected that the Epistles so edited were interpolated. It was observed, that seven Epistles only had been mentioned by EUSEBIUS; that the seven published Greek Epistles, with titles corresponding to those stated by Eusebius, did not agree with quotations from the acknowledged Epistles of Ignatius made by ancient Christian writers; and that of the remaining five no notice was taken by any ancient writer.

Nearly a hundred years after the publication of these editions, Archbishop USHER observed that some English writers had quoted passages from the Epistles of Ignatius, which did not agree with the Greek text or Latin version of the published Epistles, although they did agree with quotations made by THEODORET. It immediately occurred to his acute and inquiring mind, that some manuscript of the genuine Epistles of Ignatius might exist in England: and his inquiries led to the discovery of two Latin manuscripts, one in the Library of Caius College, Cambridge, the other in the possession of Dr. RICHARD MONTACUTE, Bishop of Norwich, which differed materially from the Greek editions hitherto published, but agreed with the quotations made by the earlier Christian writers.

With the assistance of these manuscripts, the Archbishop published, in 1644, a Greek edition of the Epistles of Ignatius, in which the additions made in the interpolated editions were distinguished by red ink.

Two years after this, in 1646, ISAAC VOSSIUS published

an edition of the genuine Epistles of Ignatius in Greek, from an ancient manuscript discovered in the Medicean Library at Florence, and closely corresponding with the ancient Latin version previously discovered.

The agreement of these shorter Epistles with the quotations in early Christian writers, added to their internal evidence, establishes their genuineness as strongly as the nature of the case appears to admit.

It is plainly shown, that the genuine Epistles of Ignatius, which had been collected by Polycarp, were probably known to Irenæus, and certainly eulogized by Eusebius, had been interpolated, it is supposed about the sixth century, by additions made in such a manner as to retain many of the sentiments of Ignatius, but in other respects to differ materially from his language. These interpolations appear also to have been made not without design, as may easily be seen by comparing the interpolated with the genuine Epistles in any of the passages which most pointedly refer to the Divine nature of our Lord.* Beside these interpolated Epistles, other spurious Epistles were ascribed to Ignatius, probably as early as the middle of the seventh century.

It must be considered a most happy circumstance, that so valuable a relic of Christian antiquity, as these Epistles of Ignatius, should have been thus recovered, after having been lost, or partially obscured, for so many years.

JUSTIN MARTYR.

The writings of Clement, Ignatius, and Polycarp are addressed to Christians, and are very interesting as

---

* As for instance, *Epist. to the Ephesians*, Introduction; Sect. 1, 7, 18, 20. There is an English translation of the Interpolated Epistles of Ignatius in Whiston's *Primitive Christianity Revived*.

showing us the feelings and sentiments of some of the earliest writers after the Apostles themselves. There is another class of Christian writings, *the Apologies*, or defences, which were addressed to the adversaries of the faith. Several of these have been preserved. And among them two of the most valuable are those of JUSTIN MARTYR and TERTULLIAN.*

JUSTIN MARTYR was born about the year 100, at Flavia Neapolis,[a] anciently called Sichem, in Samaria. His parents were Gentiles,[b] and probably Greeks. In his youth, his ardor for the acquisition of knowledge was gratified by travel: he visited Alexandria: and in the early part of his life became acquainted with the opinions of the different sects of philosophers. He attached himself[c] to the Stoics, till he found that from them he could obtain no knowledge of the nature of GOD. The covetousness of the Peripatetics, to whom he next applied, soon disgusted him. And on endeavoring to study the Pythagorean philosophy, he quickly relinquished the notion of uniting himself permanently with a sect, which required as a preliminary step an extensive acquaintance with music, astronomy, and geometry. The tenets of the Platonists[d] were more agreeable to his natural disposition. But finding no satisfaction to his mind from any of these systems of philosophy, he was led to examine Christianity, and

---

* [Mr. CHEVALLIER's volume contains a translation of the *Apology* of TERTULLIAN, which has been omitted in the present reprint, with the purpose of publishing it hereafter, with other similar writings, in a subsequent volume of this series.]

[a] *Apol.* Sect. i. ii. p. 52. [The references to pages in the writings of Justin, in this and the following notes, relate to the Paris edition of the original.]

[b] *Apol.* Sect. lxviii.   [c] *Dialogue with Trypho*, p. 218.

[d] *Apol.* II. p. 50.

found in it the certainty and adaptation to his mental wants which no other studies had afforded.[e]

The direct argument in favor of Christianity, which appears to have had the greatest weight with Justin, was the courage with which men of all ranks submitted to death in the cause of the Gospel, while no one was ever found to die in support of any philosophical opinions.[f] "While," he says,[g] "I was myself still delighted with the philosophy of Plato, I used to hear the Christians calumniated, but saw that they fearlessly encountered death, and all that is most formidable to other men. I was convinced that these men could not be living in wickedness or sinful pleasure. For what man, who was subject to his passions and to intemperance, or delighted to feed on human flesh, would dare to embrace death, which would put a period to all his delights? Such a man would strive by all means to preserve his present life; would endeavor to conceal himself from those in power: least of all would he offer himself voluntarily for punishment."

After his conversion to Christianity, Justin still continued to wear the dress of a philosopher.[h] This circumstance has been considered to imply an undue attachment to the opinions which he had renounced. It was a practice, however, far from uncommon:[i] and Justin might continue to use the dress, either as sufficiently consistent with the severity of life which Christianity required, or as a custom, in a matter of indifference, with which he might innocently comply.[k]

About the beginning of the reign of Antoninus Pius,

---

[e] *Dial.* p. 225.   [f] *Apol.* II. p. 48.
[g] *Apol.* II. p. 50. A.
[h] *Dial.* p. 217, C. EUSEBIUS, *Hist. Eccles.* iv. 11.
[i] CAVE's *Life of Justin Martyr*, c. 6.
[k] Compare TERTULLIAN, *Apol.* c. 42.

Justin Martyr fixed his abode in Rome;[1] and employed the means, which his previous studies had put into his power, in defending the purity of the Christian faith. He wrote a treatise[m] against heresies, especially against Marcion. About this time he addressed his first Apology to Antoninus Pius, Marcus Antoninus, Lucius Verus, the Senate and the people of Rome. The precise date of this Apology has been the subject of much discussion, without leading to any very satisfactory decision.

There are few internal marks of time in the Apology itself. Justin once[n] speaks, in round numbers, of the birth of CHRIST, as having occurred a hundred and fifty years before. In other places, the death and deification of Antinous,[o] the edict of Adrian against the Jews,[p] and the revolt of Barchochebas,[q] which all occurred between the years 130 and 134, are alluded to as recent events. The earliest date ascribed to the Apology is 139. Others place it as late as 150. In favor of the first date, DODWELL[r] observes, that in the introduction Marcus Antoninus is not styled Cæsar, an omission which would imply that he had not yet received the title. On the other hand, Lucius Verus was born only in the year 131; and the terms in which Justin addresses him, in conjunction with the two Antonines, could scarcely be applied to a youth of eight years of age. If the Epistle[s] to the States of Asia be properly ascribed to Antoninus Pius, and were written in his third consulship, A. D. 140, it is uncertain whether that Epistle were occasioned by Justin's Apology. EUSEBIUS[t] rather implies that it was written solely in con-

---

[1] EUSEBIUS, *Hist. Eccl.* iv. 11.   [m] *Apol.* I. Sect. xxxvi.
[n] Sect. 61.   [o] Sect. 37.   [p] Sect. 62.   [q] Sect. 39.
[r] *Dissertatio in Irenæum.* c. 14.   [s] p. 192.
[t] *Hist. Eccl.* iv. 12.

sequence of expostulations which the Emperor had received from some Christians in Asia.

The Benedictine Editors, in the preface to their edition of Justin's works, adopt the opinion of TILLEMONT and others, who assign 150 as the date of Justin's first Apology.

This Apology is very valuable, as being the earliest specimen of the manner in which the first Christians defended themselves against their Heathen adversaries. The arguments which he advances are not arranged in any very exact order.

He begins by demanding a fair hearing for the Christians, and expostulating against the injustice of punishing them unheard, or accusing all Christians of crimes, which might possibly be committed by some who bore that name.[u] He ascribes the malice of the enemies of Christianity to the agency of demons; and demands that due inquiry may be made in each individual case, and sentence passed accordingly.[x]

He shows that the doctrines of the Christians are harmless; and not derogatory to the divine nature:[y] that the Christians look for no human kingdom; but are the best and most peaceable subjects; knowing that in suffering they endure only what their LORD prophesied should come upon them.[z]

He defends the Christians from the charge of impiety; appeals to the blameless lives which they lead after their conversion; and refers to many precepts of CHRIST which teach the necessity of holiness and obedience to authority.[a]

Justin then argues on the possibility that the soul should survive death, appealing to the sentiments and

[u] Sect. 1–4.   [x] Sect. 5–7.   [y] Sect. 8–10.
[z] Sect. 11–15.   [a] Sect. 16–23.

practices of the Heathen as implying that fact; and showing that a resurrection from the dead is not so incredible as the first creation of an animated being.[b]

He shows the injustice of punishing Christians for their opinions, when poets and philosophers were permitted without molestation to support others less defensible and less rational; and all other men were allowed to choose their own objects of worship.[c] Justin appeals again to the reformation of life in Christians; whereas Simon Magus, who was honored by the Romans, and Marcion, and other heretics, were not molested, however infamous their conduct might be.[d]

Having then contrasted the purity of the lives of Christians with the cruel custom of exposing their children practised by the Heathen, Justin proceeds to the direct evidence of miracle and prophecy. He briefly alludes to the miracles of CHRIST, principally to refute the objection that they were performed by magical powers: and then alleges many prophecies of the Old Testament, which were fulfilled by CHRIST.[e] From their accomplishment he contends that other events, which are predicted but yet unfulfilled, shall assuredly come to pass; such as the conversion of the Gentiles, the resurrection of the dead, and the future judgment by CHRIST.[f]

Justin asserts that many actions ascribed to the Heathen gods were imitations of the real actions of JESUS; and that the opinions of philosophers were a concealed representation of the truths of Christianity.[g]

Justin, in conclusion, describes the manner in which the first converts were baptized;[h] and, after a di-

---

[b] Sect. 24–26.   [c] Sect. 27–32.   [d] Sect. 33–35.
[e] Sect. 36–65.   [f] Sect. 66–69.   [g] Sect. 70–78.
[h] Sect. 79, 80.

gression on the different appearances of CHRIST under the Mosaic dispensation, and on certain instances, in which the Heathen gods were made to imitate what was written by Moses,[i] he gives a most interesting account of the state of the Christians in his time; describing the administration of the Eucharist in both kinds, the assembling of Christians on Sunday, and the manner in which they conducted their public worship, and made voluntary collections for the relief of the poorer brethren.[k]

He finishes his Apology with an expression of resignation, and an appeal to the letter of Adrian in favor of the Christians.

The *Dialogue with Trypho the Jew* was certainly written after the first Apology, to which there is an allusion:[l] but the precise date is not known. It is the account of either a real or fictitious discussion with a Jew, which EUSEBIUS[m] states to have occurred at Ephesus; and is valuable as showing the state of the controversy with the Jews in the time of Justin.[n]

Justin wrote also *a second Apology*, which, in the Paris Edition, is denominated the first. According to EUSEBIUS,[o] it was addressed to Marcus Antoninus. Others suppose that it, as well as the preceding, was presented to Antoninus Pius. From expressions in the second Apology, EUSEBIUS[p] and others have concluded

---

[i] Sect. 81–84.   [k] Sect. 85–89.
[l] *Dial.* p. 349, C. *Apol.* Sect. 34.   [m] *Hist. Eccl.* iv. 18.
[n] There is a most clear and accurate analysis of the Dialogue with Trypho in the Bishop of Lincoln's [Dr. KAYE'S] *Account of the Writings and Opinions of Justin Martyr*, c. 11, and an English translation of *the Dialogue* by HENRY BROWN, M. A., London, 1755.
[o] *Hist. Eccl.* iv. 16.
[p] EUSEBIUS, *Hist. Eccl.* iv. 16, 17. JUSTIN, *Apol.* II. p. 46, E.

that it was written by Justin not long before his martyrdom.

The beginning of the Second Apology is believed to be lost: and it is in other respects imperfect. Several Christians had at that time been unjustly punished, and Justin presented the Apology in their defence; urging several of the arguments which he had used in the first Apology, and replying to objections advanced by the adversaries of Christianity.

There are several other writings attributed to Justin Martyr. Of these, the fragment *de Monarchiâ* DEI is believed to be genuine. There are doubts of the genuineness of the *Hortatory Address to the Greeks*.[q]

The ardent spirit of Justin Martyr was likely to draw upon him the indignation of those who opposed Christianity; and especially of the philosophers, whose malice, as we have seen, he anticipated. Accordingly, soon after the publication of his second Apology, about the year 165, Justin and six of his companions were brought before Rusticus, prefect of Rome. The behaviour of Justin in the hour of danger was worthy of the professions which he had previously made. He refused to worship the gods of the Romans, avowed his faith in the doctrines of Christianity, and at once declared where it was that he had been accustomed to teach the Christian religion. When threatened with torture and death, unless he sacrificed to the gods, Justin expressed his full conviction of eternal happiness, if he continued steadfast in the faith, and his determination patiently to endure all things for the sake of his LORD and Saviour. His companions assented to these courageous sentiments: and they were

---

[q] See the Bishop of Lincoln's *Account of Justin Martyr*, p. 5.

all immediately led back to prison, where, after they had been scourged, they were beheaded.

We can only briefly touch upon the doctrines and opinions which are maintained by Justin in his first Apology. Those who wish for an accurate statement of his sentiments, as deduced from a minute examination of all his genuine works, should consult the Bishop of Lincoln's admirable work upon the subject.

We find Justin distinctly acknowledging the Divinity of our LORD, representing the object of Christian worship to be the FATHER, the Creator of all things; the Divine WORD, who took our nature upon him, and died upon the cross for our sake; and the HOLY SPIRIT.[r] He maintains also the absolute Divinity of JESUS CHRIST, when he states, that it was He who appeared to Moses in the bush, and described himself as the eternal and self-existing GOD;[s] and he styles Him directly GOD.[t]

Justin does not express himself very clearly respecting the effect which the fall of man produced upon his capacity of choosing good and evil. He describes[u] the human race as having been created "intelligent, and able to choose the truth and to be happy." But he speaks "of that proneness to evil, which, although various in its kind, exists in every man,"[x] after the fall; and contrasts our first birth, in which "we were born without our knowledge or consent, by the ordinary natural means, and were brought up in evil habits," with the condition of those who by baptism "become the children of choice and judgment," and "obtain in the water remission of the sins which they have before committed."[y]

Justin is scarcely more explicit upon this point, or

---

[r] Sect. 6, 16, 77, 85, 87. See note (k,) p. 130 of this volume.
[s] Sect. 82, 83.   [t] Sect. 83, p. 186 of this volume.
[u] Sect. 36.   [x] Sect. 10.   [y] Sect. 80.

upon the subject of grace, in other parts of his works,[a] although he declares the necessity of illumination from above to be enabled rightly to understand the holy Scriptures.

It must be remembered, however, that the subject of his writings, which was, in his Apologies, to defend the Christians from the charges advanced against them by the Heathen, and, in his Dialogue with Trypho, to controvert the objections of the Jews, did not lead him to speak upon these subjects otherwise than incidentally; and that his expressions must be considered with reference rather to the whole context in which they are found, than to the words which he employs in any particular instance.

The manner in which Justin treats the difficulty of reconciling the foreknowledge of God with the moral responsibility of man, may be seen in several passages[a] of the Apology. He says[b] that God delayed the punishment of the devil, since he foreknew that some who are not yet born should be saved: but that this foreknowledge does not imply that every thing takes place by irresistible necessity.[c]

With respect to the doctrine of Justification, Justin in this Apology[d] declares that Christ "cleansed by his blood those who believe in him:" and in other parts of his works[e] constantly refers to the merits and death of Christ as the cause, and to faith as the means, by which we are justified.

When Justin speaks in his own person, he invariably maintains that the punishment of the wicked will be eternal.[f]

---

[a] See Bp. Kaye's *Account of Justin*, p. 75.
[a] Sect. 54–58.   [b] Sect. 36.   [c] Sect. 54.   [d] Sect. 41.
[e] See *Dial.* p. 229, E. 234, E. 259, A. 273, E. 322, E. 323, B. 338, D.
[f] See note (p,) p. 132 of this volume.

DOCTRINES OF JUSTIN MARTYR. liii

Justin Martyr, in the course of his first Apology, refers, on three different occasions, to the 'Memoirs[g] of the Apostles,' and in the second of those instances calls the work to which he alludes 'Gospels.' In his Dialogue with Trypho he twice[h] quotes "the Gospel;" and in several places[i] refers to the 'Memoirs of the Apostles.' In several of these passages he refers to words which are found in substance in our present Gospels. Justin describes these 'Memoirs' as having been written by the Apostles and those who followed them,[k] a description which exactly corresponds with our present Gospels, two of which were written by Apostles, and two by those who attended the Apostles. He mentions also that these writings were publicly read in the solemn assemblies of the Christians, with the Scriptures of the Old Testament, as part of their religious service.[l]

"Upon the whole," says LARDNER,[m] "it must be plain to all, that he owned and had the greatest respect for the four Gospels, written, two of them, by Apostles, and the other two by companions and followers of the Apostles of JESUS CHRIST; that is, by Matthew, Mark, Luke, and John."

The Bishop of Lincoln[n] examines at length the question which has been lately raised, whether Justin quoted our present Gospels; and, after referring to the several passages in which Justin mentions the Memoirs of the Apostles, observes, "The inference which I am

---

[g] ἀπομνημονεύματα, Sect. 43, 86, 87.   [h] p. 227, C. 326, E.
[i] p. 327, B. 328, B. 329, C. 331, B. D. 332, B. 333, B. D. E. 334, B.
[k] *Dial.* p. 331, D. ἐν γὰρ τοῖς ἀπομνημονεύμασιν, ἅ φημι ὑπὸ τῶν Ἀποστόλων αὐτοῦ καὶ τῶν ἐκείνοις παρακολουσάντων συντετάχθαι. Compare Luke i. 3. Ἔδοξε κἀμοὶ παρηκολουθηκότι ἄνωθεν κ. τ. λ.
[l] *Apol.* Sect. 87.   [m] *Credibility*, Part II. c. 10, § 3.
[n] *Account of Justin Martyr*, c. 8.

disposed to draw from the consideration of the above passages is, not that Justin quoted a Narrative of our Saviour's life and ministry agreeing in substance with our present Gospels, though differing from them in expression: but that he quoted our present Gospels from memory."—"It is moreover necessary always to bear in mind, as has been already observed, that Justin does not appeal to the New Testament as an authority: he wishes merely to give a true representation of the doctrines and precepts of the Gospel: and for this purpose it was sufficient to express the meaning without any scrupulous regard to verbal accuracy."

Justin in his Apology has but few references to the other books of the New Testament. In Sect. 63, where he states that the Jews, who had the prophecies, and always expected the CHRIST to come, not only were ignorant of him, but evil entreated him, he probably alludes to Acts xiii. 27. And in Sect. 82, he says that JESUS is called "the Apostle," an appellation which is given to him only in *Heb.* iii. 1, 2.

LARDNER shows, however, that Justin, in other parts of his works, recognises the Acts of the Apostles; the Epistle to the Romans; the Epistles to the Galatians, Ephesians, Philippians, and Colossians; the second Epistle to the Thessalonians; the Epistle to the Hebrews, and the second Epistle of Peter.

It is remarkable that the only Book which Justin expressly quotes* is the Revelation, which he ascribes to the Apostle St. John.

The most interesting part of Justin's Apology is, doubtless, the picture which he draws of the condition of the primitive Church in his time. He appeals to the

---

* *Dial.* p. 308, B. EUSEBIUS mentions this quotation, *Hist. Eccl.* iv. 18.

change which had been wrought in those who had embraced the Christian faith.* He refers directly and indirectly to the fact, that they were exposed to grievous persecution, and subject to the most atrocious calumnies; yet declares that they bore all evils with patience, not even demanding that their false accusers should be punished.† But while the believers were harassed from without, they enjoyed the privileges of Christian communion within the pale of the Church. They still continued to address one another by the apostolic title of brethren,‡ and assembled every Sunday, whether they dwelt in towns or in the country, for the purpose of public worship. Their religious services consisted in hearing the Gospels and the Scriptures of the Old Testament read and expounded. The 'President' then delivered a discourse; and after they had all stood up together to pray, the Eucharist, of bread and wine mixed with water, was administered to each; and a contribution was made for the use of the fatherless and widows, for such as were in necessity, or in bonds.

Such is the picture of the Christian Church drawn by one who had tried what the systems of Heathen philosophy could do to satisfy the anxious inquiries of his mind after spiritual things, and found them all insufficient; who dared to stand forth as the advocate of the cause of the Gospel, when to profess the faith was to expose himself to immediate persecution; and soon afterward proved the sincerity of his profession by the sacrifice of his life.§

* * * * * * * * * *

With respect to the present translations, it has already been observed, that the Epistles of Clement, Polycarp,

---

* Sect. 20. † Sect. 7. ‡ Sect. 85.

§ [A part of Mr. CHEVALLIER's Introduction, relating to the life and writings of TERTULLIAN, is omitted, for the reason stated above.]

and Ignatius, and the accounts of the Martyrdom of the two last, are in substance taken from Archbishop WAKE's Version. The language of that version has been happily styled by LARDNER "apostolical English:" and it would have been a needless affectation of originality to have injured, by any unnecessary alteration, what had already been expressed so faithfully and so well. My first intention was to have simply reprinted those Epistles, with such illustrations as they might seem to require. A comparison of the present translation with that of Archbishop WAKE will show that, with the exception of the quotations, his version has been here closely, but not servilely, followed.

In translating the Apology of Justin Martyr, my object has been to express with fidelity the sentiments of the original, in such a manner as to be intelligible to a reader who may not be able to consult the original work. Those who are best acquainted with the nature of such a task will be the most lenient in overlooking any harshness or want of fluency, which, in such a translation, it is so difficult to avoid.

THE EPISTLE OF CLEMENT TO THE CORINTHIANS.

THE Church of GOD which is at Rome to the Church of GOD which is at Corinth, called, sanctified by the will of GOD, through our Lord JESUS CHRIST; grace to you and peace from ALMIGHTY GOD, through JESUS CHRIST, be multiplied.

1. The sudden and repeated dangers and calamities which have befallen us, brethren, have, we fear, made us too slow in giving heed to those things which ye inquired of us, as well as to that wicked and detestable sedition, altogether unbecoming the elect of GOD, which a few hasty and self-willed persons have excited to such a degree of madness, that your venerable and renowned name, so worthy of the love of all men, is thereby greatly blasphemed. For who that hath sojourned among you hath not experienced the firmness of your faith, and its fruitfulness in all good works? and admired the temper and moderation of your piety in CHRIST? and proclaimed the magnificent spirit of your hospitality? and thought you happy in your perfect and certain knowledge (of the Gospel)? For ye did all things without respect of persons; and walked according to the laws of GOD; being subject to those who had the rule over you; and giving to the elders among you the honor which was due.. Young men ye commanded to think those things which are modest and grave. Women ye exhorted to perform all things with an unblameable, and seemly, and pure conscience; loving their own husbands as was fitting: ye taught them, also, to be subject to the rule of obedience, and to order their houses gravely with all discretion.

VOL. IV.—1

2. Ye were all of you humble-minded,[a] not boasting of any thing, desiring rather to be subject than to govern; to give, than to receive;[b] being content with the portion which GOD had dispensed unto you: and hearkening diligently to his word, ye were enlarged in your bowels,[c] having his sufferings always before your eyes. Thus a deep and fruitful peace[d] was given to you all, and an insatiable desire of doing good; and a plentiful effusion of the HOLY GHOST was upon all of you. And, being full of holy counsel, ye did, with great readiness of mind, and religious confidence, stretch forth your hands to ALMIGHTY GOD, beseeching him to be merciful, if in any thing ye had unwillingly sinned. Ye contended day and night for the whole brotherhood, that with compassion and a good conscience the number of his elect might be saved. Ye were sincere and without offence: not mindful of injuries one toward another. All sedition and all schism was an abomination unto you. Ye mourned over the sins of your neighbors, esteeming their defects your own. Ye were kind one to another without grudging; ready to every good work. Ye were adorned with a conversation entirely virtuous and religious; and did all things in the fear of GOD. The commandments of the LORD were written upon the tables of your heart.[e]

3. All honor and enlargement was given unto you. Then was fulfilled that which is written: "My beloved did eat and drink, he was enlarged, and waxed fat, and kicked."[f] Hence arose envy, and strife, and sedition; persecution and disorder, war and captivity. Thus they that were of no renown lifted up themselves against the honorable; those of no reputation against those that were in respect; the foolish against the wise; the young against the elders. Therefore righteousness and peace are departed from you, because every one of you hath forsaken the fear of GOD, and is become blind in his faith, and walks not by the rule of GOD's com-

---

[a] 1 Pet. v. 5.   [b] Acts xx. 35.   [c] 2 Cor. vi. 11, 12.
[d] εἰρήνη βαθεῖα καὶ λιπαρά.
  The metaphor appears to refer to a soil which is deep and fertile. Thus CHRYSOSTOM, Hom. 52 on Genesis—εἰδότες ὅτι οὐ κατὰ πετρῶν σπείρομεν, ἀλλ' εἰς λιπαρὰν καὶ βαθύγειον καταβάλλομεν τὰ σπέρματα.—Vol. I. p. 420. 37. Savile.
[e] Prov. vii. 3. 2 Cor. iii. 3.   [f] Deut. xxxii. 15.

mandments, nor regulates himself as is fitting in CHRIST. But every one follows his own wicked lusts, having taken up unjust and wicked envy, by which even death entered into the world.

4. For thus it is written; "And it came to pass, after certain days, that Cain brought of the fruit of the ground an offering unto the LORD. And Abel he also brought of the firstlings of his flock, and of the fat thereof. And GOD had respect unto Abel and unto his offering; but unto Cain and to his offering he had not respect. And Cain was very sorrowful, and his countenance fell. And GOD said unto Cain, Why art thou sorrowful? And why is thy countenance fallen? If thou shalt offer aright, but not divide aright, hast thou not sinned? Hold thy peace.ᶠ Unto thee shall be his desire; and thou shalt rule over him. And Cain said unto Abel his brother, Let us go aside into the field.ʰ And it came to pass as they were in the field that Cain rose up against Abel his brother and slew him."ⁱ Ye see, brethren, envy and jealousy wrought the murder of a brother. Through envy, our father Jacob fled from the face of his brother Esau.ᵏ Envy caused Joseph to be persecuted even unto death, and to come into bondage.ˡ Envy compelled Moses to flee from the face of Pharaoh king of Egypt; when he heard his own countryman say, Who made thee a judge and a ruler over us? wilt thou kill me, as thou killedst the Egyptian yesterday?ᵐ Through envy, Aaron and Miriamⁿ were shut out of the camp.º Envy sent Dathan and Abiram quick into the grave, because they raised up a sedition against Moses the servant of GOD.ᵖ Through envy, David was not only hated of strangers, but persecuted even by Saul, the king of Israel.ᑫ

5. But not to dwell upon ancient examples, let us come to those who in these last days have wrestled

---

ᶠ According to the version of the Septuagint. So IRENÆUS, Lib. iv. c. 34.

ʰ The Samaritan Pentateuch, Septuagint, Vulgate and other Versions supply these words, which are wanting in the Hebrew copies.

ⁱ Gen. iv. 3–8.   ᵏ Gen. xxviii.
ˡ Gen. xxxvii.   ᵐ Exod. ii. 14.
ⁿ Miriam is said to have been shut out from the camp, Numb. xii. 14, 15, but not Aaron.
º Num. xii. 14, 15.   ᵖ Num. xvi. 33.   ᑫ 1 Sam. xix.

manfully for the faith; let us take the noble examples of our own age. Through envy and jealousy, the faithful and most righteous pillars of the Church have been persecuted even to the most dreadful deaths. Let us place before our eyes the good apostles. Peter, by unjust envy, underwent not one or two but many labors; and thus having borne testimony unto death, he went unto the place of glory which was due to him. Through envy, Paul obtained the reward of patience. Seven times was he in bonds; he was scourged; was stoned.[r] He preached both in the east and in the west, leaving behind him the glorious report of his faith. And thus, having taught the whole world righteousness, and reached the furthest extremity of the west,[s] he suffered martyrdom, by the command of the governors,[t] and departed out of this world, and went to the holy place, having become a most exemplary pattern of patience.

6. To these holy apostles was added a great number of other godly men, who having through envy undergone many insults and tortures, have left a most excellent example to us. Through envy, women[u] have been persecuted; and suffering grievous and unutterable torments, have finished the course of their faith with firmness, and, though weak in body, have received a glorious reward. Envy hath alienated the minds of wives from their husbands, and changed that which was spoken by our father Adam, "This is now bone of my bone, and flesh of my flesh."[x] Envy and strife have overthrown great cities, and utterly rooted out mighty nations.

7. These things, beloved, we write unto you, not only to instruct you, but to remind ourselves: for we are enclosed in the same lists, and must engage in the same combat. Wherefore let us lay aside all vain and empty cares, and come up to the glorious and honorable rule of our holy calling. Let us consider what is good, and

---

[r] 2 Cor. xi. 25.
[s] See note (A) at the end of the Epistle.
[t] Probably of Fenius Rufus and Sofonius Tigellinus, the *two* præfects of the prætorian cohorts, appointed by Nero in the place of Burrus. TACIT. *Annal.* xiv. 51.
[u] The words, "the Danaides and Dirce," here inserted, appear to be an interpolation.
[x] Gen. ii. 23.

acceptable, and well-pleasing in the sight of him that made us.[y] Let us look steadfastly to the blood of CHRIST, and see how precious his blood is in the sight of GOD, which, being shed for our salvation, hath obtained the grace of repentance to the whole world. Let us look to all past generations, and learn that from age to age the LORD hath given place for repentance to all such as would turn to him. Noah preached repentance: and as many as hearkened to him were saved.[z] Jonah[a] denounced destruction against the Ninevites: and they, repenting of their sins, appeased the wrath of GOD by their prayers; and received salvation although they were strangers (to the covenant) of GOD.

8. The ministers of the grace of GOD have spoken by the HOLY SPIRIT, of repentance: and even the LORD of all hath himself declared with an oath concerning it, "As I live, saith the LORD, I desire not the death of a sinner, but rather that he should repent:"[b] adding also this good exhortation; "Turn from your iniquity, O house of Israel.[c] Say unto the children of my people, though your sins should reach from earth to heaven, and though they should be redder than scarlet[d] and blacker than sackcloth, yet if ye shall turn to me with all your heart, and shall say, Father![e] I will hearken to you as unto a holy people." And in another place, he saith on this wise: "Wash you, make you clean, put away the evil of your souls from before mine eyes. Cease from your wickedness: learn to do well: seek judgment: relieve the oppressed: judge the fatherless; and plead for the widow. Come now and let us reason together, (saith the LORD.) Though your sins be as scarlet, I will make them white as snow: though they be like crimson, I will make them white as wool. If ye be willing and obedient, ye shall eat the good of the land. But if ye refuse and obey not, the sword shall devour you: for the mouth of the LORD hath spoken these things."[f] GOD hath thus appointed by his almighty will, desiring that all his beloved should come to repentance.

---

[y] 1 Tim. v. 4.
[z] 2 Pet. ii. 5. Gen. vii.
[a] Jon. iii. 5.
[b] Ezek. xxxiii. 11.
[c] Ezek. xviii. 30–32.
[d] Isa. i. 18.
[e] Jer. iii. 4, 19.
[f] Isa. i. 16–20.

9. Wherefore let us obey his excellent and glorious will: and imploring his mercy and goodness, let us fall down before him, and turn ourselves to his mercy, laying aside all labor after vanities, and strife, and envy which leads to death. Let us look earnestly to those who have perfectly ministered to his excellent glory. Let us take Enoch, (for our example,) who being found righteous in obedience was translated, and his death was not known.[g] Noah being found faithful, did by his ministry preach regeneration to the world;[h] and the LORD saved by him all the living creatures, which entered with one accord into the ark.

10. Abraham, who was called the friend (of GOD),[i] was found faithful, inasmuch as he obeyed the words of GOD. He, in obedience, went out of his own country, and from his kindred, and from his father's house,[k] that by thus forsaking a small country, and a weak kindred, and a mean house, he might inherit the promises of GOD. For "(GOD) said to him: Get thee out of thy country, and from thy kindred, and from thy father's house, unto a land which I will show thee. And I will make thee a great nation: and I will bless thee, and make thy name great: and thou shalt be blessed. And I will bless them that bless thee; and curse them that curse thee: and in thee shall all families of the earth be blessed."[l] And again, when he separated himself from Lot, GOD said unto him; "Lift up now thine eyes, and look from the place where thou art, northward, and southward, and eastward, and westward. For all the land which thou seest, to thee will I give it, and to thy seed for ever. And I will make thy seed as the dust of the earth; so that if a man can number the dust of the earth, then shall thy seed also be numbered."[m]

And again he saith, "GOD brought forth Abraham and said unto him, Look now toward heaven and tell the stars, if thou be able to number them; so shall thy seed be. And Abraham believed GOD, and it was counted to him for righteousness."[n] Through faith and hospitality a son was given unto him in his old

---

[g] Gen. v. 24. Heb. xi. 5.   [h] Gen. vi. vii. viii.
[i] 2 Chron. xx. 7. Isa. xli. 8. Ja. ii. 23.
[k] Heb. xi. 8.   [l] Gen. xii. 1–3.
[m] Gen. xiii. 14–16.   [n] Gen. xv. 5, 6. Rom. iv. 3.

age: and through obedience he offered him up in sacrifice to GOD, upon one of the mountains which GOD showed unto him.

11. By hospitality and godliness, Lot was saved out of Sodom, when all the country round about was punished with fire and brimstone: the LORD thereby making it manifest, that he will not forsake those that trust in him; but will bring to punishment and correction those who decline from his ways. For his wife, who went out with him, being of a different mind, and not continuing in the same obedience, was for that reason set forth for an example, and became a pillar of salt unto this day. That all men may know, that those who are double-minded, and distrustful of the power of GOD, are prepared for condemnation, and to be a sign to all generations.

12. By faith and hospitality was Rahab the harlot saved.º For when the spies were sent by Joshua the son of Nun to search out Jericho, the king of the country knew that they were come to spy out his land, and sent men to take them and put them to death. But the hospitable Rahab received them; and hid them under the stalks of flax on the top of her house. And when the men that were sent by the king came unto her, and asked her, saying,[p] There came men unto thee to spy out the land; bring them forth, for so hath the king commanded; she answered, The two men, whom ye seek, came in unto me, but presently they departed and are gone; not discovering them unto them. Then she said to the spies, I know that the LORD your GOD hath given you this city;[q] for the fear of you, and the dread of you, is fallen upon all that dwell therein. When therefore ye shall have taken it, ye shall save me and my father's house.[r] And they said unto her, It shall be as thou hast spoken unto us. Therefore when thou shalt know that we are near, thou shalt gather all thy family together upon the house-top, and they shall be saved; but all that shall be found without thy house shall be destroyed. Moreover they gave her a sign, that she should hang out of her house a (line of) scarlet

---

º Josh. ii.
[p] Josh. ii. 3.
[q] Josh. ii. 9.
[r] Josh. ii. 13.

(thread): showing thereby, that by the blood of our LORD[a] there should be redemption to all who believe and hope in GOD. Ye see, beloved, that there was not only faith, but prophecy also in this woman.

13. Let us, therefore, be humble-minded, brethren, laying aside all pride, and boasting, and foolishness, and anger; and let us do as it is written. For thus saith the HOLY SPIRIT; "Let not the wise man glory in his wisdom; nor the strong man in his strength, nor the rich man in his riches; but let him that glorieth glory in the LORD, to seek him, and to exercise judgment and righteousness."[t] Above all, remembering the words of the Lord JESUS, which he spake, teaching us gentleness and long-suffering. For thus he said: "Be merciful, that ye may obtain mercy: forgive, that it may be forgiven unto you. As ye do, so shall it be done unto you: as ye give, so shall it be given unto you: as ye judge, so shall ye be judged: as ye show kindness, so shall kindness be showed to you. With what measure ye mete, with the same shall it be measured to you."[u] By this command, and by these rules, let us establish ourselves, that so we may always walk obediently to his holy words, being humble-minded.

---

[a] Fanciful as the illustration here given may seem, it was a favorite notion of many of the early Christian writers. JUSTIN MARTYR, in his *Dialogue with Trypho*, p. 338, says, "The sign of the scarlet thread, which the spies, sent from Joshua the son of Nun, gave to Rahab the harlot in Jericho, commanding her to hang it to the window by which she let them down that they might escape their enemies, was in like manner a sign of the blood of CHRIST, by which those of all nations, who were once harlots and sinners, are saved, receiving forgiveness of sins, and sinning no more." IRENÆUS, *Hæres.* iv. 37, makes the same use of the history. "So also Rahab the harlot, although she condemned herself as a gentile and guilty of all kinds of sin, did yet receive the three spies, who were searching the whole land, and hid them in her house, that is to say, the Father, and Son and Holy Ghost. And when all the city in which she dwelt had fallen in ruins, at the sound of the seven trumpets, Rahab the harlot was at the last saved, with all her house, by faith in the sign of the scarlet thread; as the LORD also said to the Pharisees, who received not his coming, and set at nought the crimson sign, which was the passover, the redemption and deliverance of the people out of Egypt, saying, the publicans and harlots go into the kingdom of heaven before you."
COTELERIUS [*Patr. Apostol.* annot. in loc. Clement.] refers to many other passages of the same kind.

[t] Jer. ix. 23. 1 Cor. i. 31.
[u] Luke vi. 36–38. Matt. vii. 1, 2–12.

§ 14, 15.] TO THE CORINTHIANS. 9

For thus saith the holy word, "Upon whom shall I look, but upon him that is meek and quiet, and trembleth at my words." ˣ

14. It is therefore just and holy, men and brethren, that we should become obedient unto God, rather than follow those who through pride and sedition have made themselves the leaders of a detestable emulation. For we shall undergo no ordinary harm, but exceedingly great danger, if we shall rashly give ourselves up to the wills of men, who are urgent in promoting strife and contention, to turn us aside from that which is good. Let us be kind to one another according to the compassion and sweetness of him that made us. For it is written, "The merciful shall inherit the earth; and they that are without evil shall be left upon it.ʸ But the transgressors shall perish from off (the face of) it." And again he saith, "I have seen the wicked in great power, and spreading himself like the cedars of Libanus. And I passed by, and lo, he was not: and I sought his place, but it could not be found. Keep innocency, and do the thing that is right; for there shall be a remnant to the peaceable man." ᶻ

15. Let us therefore hold fast to those who follow peace with godliness, and not to such as with hypocrisy pretend to desire it. For he saith in a certain place, "This people honoreth me with their lips, but their heart is far from me."ᵃ And again, "They bless with their mouth, but curse with their heart."ᵇ And again he saith, "They loved him with their mouth, and with their tongue they lied unto him. For their heart was not right with him, neither were they faithful in his covenant."ᶜ "Let all deceitful lips become dumb, and the tongue that speaketh proud things. Who have said, with our tongue will we prevail; our lips are our own: who is Lord over us? For the oppression of the poor, for the sighing of the needy, now will I arise, saith the Lord: I will set him in safety: I will deal confidently with him."ᵈ

ˣ Isa. lxvi. 2.
ᶻ Ps. xxxvii. 35–37.
ᵇ Ps. lxii. 4.
ᵈ Ps. xii. 4; xxxi. 18.

ʸ Ps. xxxvii. 9   Prov. ii. 21.
ᵃ Isa. xxix. 13.
ᶜ Ps. lxxviii. 36, 37.

16. For CHRIST is theirs who are humble, not theirs who exalt themselves over his flock. The sceptre of the Majesty of GOD, our Lord JESUS CHRIST, came not in the pomp of pride and arrogance, although he was able (to have done so);[*] but with humility, as the HOLY GHOST had spoken concerning him.[f] For thus he saith:[g] "LORD who hath believed our report? and to whom is the arm of the LORD revealed? We have declared before him as (if he were) a child: as a root in a thirsty ground. For there is no form in him, nor glory. Yea we saw him, and he had no form nor comeliness: but his form was without honor, marred more than the sons of men. He is a man in stripes and sorrow, and acquainted with the endurance of infirmity. For his face was turned away; he was despised, and esteemed not. He beareth our sins, and is put to grief for us; and we did esteem him to be in sorrow, and in stripes, and in affliction. But he was wounded for our transgressions; and bruised for our iniquities. The chastisement of our peace was upon him; with his stripes we are healed. All we, like sheep, have gone astray: man hath gone astray in his way; and the LORD hath given him up for our sins; and he opened not his mouth through his suffering. He was led as a sheep to the slaughter, and like a lamb dumb before his shearer, so opened he not his mouth. In his humiliation his judgment was taken away: and who shall declare his generation; for his life is taken from the earth. For the transgressions of my people he cometh to death. And I will give the wicked for his tomb, and the rich for his death. Because he did no iniquity, neither was guile found in his mouth. And the LORD is pleased to purify him with stripes. If ye make an offering for sin, your soul shall see a long-lived seed. And the LORD is pleased to lighten the travail of his soul, to show him light, to form him in understanding, to justify the just one who ministereth well to many: and he himself shall bear their sins. For this cause he shall inherit many: and

---

[*] JEROME, who translated this Epistle into Latin, appears to have read καίπερ πάντα δυνάμενος, 'although he was able to do all things.' HIERON. *ad Isa. c. liii.* Opera, Tom. III. p. 382.

[f] See note (B) at the end of the Epistle.

[g] Isa. liii. according to the Septuagint.

shall divide the spoil of the strong; because his soul was given up to death, and he was numbered with the transgressors: and he bare the sins of many, and was given over for their sins." And again he himself saith; "But I am a worm and no man, a reproach of men, and despised of the people. All they that see me laugh me to scorn: they shoot out their lips, they shake their head, (saying,) He trusted in the Lord, let him deliver him, let him save him, seeing he delighteth in him."[h] Ye see, beloved, what the pattern is which hath been given unto us. For if the Lord was so humble-minded, what should we do, who are brought by him under the yoke of his grace?

17. Let us be followers of those also, who went about in goat-skins and sheep-skins,[i] preaching the coming of Christ. Such were Elijah and Elisha, and Ezekiel the prophets, and moreover those who have received the like testimony. Abraham was honored with a good report, and was called the friend of God:[k] and he, steadfastly beholding the glory of God, saith with all humility, I am dust and ashes.[l] Again, of Job it is thus written, "Job was just, and blameless, true, one that served God, and eschewed all evil."[m] Yet he, accusing himself, saith, "No man is free from pollution, no, not though he should live but one day."[n] Moses was called faithful in all God's house,[o] and by his conduct the Lord punished Israel by stripes and plagues. And even this man so greatly honored, spake not greatly of himself, but when the oracle of God was delivered to him out of the bush, he said, "Who am I that thou dost send me? I am of a slender voice and of a slow tongue."[p] And again he saith: "I am as the smoke of the pot."[q]

18. Again, what shall we say of David who hath

---

[h] Ps. xxii. 6.   [i] Heb. xi. 37.
[k] 2 Chron. xx. 7. Isa. xli. 8. Ja. ii. 23.
[l] Gen. xviii. 27.   [m] Job i. 1.
[n] Job xiv. 4. Septuagint. Thus Cyprian, *Test. ad Quirinum*, l. iii. c. 54. "Apud Job; Quis enim mundus à sordibus? Nec unus, etiamsi unius diei sit vita ejus in terrâ."—Jerome, on Isai. liii. and on Ps. li. quotes the passage in the same manner.
[o] Num. xii. 7. Heb. iii. 2.   [p] Exod. iii. 11; iv. 10.
[q] These words are not found in the Pentateuch. See Ps. cxix. 83. Hos. xiii. 3.

obtained so good a report? to whom GOD said, "I have found a man after mine own heart, David the son of Jesse: with my holy oil have I anointed him."[r] But yet he himself saith unto GOD; "Have mercy upon me, O GOD, according to thy great kindness, and according unto the multitude of thy tender mercies, blot out my transgression. Wash me thoroughly from mine iniquity, and cleanse me from my sin. For I acknowledge mine iniquity, and my sin is ever before me. Against thee only have I sinned, and done this evil in thy sight, that thou mightest be justified when thou speakest, and overcome when thou judgest. For, behold, I was shapen in wickedness, and in sin did my mother conceive me. For behold thou lovedst truth; the secret and hidden things of wisdom hast thou revealed unto me. Thou shalt purge me with hyssop, and I shall be clean: thou shalt wash me, and I shall be whiter than snow. Thou shalt make me to hear joy and gladness; the bones which have been broken shall rejoice. Turn thy face from my sins, and blot out all mine iniquities. Create in me a clean heart, O GOD, and renew a right spirit within me. Cast me not away from thy presence, and take not thy HOLY SPIRIT from me. Restore unto me the joy of thy salvation, and establish me with the guidance of thy Spirit. I will teach sinners thy ways, and the ungodly shall be converted unto thee. Deliver me from blood, O GOD, thou GOD of my salvation. My tongue shall rejoice in thy righteousness. O LORD, open thou my lips, and my mouth shall show forth thy praise. For if thou hadst desired sacrifice, I would have given it; thou delightest not in burnt offerings. The sacrifices of GOD are a broken spirit: a broken and contrite heart GOD will not despise."[s]

19. Thus the humility and godly fear of such great and excellent men, whose praise is in the Scriptures, hath, by means of their obedience, improved not only us, but generations before us, even as many as have received his holy oracles in fear and truth. Having therefore so many, and great, and glorious examples

---

[r] Ps. lxxxix. 20. Compare Acts. xlii. 22. 1 Sam. xiii. 14.
[s] Ps. li.

transmitted to us, let us turn again to that mark of peace which from the beginning was set before us: let us look steadfastly up to the Father and Creator of the universe, and hold fast by his glorious and exceeding gifts, and benefits of peace. Let us see him with our understanding, and look with the eyes of our soul to his long-suffering will: calling to mind how gentle and slow to anger he is toward his whole creation.

20. The heavens, peaceably revolving by his appointment, are subject unto him. Day and night perform the course appointed by him, in no wise interrupting one another. By his ordinance, the sun and moon, and all the companies of stars, roll on, in harmony, without any deviation, within the bounds allotted to them. In obedience to his will, the pregnant earth yields her fruit plentifully in due season to man and beast, and to all creatures that are therein; not hesitating nor changing any thing which was decreed by him. The unsearchable secrets of the abyss, and the untold judgments of the lower world, are restrained by the same commands. The hollow depth of the vast sea, gathered together into its several collections by his word, passes not its allotted bounds; but as he commanded, so doth it. For he said, "Hitherto shalt thou come, and thy waves shall be broken within thee."[1] The ocean impassable to mankind, and the worlds which are beyond it, are governed by the same commands of their master. Spring and summer, and autumn and winter, give place peaceably to one another. The winds, in their stations, perform their service without interruption, each in his appointed season. The ever-flowing fountains, ministering both to pleasure and to health, without ceasing put forth their breasts to support the life of man. Nay, the smallest of living creatures maintain their intercourse in concord and peace. All these hath the great Creator and LORD of all things ordained to be in peace and concord; for he is good to all; but above measure to us, who flee to his mercy, through our Lord JESUS CHRIST, to whom be glory and majesty, for ever and ever; Amen.

[1] Job xxxviii. 11.

21. Take heed, beloved, that his many blessings be not turned into condemnation to us all. (For thus it will surely be) unless we walk worthy of him, and with one consent do that which is good and well-pleasing in his sight. For he saith in a certain place, "The Spirit of the Lord is a candle, searching out the inward parts of the belly."[u] Let us consider how near he is, and that none of our thoughts or reasonings which we frame within ourselves are hid from him. It is therefore just that we should not desert our ranks, (by declining) from his will. Let us choose to offend men, who are foolish and inconsiderate, lifted up, and glorying in the pride of their reasoning, rather than God. Let us reverence our Lord Jesus Christ, whose blood was given for us. Let us honor those who are set over us; let us respect our elders, let us instruct our young men in the discipline and fear of the Lord. Our wives let us direct to that which is good. Let them show forth the lovely habit of purity (in all their conversation) with a sincere affection of meekness. Let them make manifest the government of their tongues by their silence. Let their charity be without partiality,[x] exercised equally to all who religiously fear God. Let our children partake of the instruction of Christ; let them learn of how great avail humility is before God, what power a pure charity hath with him, how excellent and great his fear is, saving such as live in it with holiness and a pure conscience. For he is a searcher of the thoughts and counsels (of the heart): whose breath is in us, and when he pleases, he takes it away.

22. All these things the faith which is in Christ confirms. For he himself, by the Holy Ghost thus speaks to us:[y] "Come, ye children, hearken unto me; I will teach you the fear of the Lord. What man is he that desireth life, and loveth to see good days? Keep thy tongue from evil, and thy lips from speaking guile. Depart from evil, and do good; seek peace, and ensue it. The eyes of the Lord are upon the righteous; and his ears are open unto their prayer. But the face of the Lord is against them that do evil, to cut off the remembrance of them from the earth. The righteous

---

[u] See Prov. xx. 27.   [x] 1 Tim. v. 21.   [y] Ps. xxxiv. 11–17.

cried, and the LORD heard him; and delivered him out of all his troubles." "Many are the plagues of the wicked: but they that trust in the LORD, mercy shall compass them about."[a]

23. Our all-merciful and beneficent Father hath bowels of compassion toward them that fear him; and kindly and lovingly bestows his graces upon such as come to him with a simple mind. Wherefore let us not be double-minded, neither let us have any doubt in our hearts, of his excellent and glorious gifts. Let that be far from us which is written, "Miserable are the double-minded, and those who are doubtful in their hearts;[a] who say, These things have we heard, even from our fathers; and lo, we are grown old, and nothing of them hath happened unto us. O fools! Compare yourselves unto a tree: take the vine, (as an example to you.) First it sheds its leaves; then comes forth the bud, then the leaf, then the flower; after that the unripe grape, and then the perfect fruit." Ye see how, in a little time, the fruit of a tree comes to maturity. Of a truth, yet a little while, and his will shall suddenly be accomplished: the Scripture also bearing witness, "That He shall quickly come, and shall not tarry: and that the LORD shall suddenly come to his temple, even the Holy One, whom ye look for."[b]

24. Let us consider, beloved, how the LORD doth continually show us, that there shall be a future resurrection, of which he hath made our Lord JESUS CHRIST the first fruits, raising him from the dead. Let us contemplate, beloved, the resurrection which is continually taking place. Day and night declare to us a resurrection.[c] The night lies down, the day arises: again, the day departs, and the night comes on. Let us behold the fruits (of the earth). Every one sees how the seed is sown. The sower goes forth, and casts it upon the earth, and the seed which, when it was sown, fell upon the earth dry and naked, in time is dissolved; and from this dissolution the mighty power of the providence of the LORD raises it, and out of one seed many arise and bring forth fruit.

---

[a] Ps. xxxii. 10.   [a] James i. 8.   [b] Hab. ii. 3. Mal. iii. 1.
[c] See TERTULLIAN, *Apology*, chap. 48.

25. Let us consider that wonderful sign, which occurs in the regions of the East, in Arabia. There is a certain bird, called a Phœnix.[d] It is the only individual of its kind, and lives five hundred years. When the time of its dissolution draws near, that it must die, it makes itself a nest of frankincense, and myrrh, and other spices, into which, when its time is fulfilled, it enters, and dies. But as the body decays, a certain kind of worm is produced, which nourished by the juices of the dead bird, puts forth feathers. And when it is at length grown to a perfect state, it takes up the nest in which the bones of its parent lie, and carries it from Arabia into Egypt, to the city called Heliopolis; and, in open day, flying in the sight of all men, places them upon the altar of the sun, and, having done this, hastens back to his abode. The priests, then, search the records of the time, and find that it hath come at the completion of the five hundredth year.

26. Shall we then think it to be any very great and strange thing, for the Maker of all things to raise up those that religiously serve him in the assurance of a good faith, when even by a bird he shows us the greatness of his (power to fulfil his) promise. For he saith in a certain place, "Thou shalt raise me up, and I shall confess unto thee." And again, "I laid me down and slept, and awaked, because thou art with me."[e] And

---

[d] The application, which CLEMENT here makes of the supposed history of the Phœnix, has given rise to more discussion than the question deserves. He was not likely to be better informed upon a fact of natural history, than his contemporaries, TACITUS and PLINY: (TACITUS, *Annal.* vi. 28. PLINIUS, *Hist. Nat.* x. 2.) Historians, from HERODOTUS, (ii. 73,) downward, have related particulars of this imaginary bird, with circumstances more or less fanciful: and CLEMENT might, without impropriety, employ an illustration founded upon an alleged fact, which was generally credited in the age in which he lived: his object being, not to prove the *fact* of the resurrection, but to show that it is possible. TERTULLIAN, AMBROSE, (*De fide Resurrect.* c. 8,) and many other Christian writers allude to the phœnix in the same manner. See JUNIUS' note on Clem. Rom. It does not appear that CLEMENT applied to the *phœnix* what is said of the *palm-tree*, Ps. xcii. 12. Job xxix. 18;—as TERTULLIAN (*De Resurrect. Carnis*, c. 13,) and others did, being misled by the circumstance that, in the Greek translation, the same word, φοίνιξ, expressed both. Compare TERTULLIAN, *Apol.* c. 48. *De Resurrect. Carnis*, c. 12. THEOPHILUS *ad Autolycum*, Lib. i. p. 77, D. See PEARSON *on the Creed*, Art. XI. p. 376.

[e] Ps. iii. 5.

again Job saith, "Thou shalt raise up this my flesh, which hath suffered all these things."ᶠ

27. Having therefore this hope, let us hold fast to him who is faithful in his promises, and righteous in his judgments. He who hath commanded us not to lie, much more will he not himself lie. For nothing is impossible with GOD,ᵍ but to lie.ʰ Let his faith therefore be stirred up again in us, and let us consider that all things are near unto him. By the word of his power he made all things; and by his word he is able to destroy them. Who shall say unto him, What hast thou done? or who shall resist the power of his might?ⁱ He hath done all things when he pleased, and as he pleased; and nothing shall pass away of all that hath been determined by him. All things are open before him, and nothing is hid from his counsel. "The heavens declare the glory of GOD, and the firmament showeth his handy work. Day unto day uttereth speech, and night unto night showeth knowledge. There is no speech nor language where their voices are not heard."ᵏ

28. Since, then, all things are seen and heard (by GOD), let us fear him, and lay aside the wicked works which proceed from impure desires, that through his mercy we may be delivered from the condemnation which is to come. For whither can any of us escape from his mighty hand? Or what world shall receive any of those who flee from him? For thus saith the Scripture in a certain place: "Whither shall I flee, or where shall I hide myself from thy presence? If I go up to heaven, thou art there; if I go to the uttermost parts of the earth, there is thy right hand. If I shall make my bed in the deep, there is thy spirit." ˡ Whither then shall any one go, or whither shall he flee from Him who comprehends all things in himself.

29. Let us therefore come to him with holiness of mind, lifting up pure and undefiled hands unto him:ᵐ loving our gracious and merciful Father, who hath made us partakers of his election. For thus it is written,ⁿ

ᶠ Job xix. 26. ᵍ Mark x. 27. ʰ Heb. vi. 18.
ⁱ Wisd. xii. 12. ᵏ Ps. xix. 1, 2, 3. ˡ Ps. cxxxix. 7.
ᵐ 1 Tim. ii. 8. ⁿ Deut. xxxii. 8, 9. Septuagint.

"When the most High divided the nations, when he separated the sons of Adam, he set the bounds of the nations according to the number of his angels. His people Jacob became the portion of the LORD, and Israel the lot of his inheritance." And in another place he saith, "Behold the LORD taketh unto himself a nation from the midst of the nations, as a man taketh the first-fruits of his flour; and the most Holy shall come out of that nation."

30. Wherefore we being a part of the Holy One, let us do all things which pertain unto holiness, fleeing all evil-speaking against one another, all filthy and impure embraces, together with all drunkenness, youthful lusts, abominable concupiscence, detestable adultery, and execrable pride. "For GOD," saith he, "resisteth the proud, but giveth grace unto the humble." Let us therefore cleave to those to whom GOD hath given his grace. And let us be clothed with concord, humble-minded, temperate, free from all whispering and detraction, justified by our actions not by our words. For he saith, "He that speaketh much, shall hear much in answer. Doth he who is of fair speech count himself righteous? Doth he that is born of woman and liveth but a few days think himself blessed? Be not a man of many words." Let our praise be of GOD, not of ourselves. For those that praise themselves GOD hates. Let the testimony of our good works be given by others, as it was given to the holy men, our fathers. Boldness, and arrogance, and confidence belong to them who are accursed of GOD: but moderation, and humility and meekness to those who are blessed by him.

31. Let us then lay hold on his blessing, and consider by what means we may attain unto it. Let us revolve in our minds those things which have happened from the beginning. Wherefore was our father Abraham blessed? Was it not that through faith he wrought righteousness and truth? Isaac, being fully persuaded of that which he knew was to come, cheerfully yielded

---

* Deut. iv. 34.   p Greek, 'the holy of holies.'
q James iv. 6.   1 Pet. v. 5.   r Job xi. 2, 3. Septuagint.
s Greek, 'Be not much in words.'

himself up for a sacrifice.[t] Jacob with humility departed out of his own country, fleeing from his brother, and went unto Laban, and served him: and so the sceptre of the twelve tribes of Israel was given unto him.

32. Whoever will carefully consider each particular, will understand the greatness of the gifts, which were given through him. For from him came all the priests and Levites, who ministered at the altar of GOD. From him came our Lord JESUS CHRIST, according to the flesh.[u] From him came the kings and princes and rulers in Judah. And the rest of his tribes were in no small glory; since GOD had promised, "Thy seed shall be as the stars of heaven."[x] They were all, therefore, glorified and magnified, not for their own sake or for their works, or for the righteous deeds which they had done, but through his will. And we also, being called by his will in CHRIST JESUS, are not justified by ourselves, neither by our own wisdom, or knowledge, or piety, or the works which we have done in holiness of heart; but by that faith by which ALMIGHTY GOD hath justified all men from the beginning: to whom be glory for ever and ever; Amen.

33. What shall we do, then, brethren? Shall we grow weary in well-doing, and lay aside charity? GOD forbid that any such thing should be done by us. Rather let us hasten with all earnestness and readiness of mind to perfect every good work. For even the Creator and LORD of all things himself rejoices in his own works. For by his almighty power he established the heavens; and by his incomprehensible wisdom he adorned them. He also divided the earth from the water which encompasses it, and fixed it as a firm tower, upon the foundation of his own will. By his appointment also he commanded all the living creatures, that are upon it, to exist. He created the sea and all the creatures that are therein, and by his power enclosed them within their proper bounds. Above all, with his holy and

---

[t] This assertion may appear to disagree with Gen. xxii. 7. The faith of Isaac in blessing "Jacob and Esau concerning things to come," is commemorated, Heb. xi. 20.—CHRYSOSTOM, in his 47th Homily on Genesis, notices the willing obedience of Isaac.

[u] Rom. ix. 5.   [x] Gen. xv. 5; xxii. 17; xxviii. 14.

pure hands, he formed man, the most excellent of his creatures, and the greatest, as endowed with reason; the impress of his own image. For thus GOD saith: "Let us make man after our image and likeness."ʸ So GOD made man, male and female created he them. Having thus furnished all these things, he pronounced them good, and blessed them, and said, Be fruitful and multiply.ᶻ We see how all righteous men have been adorned with good works. Wherefore even the LORD himself, having adorned himself with his works, rejoiced. Having therefore such an example, let us diligently fulfil his will: and with all our strength work the work of righteousness.

34. The good workman receives with confidence the bread of his labor: the idle and negligent cannot look his employer in the face. We must therefore be ready and active in well-doing; for from him are all things. And thus he foretells us: "Behold the LORD cometh, and his reward is before his face, to render to every man according to his work."ᵃ He warns us therefore beforehand with all his heart to this end, that we should not be slothful and negligent in well-doing.ᵇ Let our boasting and our confidence be in GOD. Let us submit ourselves to his will. Let us consider the whole multitude of his angels, how ready they stand to minister unto his will. For the Scripture saith, "Ten thousand times ten thousand stood before him, and thousands of thousands ministered unto him. And they cried, saying, Holy, holy, holy, is the LORD of Sabaoth; all creation is full of his glory."ᶜ Wherefore let us also, being conscientiously gathered together in concord with one another, as with one mouth cry earnestly unto him, that we may be partakers of his great and glorious promises. For he saith; "Eye hath not seen, nor ear heard, neither have entered into the heart of man the things which he hath prepared for them that wait for him."ᵈ

35. How blessed and wonderful, beloved, are the gifts of GOD! Life in immortality! brightness in righte-

---

ʸ Gen. i. 26, 27.   ᶻ Gen. i. 28.
ᵃ Isa. xl. 10; lxii. 11.   Rev. xxii. 11.
ᵇ Gal. vi. 9.   2 Thes. iii. 13.   ᶜ Dan. vii. 10.   Isa. vi. 3.
ᵈ 1 Cor. ii. 9.   Isa. lxiv. 4.

ousness! truth in full assurance! faith in confidence! temperance in holiness! And all these hath God subjected to our understandings. What therefore shall those things be which he hath prepared for them that wait for him? The Creator and Father of the worlds,* the most Holy, He (only) knows both the greatness and beauty of them. Let us therefore strive with all earnestness, that we may be found in the number of those that wait for him, that we may receive the gifts which he hath promised. And how shall this be, beloved? by fixing our minds through faith toward God, and seeking the things which are pleasing and acceptable unto him: by acting conformably to his holy will; and following the way of truth, casting away from us all unrighteousness and iniquity, covetousness, strife, evil manners, deceit, whispering, detraction; all hatred of God, pride and boasting, vain-glory and ambition.[f] For they that do these things are hateful to God; and not only they that do them, but also all such as have pleasure in them that do them.[g] For the Scripture saith,[h] "But to the ungodly said God, Why dost thou preach my laws, and takest my covenant in thy mouth; whereas thou hatest to be reformed, and hast cast my words behind thee. If thou sawest a thief, thou didst run with him, and with the adulterers thou didst cast in thy lot. Thy mouth abounded in wickedness, and thy tongue contrived deceit. Thou satest, and spakest against thy brother and hast slandered thine own mother's son. These things hast thou done, and I held my tongue, and thou thoughtest wickedly that I should be like unto thee. But I will reprove thee, and set thyself before thee. Consider, then, this, ye that forget God, lest he tear thee in pieces, like a lion, and there be none to deliver you. The sacrifice of praise, that shall honor me; and there is the way, by which I will show to him the salvation of God."

36. This is the way, beloved, in which we find the means of our salvation, JESUS CHRIST, the high-priest of all our offerings, the defender and helper of our weakness. By him we look up to the highest heavens,

* τῶν αἰώνων.
[f] 2 Cor. xii. 20. Rom. i. 29.
[g] Rom. i. 32.
[h] Ps. l. 16–23. Septuagint.

and behold, as in a glass, his spotless and most excellent countenance. By him are the eyes of our hearts opened; by him our foolish and darkened understanding rejoices (to behold) his wonderful light. By him would God have us to taste the knowledge of immortality, "Who being the brightness of his glory, is by so much greater than the angels, as he hath by inheritance obtained a more excellent name than they."¹ For so it is written, "Who maketh his angel spirits, and his ministers a flame of fire."ᵏ "But to his Son, thus saith the Lord, Thou art my Son, this day have I begotten thee. Ask of me, and I will give thee the heathen for thine inheritance, and the utmost parts of the earth for thy possession."ˡ And again he saith unto him, "Sit thou on my right hand, until I make thine enemies thy footstool."ᵐ And who then are his enemies? the wicked, and such as oppose their own wills to the will of God.

37. Let us, therefore, wage (our heavenly) warfare, men and brethren, with all earnestness according to his holy commands. Let us consider those who fight under our (earthly) governors, how orderly, how readily, how obediently they perform the commands which each receives. All are not captains of the host, all are not commanders of a thousand, nor of a hundred, nor of fifty, nor the like. But each one, in his respective rank, performs what is commanded him by the King, and those who are in authority. They who are great cannot subsist without those who are small; nor the small without the great. There must be a mixture in all things, and hence arises their use. Let us take our body as an example.ⁿ The head without the feet is nothing: so neither the feet without the head: and the smallest members of our body are necessary, and useful to the whole body. But all conspire together, and are subject to one common use, the preservation of the whole body.

38. Let, therefore, our whole body be saved in Christ Jesus; and let each one be subject to his neighbor,º according to the order in which he is placed

---

ⁱ Heb. i. 2, 3.   ᵏ Ps. civ. 4.   Heb. i. 7.   ˡ Ps. ii. 7, 8.
ᵐ Ps. cx. 1. Heb. i. 13.   ⁿ 1 Cor. xii. 13.   º 1 Pet. v. 5. Eph. v. 21.

by the gift of God. Let not the strong man despise the weak; and let the weak reverence the strong. Let the rich man distribute to the necessities of the poor; and let the poor bless God, that he hath given him one by whom his want may be supplied. Let the wise man show forth his wisdom, not in words, but in good works. Let him that is of humble mind not bear witness to himself, but leave it to another to bear witness of him. Let him, that is pure in the flesh, glory not therein, knowing that it was another who gave him the gift of continence. Let us consider, therefore, brethren, whereof we are made; who, and what manner of beings, we came into this world, as it were out of a sepulchre, and darkness. He, who made us and formed us, brought us into his own world. He prepared his benefits for us, even before we were born. Having, therefore, received all these blessings from him, we ought in every thing to give thanks unto him: to whom be glory for ever and ever; Amen.

39. Foolish and unwise men, who have neither prudence nor learning, may mock and deride us, wishing to set up themselves in their own conceits. But what can mortal man do? or what strength is there in him that is made of the dust? For it is written,[p] "There was no shape before mine eyes; only I heard a sound and a voice. For what? shall man be pure before the Lord? shall he be blameless in his works, if He trusteth not in his servants, and hath charged his angels with folly? Yea the heaven is not clean in his sight. How much less they that dwell in houses of clay; of which also we ourselves were made. He smote them as a moth; and from morning even unto the evening they endure not. Because they were not able to help themselves, they perished. He breathed upon them, and they died; because they had no wisdom. Call now, if there be any that will answer thee: and if thou wilt look to any of the angels. For wrath killeth the foolish man; and envy slayeth him that is in error. I have seen the foolish taking root, but lo their habitation was presently consumed. Be their children far from safety;

---

[p] Job iv. 16; xv. 15; iv. 19.

may they perish at the gates of those who are less than themselves; and let there be no man to deliver them. For what was prepared for them, the righteous shall eat! and they shall not be delivered from evil."

40. Seeing, then, that these things are manifest unto us, we ought to take heed, that, looking into the depths of divine knowledge, we do all things in order, whatsoever our LORD hath commanded us to do. That we perform our offerings [q] and service to GOD, at their appointed seasons; for these he hath commanded to be done not rashly and disorderly, but at certain determinate times and hours. He hath himself ordained by his supreme will both where and by what persons they are to be performed, that all things being piously done unto all well-pleasing, they may be acceptable unto his will. They therefore who make their oblations at the appointed seasons are accepted and happy: for they sin not, inasmuch as they obey the commandments of the LORD. For to the chief-priest his peculiar offices are given, and to the priests their own place is appointed, and to the Levites appertain their proper min-

---

[q] In the early ages of the Church there was not only a pecuniary collection made every Lord's day, for the benefit of the poor, in compliance with the command of St. Paul, 1 Cor. xvi. 1, 2, but certain *offerings* were placed upon the holy table by the minister. This was done, after the service of the Catechumens, and before the service of the faithful began. JUSTIN MARTYR speaks of them in his *First Apology*, Sect. 16 and 87. IRENÆUS, *Adv. Hæres.* iv. 32, says, "The LORD gave his disciples command to offer unto GOD the first-fruits of his creatures, not as if he needed them, but that they themselves might be neither unfruitful nor ungrateful. He took that which by its created nature was bread, and gave thanks, saying, This is my body. In like manner also he declared that, which by its present created nature is the cup, to be his blood: and taught them to make a new offering of the New Testament."

Hence the term oblation, προσφορά, is frequently used for the celebration of the Eucharist itself; and sometimes for the offerings thus made. Every one made these offerings, according to his ability, as the first-fruits of his increase. They were applied to the general uses of the Church, to the support of the ministry and of the poor. The common entertainment, or feast of love, in which the rich and the poor met together at the same table, either before, or soon after the celebration of the Holy Sacrament, was probably furnished from this source.

In reference to these offerings, bishops are described, in this Epistle, c. 44, as those who "offer the gifts."

istries. And the layman[r] is confined within the bounds of what is commanded to laymen.

41. Let every one of you, brethren, bless GOD, in his proper station, with a good conscience, and with all gravity, not exceeding the rule of his service that is appointed to him. The daily sacrifices are not offered every where, nor the peace-offerings, nor the sacrifices appointed for sins and transgressions, but only in Jerusalem. And even there, they are not offered in every place, but only at the altar before the temple: that which is offered being first diligently examined [s] by the high-priest, and the other ministers before mentioned. They, then, who do any thing which is not agreeable to his will, are punished with death. Consider, brethren, that the greater the knowledge is, which hath been vouchsafed to us, the greater is the danger to which we are exposed.

42. The apostles have preached to us from our Lord JESUS CHRIST: JESUS CHRIST from GOD. CHRIST therefore was sent by GOD; and the apostles by CHRIST. Thus both were orderly sent according to the will of GOD. For having received their command, and being thoroughly assured by the resurrection of our Lord JESUS CHRIST,[t] and convinced by the word of GOD, with the fulness of the HOLY SPIRIT, they went forth, proclaiming, that the kingdom of GOD was at hand. And thus preaching through countries and cities, they appointed

---

[r] ὁ λαϊκὸς ἄνθρωπος.

There are no instances, among the few remains of the writings of the Hellenistic Jews, in which the priests and Levites are called κλῆρος and κληρικοί, as distinguished from the rest of the people, λαϊκοί. The word λαϊκὸς is used, however, in Hellenistic Greek, to indicate that which is not consecrated; as 1 Sam. xxi. 4, ἄρτοι λαϊκοί implies "common bread," in contradistinction to "hallowed bread," in Aquila, Symmachus, and Theodotion. And in Ezek. xlviii. 15, Symmachus and Theodotion have λαϊκὸν where Aquila has βέβηλον. LE CLERC mentions these and several other instances, in which this word, and even λαϊκόω, are used in a corresponding sense.

CLEMENT here uses the word λαϊκὸς in a manner which shows that the distinction between the clergy and the laity was familiar to him.

[s] Μωμοσκοπηθέν. This word was used to signify peculiarly the strict examination to which victims were subjected, both under the Jewish law and by the customs of the Gentiles. See POLYCARP's *Epistle*, Sect. 4.

[t] 1 Thes. i. 5.

the first fruits (of their conversions) to be bishops and ministers over such as should afterward believe, having first proved them by the Spirit. Nor was this any new thing: seeing that long before it was written concerning bishops and deacons. For thus saith the Scripture in a certain place, "I will appoint their overseers[u] in righteousness, and their ministers[x] in faith."[y]

43. And what wonder, if they to whom such a work was committed by GOD in CHRIST, established such an order of men, as hath been mentioned, since even Moses, that happy and faithful servant in all his house,[z] set down in the holy Scriptures all things that were commanded him. Whom also all the other prophets followed, bearing witness with one consent to what was written by him in the law. For when a strife arose concerning the priesthood, and the tribes contended which of them should be adorned with that glorious name, he commanded their twelve captains to bring him rods, inscribed each according to the name of its tribe. And he took and bound them, and sealed them with the seals of the twelve princes of the tribes, and laid them up in the tabernacle of witness, upon the table of GOD. And when he had shut (the door of) the tabernacle, he sealed up the keys of it, in like manner as he had sealed the rods: and said unto them, Men and brethren; whichsoever tribe shall have its rod blossom, that tribe hath GOD chosen, to be priests and ministers before him. And when the morning was come, he called together all Israel, six hundred thousand men, and he showed the seals to the princes of the tribes, and opened the tabernacle of witness, and brought forth the rods. And the rod of Aaron was found not only to have blossomed, but also to have brought forth fruit.[a] What think ye, beloved? Did not Moses know beforehand, that thus it would be? Yes, verily. But that there might be no division nor tumult in Israel, he did in this manner, that the name of the true and only GOD might be glorified: to him be honor for ever and ever; Amen.

---

[u] ἐπισκόπους. [x] διακόνους.
[y] See Isa. lx. 17.   [z] Heb. iii. 2. Num. xii. 7.
[a] Num. xvii.

44. So likewise our apostles knew by our Lord JESUS CHRIST, that contentions should arise on account of the ministry. And therefore, having a perfect foreknowledge of this, they appointed persons as we have before said, and then gave a direction[b] in what manner, when they should die, other chosen and approved men should succeed in their ministry. Wherefore, we cannot think that those may justly be thrown out of their ministry, who were appointed by them, or afterward chosen by other eminent men, with the consent of the whole Church,[*] and who have with all lowliness and innocency ministered to the flock of CHRIST in peace, and without self-interest, and have been for a long time commended by all. For it would be no small sin in us, should we cast off those from the ministry, who holily and without blame

---

[b] ἐπινομή. JUNIUS conceives this word to imply a description of the duties attached to each office; SALMASIUS renders it, "a precept;" Archbishop USHER, "a prescribed order;" MARCA, "a form;" HAMMOND gives it the sense of "a catalogue, or a series and order of succession." LE CLERC imagines the meaning of Clement to be, that the apostles not only appointed the first bishops, but selected, from the whole body of the Church, those who should succeed them.

[*] A clear intimation is here given of the different parts which the clergy and people took in the ordination of a bishop. The first appointment rested with the apostles and bishops, but the consent of the people was necessary. CYPRIAN, *Epist.* lxviii. plainly shows that this was the case. "In compliance with divine tradition and apostolical usage, the custom must diligently be observed and maintained, which is established among us and in almost all other provinces; that, for the due celebration of ordinations, the bishops of all the adjoining provinces are to repair to the people, over whom a bishop is to be ordained; and then a bishop shall be chosen, in the presence of the people, who have had the fullest knowledge of the life of each one, and been thoroughly acquainted with their manners and whole conversation." In his lvth Epistle he says also, "(Cornelius) was ordained bishop by many of our colleagues who were there present in Rome: he was ordained bishop by the judgment of GOD and of CHRIST, by the testimony of almost all the clergy, with the assent of the people who were there present, and by the assembly of ancient priests and holy men."

ORIGEN, in his 6th *Homily upon Leviticus,* says, "That the presence of the people is necessary in the ordination of a bishop, that all may know and be well assured, that he who is chosen to that office is distinguished among all the people for his pre-eminence in learning, and holiness, and a virtuous life: and this is done in the presence of the people, that there may be no room for mistake or objection."

Bishop FELL, who gives two of these references, shows, in his note, how exactly this primitive usage agrees with the custom of the Church of England.

fulfil the duties [d] of it. Blessed are those priests, who having finished their course before these times, have obtained a fruitful and perfect dissolution. For they have no fear lest any one should remove them from the place appointed for them. But we see how you have put out some, who conducted themselves well, from the ministry which by their innocence they had adorned.

45. Ye are contentious, brethren, and zealous for things which pertain not unto salvation. Look into the holy Scriptures, which are the true words of the HOLY GHOST. Ye know that nothing unjust or counterfeit is written in them. There you shall not find that righteous men were ever cast off by those who were holy themselves. The just were persecuted; but it was by the unjust: they were cast into prison; but it was by the unholy: they were stoned; but it was by transgressors: they were slain; but it was by the wicked, and by such as had taken up unjust envy against them. All these sufferings they endured gloriously. For what shall we say, brethren? Was it by those who feared GOD that Daniel was cast into the den of lions? Was it by men, who worshipped the most High with excellent and glorious worship, that Ananias, Asarias, and Misael, were shut up in the fiery furnace? GOD forbid. What manner of men, therefore, were they who did these things? they were men abominable, full of all wickedness: men so incensed as to afflict those who served GOD with a holy and unblameable purpose of mind: knowing not that the most High is the protector and defender of all those who with a pure conscience serve his holy name: to whom be glory for ever and ever; Amen. And they who in the fulness of faith have endured, are become inheritors of glory and honor; and are exalted and lifted up by GOD in their memorial for ever and ever; Amen.

46. It is, therefore, brethren our duty to cleave to such examples as these. For it is written "Hold fast to such as are holy; for they that do so shall be sanc-

---

[d] προσενέγκοντας τὰ δῶρα, offering the gifts. See note on Sect. 40. The Eucharist itself was also styled "munus consecratum," "munera sancta," "ἡ μυστικὴ δωροφορία," and by the Ethiopians, expressly, 'Corban,' that is to say, a *gift*; Mark vii. 11.

tified."[e] And again in another place he saith, "With the pure thou shalt be pure, and with the elect thou shalt be elect, but with the perverse man thou shalt be perverse."[f] Let us therefore cleave to the innocent and righteous; for such are the elect of God. Wherefore are there strifes, and anger, and divisions, and schisms, and wars among us? Have we not all one God, and one CHRIST?[g] Is not one Spirit of grace poured upon us all? Have we not one calling in CHRIST? Wherefore, then, do we rend and tear in pieces the members of CHRIST: and raise seditions against our own body? And are come to such a height of madness, as to forget that "we are members one of another."[h] Remember the words of our Lord JESUS. For he said;[i] "Wo to that man (by whom offences come): it were better for him that he had never been born, than that he should have offended one of mine elect. It were better for him, that a millstone should be hanged about his neck, and he should be cast into the sea, than that he should offend one of my little ones." Your schism hath perverted many, hath discouraged many: it hath thrown many into doubt, and all of us into grief. And yet your sedition continues to prevail.

47. Take into your hands the epistle of the blessed Paul the apostle. What did he first write to you at the beginning of the Gospel.[k] Verily he did by the Spirit admonish you concerning himself, and Cephas, and

---

[e] See Wisd. vi. 25. 1 Cor. vii. 14. [f] Ps. xviii. 26.
[g] Eph. iv. 4. 1 Cor. xii. [h] Rom. xii. 5.
[i] Matt. xxvi. 24. Mark ix. 42. Luke xvii. 2. Matt. xviii. 6.
[k] The phrase, "in the beginning of the Gospel," which is used by St. Paul, Phil. iv. 15, denotes either the period when the Gospel was first preached, or the time when it was first made known to any particular Church. The Corinthian Church is here, then, called ancient, as having been founded in the first ages of the Christian religion. The Churches which were first established, were always held in the highest honor. Thus, IRENÆUS, Adv. Hæres. iii. 3, eulogizes the Church of Rome, as "the greatest and most ancient and well known Church, founded and established by the two most glorious apostles, Peter and Paul." TERTULLIAN, de Virginibus Velandis, c. 2, describes the apostolic Churches, as those "which were avowedly founded by the apostles, which ascribed their origin to one of the apostles: which were taught by them; and to which any Epistles of the apostles were addressed." See TERTULLIAN, Præscrip. Hæret. 32. Adv. Marcion. iv. 5.—COTELERIUS.

Apollos,[1] because that even then ye had formed parties, and divisions among yourselves. Nevertheless your partiality then led you into less sin. For you were favorably inclined toward apostles, men of eminent reputation in the Church ; and toward another who had been approved of by them. But consider, who they are that have now led you astray, and lessened the reputation of that brotherly love which was so celebrated among you. It is shameful, beloved, it is exceedingly shameful, and unworthy of your Christian profession, to hear, that the most firm and ancient Church of the Corinthians, should by one or two persons be led into a sedition against its priests. And this report is come, not only unto us, but to those also whose minds are unfavorably affected toward us. Insomuch that the name of the LORD is blasphemed through your folly; and ye yourselves are brought into danger by it.

48. Let us, therefore, with all haste take away this cause of offence ; and let us fall down before the LORD, and beseech him with tears, that he would be favorably reconciled to us, and restore us again to a grave and holy course of brotherly love. For this is the gate of righteousness, opening into everlasting life: as it is written, "Open to me the gates of righteousness; I will go in unto them and praise the LORD. This is the gate of the LORD: the righteous shall enter into it."[m] Although, therefore, many gates are opened, yet this gate, which is in righteousness, the same is that gate in CHRIST, into which blessed are all they that enter, and direct their way in holiness and righteousness, doing all things without disorder. Let a man be faithful; let him be powerful in the utterance of knowledge ; let him be wise in making an exact judgment of words ; let him be pure in all his actions: still, he ought to be so much the more humble-minded as he seems to be superior to others ; and to seek that which is profitable to all men, and not his own advantage.

49. He that hath the love that is in CHRIST, let him keep the commandments of CHRIST. Who is able to express the obligation of the love of GOD ? What man is sufficiently worthy to declare the excellency of its

---

[1] 1 Cor. i. 12.   [m] Ps. cxviii. 19, 20.

beauty? The height to which charity leads is inexpressible. Charity unites us to God: charity "covereth the multitude of sins:"[a] "charity endureth all things;"[o] is long-suffering in all things. There is nothing sordid in charity, nothing proud. Charity hath no schism; charity is not seditious; charity doth all things in peace and concord. In charity were all the elect of God made perfect; without charity nothing is well-pleasing to God. In charity did the Lord take us to himself: through the love which he bare toward us, Christ our Lord gave his blood for us, by the will of God: and his flesh for our flesh: and his soul for our souls.[p]

50. Ye see, beloved, how great and wonderful charity is: and its perfection cannot be expressed. Who is fit to be found in it, except those whom God shall vouchsafe to make so? Let us therefore pray to him and beseech him, that we may be worthy of it: that we may live in charity, without human partiality, unblameable. All generations from Adam until this day have passed away: but they who have been made perfect in love, according to the grace of Christ, have a place among the righteous, and shall be made manifest in the judgment of the kingdom of Christ. For it is written, "Enter into thy chamber for a little space, until mine anger and indignation shall pass away.[q] And I will remember the good day, and will raise you up out of your graves." Happy, then, are we, beloved, if we shall have performed the commandments of God in the unity of love, that so, through love, our sins may be forgiven us. For so it is written; "Blessed are they whose iniquities are forgiven, and whose sin is covered. Blessed is the man to whom the Lord imputeth no sin, and in whose mouth there is no guile."[r] This blessing is upon those who are chosen of God, through Jesus

---

[a] 1 Pet. iv. 8. [o] 1 Cor. xiii. 7.

[p] τὴν ψυχὴν ὑπὲρ τῶν ψυχῶν ἡμῶν. Irenæus, Lib. v. 1, uses the same expression: "The Lord, therefore, having redeemed us by his own blood, and having given his soul for our souls, and his flesh for our flesh, and having poured forth the Spirit of the Father, for the purpose of uniting God and man."

[q] Isa. xxvi. 20. [r] Ps. xxxii. 1.

Christ our Lord; to whom be glory for ever and ever; Amen.

51. Let us, therefore, as many as have transgressed by any of the suggestions of the adversary, pray for forgiveness: and let those, who have been the leaders of the sedition and dissension among you, look to the common object of our hope. For as many as have their conversation in fear and charity, would rather they themselves should fall into trials than their neighbors: and choose to be condemned themselves, rather than to violate that good and equitable concord which hath been transmitted to us. For it is good for a man to confess wherein he hath transgressed, rather than to harden his heart, as the hearts of those were hardened, who raised up sedition against Moses the servant of God: whose punishment was manifest to all men; for they went down alive into the grave; death swallowed them up.* Pharaoh and his host,ᵗ and all the rulers of Egypt, their chariots also and their horsemen, were overwhelmed in the Red Sea and perished, for no other reason than because they hardened their foolish hearts, after so many signs had been done in the land of Egypt, by Moses the servant of God.

52. Beloved, the Lord is in want of nothing: neither requires he any thing of us, but that we should confess our sins unto him. For so saith the holy David: "I will confess unto the Lord, and it shall please him better than a young bullock, that hath horns and hoofs. Let the poor see it, and be glad."ᵘ And again he saith, "Offer unto God the sacrifice of praise; and pay thy vows unto the most Highest. And call upon me in the day of trouble, and I will deliver thee, and thou shalt glorify me."ˣ "The sacrifice of God is a broken spirit."ʸ

53. Ye know, beloved, ye know full well the holy Scriptures; and have thoroughly searched into the oracles of God. Call them, therefore, to your remembrance. For when Moses went up into the mount, and tarried there forty days and forty nights, in fasting and humiliation, God said unto him,ᶻ "Arise, Moses, get

---

* Num. xvi.   ᵗ Exod. xiv.   ᵘ Ps. lxix. 31.   ˣ Ps. l. 14.
ʸ Ps. li. 17.   ᶻ Exod. xxxii. Deut. ix. 12.

thee down quickly from hence, for thy people have committed wickedness: they whom thou hast brought out of the land of Egypt have quickly turned aside from the way which I commanded them, and have made to themselves molten images. And the LORD said unto him, I have spoken unto thee once and again, saying, I have seen this people, and behold it is a stiff-necked people. Let me therefore destroy them, and I will blot out their name from under heaven, and I will make of thee a nation mighty and wonderful, and much greater than they. But Moses said, not so, LORD: forgive now this people their sin; and if not, blot me also out of the book of the living." O admirable charity! O insuperable perfection! The servant speaks boldly to his LORD; he beseeches him either to forgive the people, or that he himself may also be destroyed with them.

54. Who, then, is there among you that is generous? who, that is compassionate? who, that is filled with charity? let him say, if this sedition, and strife and schism be upon my account,* I am ready to depart, to go away whithersoever ye please; and to do whatso-

---

* CLEMENT here professes* no more than he practised. It is highly probable, as EPIPHANIUS asserts, that he was appointed, by St. Peter, to be Bishop of Rome, but declined accepting the office as long as Linus and Cletus (or Anencletus) lived. This seems the most probable cause of the difficulty of ascertaining the succession of the first bishops of Rome.

CHRYSOSTOM, in his 11th *Homily on the Epistle to the Ephesians*, (Vol. iii. p. 824. Savile.) expresses his readiness to act up to this precept; "If you entertain," he says, "such suspicions respecting me, I am ready to resign my office, and to retire whithersoever ye will, only so that the unity of the Church may be preserved."

GREGORY NAZIANZEN actually resigned the see of Constantinople, rather than be the cause of disputes in the Church. See CAVE's *Life* [of Gregory.] Sect 6.

* [What does Clement *profess*? The probability of his *practice* of the resignation of a bishopric, is extremely slight—scarcely any; as will be apparent if the value of EPIPHANIUS' single testimony to an event so far removed from his own knowledge be duly estimated, and placed in counterpoise with the discrepant accounts of earlier and more trustworthy writers.—But it is astonishing that this passage should have been thought to bear on the question, when the least attention to the context might suffice to convince the reader that Clement has not the slightest reference to himself in his *recommendations* for others; and that those recommendations (being addressed distributively to members of a Church which could have had *but one* bishop) were adapted to the circumstances of persons filling inferior office in the Church, not to the different obligations and responsibilities of *a bishop*.]

ever the multitude command me; only let the flock of CHRIST be in peace, with the elders that are set over it. He that shall do this, shall obtain to himself a very great honor in the LORD: and every place will be ready to receive him. "For the earth is the LORD's, and the fulness thereof.' [b] These things they who have their conversation toward GOD not to be repented of, both have done, and will always be ready to do.

55. Nay, to produce examples even of the Gentiles: many kings and rulers, in times of pestilence, being warned by their oracles, have given themselves up to death, that they might, by their own blood, deliver their country. Many have forsaken their cities, that seditions might no longer continue. We know how many[c] among ourselves have given themselves up into bonds that thereby they might free others. Many have sold themselves into bondage, and received the price, that with it they might feed others. Nay, even women, strengthened by the grace of GOD, have performed many manly actions. The blessed Judith,[d] when her city was besieged, desired the elders that they would suffer her to go into the camp of their enemies. Thus she went out, and exposed herself to danger for the love she bare to her country, and her people that were besieged: and the LORD delivered Holofernes into the hand of a woman. Again, Esther,[e] being made perfect in the faith, exposed herself to a danger equally great, that she might deliver the twelve tribes of Israel, who were in danger of being destroyed. For by fasting and humbling herself she entreated the great maker of all

---

[b] Ps. xxiv. 1.

[c] St. Paul mentions "Priscilla and Aquila, my helpers in CHRIST JESUS, who have for my life laid down their own necks." Rom. xvi. 3, 4, and Epaphroditus, who "for the work of CHRIST was nigh unto death not regarding his life." Phil. ii. 30. BARONIUS relates that St. Alban, the proto-martyr of Britain, gave himself up and was put to death under Diocletian, A. D. 303, instead of a fugitive who had taken refuge from persecution under his roof.

In the early ages of Christianity many, under the designation of *Parabolani*, gave themselves up to the care of the sick, at the peril of their own lives. These were so numerous, that a law was passed to limit their number. *Codex Theodos.* Lib. xvi. Tit. 2. leg. 42. (FELL.)

[d] Judith viii. ix. x. xi.   [e] Esth. vii. viii.

things, the God of the worlds;' so that beholding the humiliation of her soul, he delivered the people, for whose sake she was in peril.

56. Let us, therefore, pray for those who are fallen into any sin; that meekness and humility may be given unto them, so that they may submit not unto us, but unto the will of God. For by these means they shall obtain a fruitful and perfect remembrance, with mercy, both in our prayers to God, and in our mention of them before his saints. Let us receive correction, at which no man ought to repine. Beloved, the admonition which we exercise toward one another is good, and exceedingly profitable: for it unites us the more closely to the will of God. For thus saith the holy Scripture: "The Lord chastened and corrected me; but he did not give me over unto death." ᵍ "For whom the Lord loveth, he chasteneth, and scourge the very son whom he receiveth." ʰ "The righteous," saith he, "shall instruct me in mercy, and reprove me: but let not the oil of sinners anoint my head with its fatness." ⁱ And again he saith, ᵏ "Happy is the man whom God correcteth: but despise not thou the chastening of the Almighty. For he maketh sore, and again restoreth; he woundeth, and his hands make whole. Six times out of trouble he shall deliver thee: yea, in seven there shall no evil touch thee. In famine, he shall redeem thee from death; and in war he shall defend the from the hand of iron. He shall hide thee from the scourge of the tongue: neither shalt thou be afraid of evils when they come. Thou shalt laugh at the wicked and sinners; neither shalt thou be afraid of the beasts of the earth. For the wild beasts shall be at peace with thee. Then shalt thou know that thy house shall be in peace; and the habitation of thy tabernacle shall not err. Thou shalt also know that thy seed shall be great; and thy offspring as all the grass of the field. And thou shalt come to the grave as ripe corn, that is taken in due time, like as a shock of corn cometh in, in its season." Ye see, beloved, that there is a protection to those who are corrected of the Lord. For he is a good instructer; and is

---

ᶠ Θεὸς τῶν αἰώνων.   ᵍ Ps. cxviii. 18.   ʰ Prov. iii. 11.
ⁱ Ps. cxl. 5. Septuagint.   ᵏ Job v. 17.

willing that we should be admonished by his holy discipline.

57. Do ye, therefore, who laid the foundation of the sedition, submit yourselves unto your elders;[1] and be instructed unto repentance, bending the knees of your hearts. Learn to be subject; laying aside all proud and arrogant boasting of your tongues. For it is better for you to be found in the sheep-fold of CHRIST little and approved, than to appear superior to others, and to be cast out of his hope.[m] For thus speaks the excellent and all-virtuous Wisdom,[n] "Behold I will pour out the word of my spirit upon you; I will make known my speech unto you. Because I called, and ye would not hear: I stretched out my words, and ye regarded not: but ye set at nought all my counsel, and disobeyed my reproof; therefore I also will laugh at your calamity, and exult when your desolation cometh; and when trouble cometh suddenly upon you, and destruction as a whirlwind, or when persecution or siege cometh upon you. For it shall come to pass, when ye call upon me, I will not hear you: the wicked shall seek me; but they shall not find me. For they hated knowledge, and did not seek the fear of the LORD: neither would they take heed to my counsels, but laughed my reproofs to scorn. Therefore shall they eat of the fruit of their own ways; and shall be filled with their own wickedness."

---

58. Now GOD, the inspector of all things, the Father of spirits, and the LORD of all flesh,[o] who hath chosen our Lord JESUS CHRIST, and us, by him, to be his peculiar people, grant to every soul of man that calleth upon his glorious and holy name, faith, fear, peace, patience, long-suffering, temperance, holiness, and sobriety, unto all well-pleasing to his name: through our high priest and protector JESUS CHRIST; by whom be glory and majesty, and power, and honor, unto Him now and for evermore. Amen.

---

[1] 1 Pet. v. 5.

[m] ἐκ τῆς ἐλπίδος αὐτοῦ—perhaps we should read ἐκ τῆς ἐπαύλιδος—'out of his fold.'

[n] Prov. i. 23. The book of Proverbs is often quoted by this title, by the early Christian writers.

[o] δεσπότης.

59. The messengers, whom we have sent unto you, Claudius Ephebus, and Valerius Bito, with Fortunatus, send back to us again with all speed in peace and with joy, that they may the sooner acquaint us with your peace and concord, so much prayed for and desired by us; and that we may rejoice in your good order.

60. The grace of our Lord JESUS CHRIST be with you, and with all that are any where called by GOD and through him; to whom be honor and glory, and might and majesty, and eternal dominion, by CHRIST JESUS,[p] from everlasting to everlasting. Amen.

[p] δι οὗ αὐτῷ δόξα. κ. τ. λ.

NOTES

ON THE

EPISTLE OF CLEMENT TO THE CORINTHIANS.

Note A. on § 5. p. 4.

On the Preaching of St. Paul in the West.

This is the earliest account of the preaching of St. Paul, after the close of that part of his history, which is recorded in the Acts of the Apostles. The testimony of Clement, the fellow laborer of St. Paul in the work of the Gospel, (*Phil.* iv. 3.) is very valuable, and proves that at least a part of the Apostle's labors was directed to the West of Europe.

To form a judgment respecting the extent of his travels, it is necessary to consider what time probably elapsed between the termination of his two years' residence in Rome, (*Acts* xxiv. 10.) and his martyrdom: and, consequently, to fix the date of his first visit to Rome, which took place nearly at the time when Felix was recalled from the government of Judea. (*Acts* xxiv. 27.)

To this journey different dates are assigned by different writers.

Eusebius and Jerome, (Eusebius, *Chronicon*; Jerome, *Catalogus Script. Eccles.* Tom. IV. Part II. p. 103. Benedict. Edit.) who are followed by Scaliger, Cave, Stillingfleet and others, fix upon the second year of Nero, A.D. 56. Bp. Pearson, in his *Annales Paulini*, places this visit in the sixth year of Nero, A.D. 60. Hale, in his *Analysis of Chronology*, fixes upon the seventh of Nero, A.D. 61. And Abp. Usher places the event as late as the ninth year of Nero, A.D. 63.

The earliest of these dates appears to correspond very well with the period of the recall of Felix. Josephus (*Ant.* xx. c. 8, 9.) says that Felix would have been punished for his misconduct, had he not been pardoned at the intercession of his brother Pallas, who was then at the height of his favor with Nero. Tacitus (*Annal.* xii. 54.) shows how dependent Felix was upon the power of his brother.

Now Pallas was himself dismissed by Nero, in the second year of his reign; (Tacit. *Ann.* xiii. 14.) was soon after brought to trial for treason; (*Ibid.* c. 23.) and was put to death in the ninth year of Nero. (Tacit. *Ann.* xiv. 65.) It is probable that Pallas, who was intimate with Agrippina, (Tacit. *Ann.* xii. 25. xiv. 2.) was not restored to the favor of Nero, until after her death, in the fifth year of Nero. If, therefore, the pardon of Felix was obtained by the intercession of Pallas with Nero, his recall probably took place as early as the second year of Nero.

If we assume, however, that Eusebius and Jerome were correct in assigning the second year of Nero as the date of St. Paul's first journey to Rome, his release would take place about the fifth year of Nero, probably in consequence of favors shown to prisoners and exiles, after the murder of Agrippina. (Massutius *de Vitâ Pauli*,

l. 13. c. 1.) And he was put to death during the persecution which began in the eleventh year of Nero, and continued four years. EUSEBIUS and JEROME say that he suffered in the fourteenth year of Nero.

This computation would leave a space of about eight years for the labors of St. Paul, after his first imprisonment at Rome; an opportunity which he doubtless employed with his characteristic energy and activity.

It was during these years, then, that St. Paul, according to CLEMENT, visited "the furthest extremity of the West."

HALES, in his *Chronology* (Vol. III. p. 546. edit. 2.) thinks that CLEMENT here "speaks rather rhetorically of St. Paul's travels to the western extremity of Europe." And BASNAGE (*Exercitationes Historico-criticæ*, p. 511.) conceives that he means no more than St. Paul visited Italy. "Mihi certum non Hispaniam, sed Italiam à Clemente designari." Considering, however, that CLEMENT wrote at Rome, we cannot but consider his words as referring to some country included under the Western provinces with respect to Rome. And the general current of ecclesiastical history plainly points to Spain, as one of the countries which he visited, in compliance with an intention which he himself expressed. (*Rom.* xvi. 24, 28.)

The evidence in favor of St. Paul having visited Spain appears quite conclusive.

CAIUS, the presbyter, in the beginning of the third century, says that "writings not included in the canon of Scripture expressly mention the journey of St. Paul from Rome into Spain."[a] HIPPOLYTUS, in the same century, says, that "St. Paul went as far as Illyricum, and Italy, and Spain, preaching the Gospel."[b] ATHANASIUS, in the fourth century, that St. Paul "did not hesitate to go to Rome and to Spain."[c] JEROME, in the same century, says, that "St. Paul, after his release from his trial before Nero, preached the Gospel in the Western parts."[d] And THEODORET, in the fifth century, that "when, in con-

---

[a] Sicut et semota passionem Petri evidenter declarant, sed et profectionem Pauli ab urbe ad Spaniam proficiscentis.—CAII Presbyteri fragmentum: *Reliquiæ Sacræ*, [à ROWTH.] Vol. IV. pp. 4, 37.

[b] Παῦλος δὲ μετ' ἐνιαυτὸν ἕνα τῆς τοῦ Χριστοῦ ἀναλήψεως εἰσῆλθεν εἰς τὴν ἀποστολὴν, καὶ ἀρξάμενος ἀπὸ 'Ιερουσαλὴμ, προῆλθεν ἕως τοῦ 'Ιλλυρικοῦ καὶ 'Ιταλίας καὶ Σπανίας κηρύσσων τὸ Εὐαγγέλιον ἔτη λέ. 'Επὶ δὲ Νέρωνος, ἐν 'Ρώμῃ τὴν κεφαλὴν ἀποτμηθεὶς, θάπτεται ἐκεῖ.

HIPPOLYTUS *de xii Apostolis*, Appendix, p. 31. Edit. Fabricii. There is some doubt whether this tract was written by HIPPOLYTUS the Martyr. At all events, it contains little more information than could be collected or conjectured from the Acts of the Apostles, and the Epistle to the Romans. The same remark applies to the subsequent passage of ATHANASIUS.

[c] Διὰ τοῦτο καὶ σπουδῇ τῶν ἁγίων μέχρι τοῦ 'Ιλλυρικοῦ κηρύττει, καὶ μὴ ὀκνεῖ, μηδὲ εἰς τὴν 'Ρώμην ἀπελθεῖν, μηδὲ εἰς τὰς Σπανίας ἀναβῆναι.

ATHANAS. *Epist. ad Dracontium*, Tom. I. p. 956. A. Edit. Paris, 1627.

[d] Sciendum autem in primâ satisfactione, necdum Neronis imperio roborato, nec in tanta erumpente scelera, quanta de eo narrant historiæ, Paulum à Nerone dimissum, ut Evangelium CHRISTI in Occidentis quoque partibus prædicaretur, sicut ipse scribit in secundâ Epistolâ ad Timotheum, eo tempore quo et passus est, de vinculis dictans Epistolam. (2 Tim. iv. 16.)

HIERON. *Catalogus Scriptor. Eccles.* Num. v. Tom. IV. Par. II. p. 105. Edit. Benedict.

sequence of his appeal to Cæsar, he (St. Paul) was sent to Rome by Festus, and was acquitted on his defence, he went to Spain, and carried the light of the Gospel to other nations."[*]

The expressions of CLEMENT, however—ἐπὶ τὸ τέρμα τῆς δύσεως ἐλθών—have been supposed to imply that the Apostle's preaching did not terminate in Spain, but extended to the British Islands. Those who entertain this opinion observe, that in the language of that period, Britain is often called the extremity of the West. Thus PLUTARCH, in his life of Cæsar, denominates the sea between Gaul and Britain, "the Western Ocean:" EUSEBIUS and NICEPHORUS give the same name to the British Ocean: (EUSEB. *Vita Constant.* I. cc. 25, 41. II. c. 28. NICEPH. *Hist.* Lib. i. c. 1.) and EUSEBIUS elsewhere (*De Martyr. Palæstin.* c. 13.) describes Britain under the appellation of the Western parts beyond Gaul. THEODORET also, speaking of the visiters attracted by the fame of Simeon Stylites, enumerates the inhabitants of Spain, Britain, and Gaul, which he says lies between the other two, and describes them all as dwelling in the extreme bounds of the west.[†] In the language of CATULLUS, Britain is "Ultima Britannia," and "Ultima Occidentis Insula." (*Carm.* xxix.) He speaks of the inhabitants as "horribilesque ultimosque Britannos;" (*Carm.* xi.) as HORACE afterward calls them "Ultimos orbis Britannos." (*Carm.* i. 35.)

The language of CLEMENT might very well therefore imply that St. Paul went not only to Spain, but to the most remote of the three Western provinces, Spain, Gaul, and Britain.

There is distinct evidence that the Gospel was preached in the British Islands by *some of the Apostles*. Thus TERTULLIAN, in the second century, speaks of "all the extremities of Spain, and the different nations of Gaul, and parts of Britain inaccessible to the Romans, but subject to CHRIST." See TERTULLIAN's *Apology*, c. 37. p. 430. [of CHEVALLIER's translation, Eng. ed.] note. The testimony of EUSEBIUS to the same fact is peculiarly valuable. As the favorite of Constantine, the first Christian Emperor, who was born in Britain and there proclaimed Emperor, he may be supposed to have been well acquainted with the manner in which Christianity was introduced into Britain. And the remarkable passage in his *Demonstratio Evangelica*, in which he not only asserts the fact, that some of the apostles preached in Britain, but argues upon the fact, may be regarded as a deliberate assertion, founded upon actual inquiry. His object is to prove that the first preachers of Christianity were not deceivers nor impostors. "Observe," he says, "this also. If they were impostors and deceivers, and also uninstructed and entirely ignorant men, nay, rather barbarians, acquainted with no other than the Syrian language, how could they ever go through the whole world? How could so bold an undertaking enter their thoughts? and by what power could

---

[*] Ἡνίκα τῇ ἐφέσει χρησάμενος εἰς τὴν Ῥώμην ὑπὸ τοῦ Φήστου παρεπέμφθη, ἀπολογησάμενος ὡς ἀθῶος ἀφείθη, καὶ τὰς Σπανίας κατέλαβε, καὶ εἰς ἕτερα ἔθνη ἐδράμων, τὴν τῆς διδασκαλίας λαμπάδα προσήνεγκε.
THEODORET *in Epist.* ii. *ad Timoth.* iv. 7.
[†] Ἀφίκοντο δὲ πολλοί, τὰς τῆς ἑσπέρας οἰκοῦντες ἐσχατιάς, Σπάνοι τε καὶ Βρεττανοί, καὶ Γαλάται, οἱ τὸ μέσον τούτων κατέχοντες.
THEODORET. *Religiosa Hist.* c. 26. Tom. III. p. 881. D. Edit. Paris, 1642.

they effect their purpose? For, supposing it possible for rustic men, wandering about in their own country, to deceive and be deceived, and not to waste their labor in vain; yet, that they should preach the name of JESUS to all mankind, and teach his miraculous works in country and city,—that some of them should visit the Roman Empire, and the imperial city itself, and others severally the nations of the Persians, and Armenians, and Parthians, and Scythians—nay, further, that some should proceed to the very extremities of the inhabited world, and reach the country of the Indians, *and others again pass over the Ocean to those which are called the British Islands*—all this I conceive to be beyond the power of any human being, not to say of ordinary and uninstructed men, and, still less, of deceivers and impostors."[g]

THEODORET goes further than this, asserting that St. Paul preached in islands beyond the Ocean, with respect to Spain; which can scarcely refer to any other than the British Islands. "The blessed apostle St. Paul teaches us, in a few words, to how many nations he carried the sacred doctrines of the Gospel; so that from Jerusalem, and round about unto Illyricum, he fully preached the Gospel of CHRIST. He went afterward also to Italy and Spain, and carried salvation to islands which lie in the Ocean."[h]

JEROME also, beside the passage quoted above, appears to allude, though with less precision than THEODORET, to St. Paul's preaching beyond the ocean; when he says, that "St. Paul, having been in Spain, went from one ocean to another, imitating the motion and course of the Sun of righteousness, of whom it is said, His going forth is from the end of heaven and his circuit unto the ends thereof; and that his diligence in preaching extended as far as the earth itself."[i]

---

[g] Ἔτι δὲ καὶ τούτῳ πρόσχες. Εἰ δὴ καὶ αὐτοὶ πλανοὶ καὶ ἀπατεῶνες ἐτύγχα-
νον, προσθὲς δ' ὅτι καὶ ἀπαίδευτοι καὶ παντελῶς ἰδιῶται, μᾶλλον δὲ ὅτι καὶ βάρ-
βαροι, καὶ τῆς Σύρων οὐ πλέον ἐπαίοντες φωνῆς, καὶ πῶς ἐπὶ πᾶσαν προῆλθον τὴν
οἰκουμένην; ἢ ποίᾳ τοῦτο διανοίᾳ ἐφαντάσθησαν τολμῆσαι; ποίᾳ δὲ δυνάμει τὸ
ἐπιχειρηθὲν κατωρθώσαν: Ἔστω γὰρ ἐπὶ τῆς οἰκείας γῆς καλινδουμένους ἀγροί-
κους ἄνδρας πλανᾶν καὶ πλανᾶσθαι, καὶ μὴ ἐφ' ἡσυχίας βάλλεσθαι τὸ πρᾶγμα.
Κηρύττειν δ' εἰς πάντας τὸ τοῦ Ἰησοῦ ὄνομα, καὶ τὰς παραδόξους πράξεις αὐτοῦ
κατά τε τοὺς ἀγροὺς καὶ κατὰ πόλιν διδάσκειν, καὶ τοὺς μὲν αὐτῶν τὴν Ῥωμαίων
ἀρχὴν, καὶ αὐτήν τε τὴν βασιλικωτάτην πόλιν νείμασθαι, τοὺς δὲ τὴν Περσῶν,
τοὺς δὲ τὴν Ἀρμενίων, ἑτέρους δὲ τὸ Πάρθων ἔθνος, καὶ αὖ πάλιν τὸ Σκυθῶν,
τινὰς δὲ ἤδη καὶ ἐπ' αὐτὰ τῆς οἰκουμένης ἐλθεῖν τὰ ἄκρα, ἐπί τε τὴν Ἰνδῶν φθά-
σαι χώραν, καὶ ἑτέρους ὑπὲρ τὸν Ὠκεανὸν παρελθεῖν ἐπὶ τὰς καλουμένας Βρετ-
τανικὰς νήσους, ταῦτα οὐκ ἔτ' ἐγώ γε ἡγοῦμαι κατὰ ἄνθρωπον εἶναι, μήτιγε
κατὰ εὐτελεῖς καὶ ἰδιώτας, πολλοῦ δεῖ κατὰ πλάνους καὶ γόητας.
EUSEB. *Demonst. Evang.* Lib. iii. p. 112. D. Coloniæ, 1688.

[h] Ὁ δὲ μακάριος Παῦλος διδάσκει συντόμως, ὅσοις ἔθνεσι προστήνοχε τὰ θεῖα
κηρύγματα· ὥστε ἀπὸ Ἱερουσαλὴμ κύκλῳ μέχρι τοῦ Ἰλλυρικοῦ πεπληρωκέναι τὸ
εὐαγγέλιον τοῦ Χριστοῦ.——— ὕστερον μέντοι καὶ τῆς Ἰταλίας ἐπέβη, καὶ εἰς
τὰς Σπανίας ἀφίκετο, καὶ ταῖς ἐν τῷ πελάγει διακειμέναις νήσοις τὴν ὠφελείαν
προσήνεγκε. He then refers to St. Paul's Epistle to the Romans, xv.
THEODORET *in Psalm* cxvi. Tom. I. pp. 870. D. 871. A.

[i] "Paulus Apostolus ——— qui vocatus à DOMINO effusus est super faciem universæ terræ, ut prædicaret Evangelium de Jerosolymis usque ad Illyricum, et ædificaret non super alterius fundamentum, ubi jam fuerit prædicatum, sed usque ad Hispanias tenderet, et mari rubro iind ab Oceano usque ad Oceanum curreret, imitans DOMINUM suam et solem justitiæ, de quo

The earliest writer, however, who in express terms asserts that St. Paul visited Britain, is VENANTIUS FORTUNATUS, an Italian poet of the sixth century. In the third book of his *Life of St. Martin*, he thus describes the preaching of St. Paul:

> Transit et Oceanum, vel quâ facit insula portum,
> Quasque Britannus habet terras, quasque ultima Thule.

This is plainly, however, a poetical expression, on which no stress whatever can be laid. And very little more weight can be attached to the testimony of SOPHRONIUS, Patriarch of Jerusalem, in the seventh century, as quoted by GODWIN, asserting that St. Paul visited Britain.[a]

Upon the whole, it seems clear, that St. Paul preached "in the West," including Spain, in the interval between the termination of his imprisonment in Rome and his martyrdom; that the Gospel was preached *in Britain* by *some* of the apostles; that the terms in which the field of St. Paul's preaching is described, may include the British Islands, and that there was probably time for his visiting them. But whether he actually did so, may reasonably admit of much doubt. Archbishop USHER, in his *Britannicarum Ecclesiarum Antiquitates*, and Bishop STILLINGFLEET, in his *Origines Britannicæ*, maintain the opinion that St. Paul preached in Britain. The same side of the question has lately found a learned and zealous advocate in the Bishop of Salisbury, [Dr. BURGESS]. His tracts on the *Origin and Independence of the Ancient British Church*, and his two Sermons, the one preached at the Anniversary Meeting of the Society for Promoting Christian Knowledge and Church Union in the Diocese of St. David's, in the year 1813; the other preached, in the year 1821, before the Royal Society of Literature, contain the principal facts and arguments connected with the question.

The Bishop of London, [Dr. BLOMFIELD,] in his 7th *Lecture on the Acts of the Apostles*, leans to the opinion of JABLONSKI, (*Opusc.* Tom. III. p. 301.) that the preaching of St. Paul in Britain is extremely improbable.

NOTE B. § 16. p. 10.

As early as the middle of the ninth century, PHOTIUS, Patriarch of Constantinople, objected to CLEMENT of Rome that he had not used terms sufficiently elevated and sufficiently significative, in speaking of the divine nature of CHRIST, although he nowhere speaks decidedly against it. (ὅτι ἀρχιερέα καὶ προστάτην τὸν Κύριον ἡμῶν Ἰησοῦν Χριστὸν ὀνομάζων, οὐδὲ τὰς θεοπρεπεῖς καὶ ὑψηλοτέρας ἀφῆκε περὶ αὐτοῦ φωνάς· οὐ μὴν οὐδ' ἀπαρακαλύπτως αὐτὸν οὐδαμῇ ἐν τούτοις βλασφημεῖ.) PHOTIUS *Bibliothec.* Cod. 126.) Assertions of the same nature have been more strongly repeated by later writers.

---

egimus, A summo cœlo egressio ejus, et occursus ejus usque ad summum ejus: ut antè eum terra deficeret quàm studium prædicandi."
HIERON. *in Amos Prophet.* c. v. Tom. III. p. 1412. Edit. Benedict.
[a] "Sophronius Patriarcha Hierosolymitanus disertis verbis asserit, Britanniam nostram eum invisisse."—GODWIN *de Præsul. Anglican.* p. 8.

It was scarcely to be expected that the language of CLEMENT upon this point should be so guarded, as that which was used after controversies had arisen upon the question. But,—without referring to his second Epistle, which is certainly free from any such objection— there are passages enough in his first Epistle to show that PHOTIUS does not accurately represent the sentiments of CLEMENT, if indeed he intended to imply a doubt of his belief of the divine nature of CHRIST.

Thus in c. 2. of this Epistle we find the words—τοῖς ἐφοδίοις τοῦ Θεοῦ ἀρκούμενοι, καὶ προσέχοντες τοὺς λόγους αὐτοῦ ἐπιμελῶς, ἐστερνισμένοι ἦτε τοῖς σπλάγχνοις, καὶ τὰ παθήματα αὐτοῦ ἦν πρὸ ὀφθαλμῶν ὑμῶν. c. 2. (Compare Acts xx. 28. ποιμαίνειν τὴν ἐκκλησίαν τοῦ Θεοῦ, ἣν περιεποιήσατο διὰ τοῦ ἰδίου αἵματος.) In c. 36. CLEMENT denominates CHRIST, ἀπαύγασμα τῆς μεγαλωσύνης αὐτοῦ (Θεοῦ) c. 36. In c. 32. he thus distinguishes the divine nature of CHRIST from his human nature, ἐξ αὐτοῦ ('Ισραὴλ) ὁ Κύριος Ἰησοῦς τὸ κατὰ σάρκα.—Compare Rom. ix. 5. And, in the passage above, c. 16. CLEMENT expressly says of CHRIST, perhaps with an allusion to Phil. ii. 5—8. Τὸ σκῆπτρον τῆς μεγαλωσύνης τοῦ Θεοῦ, ὁ Κύριος ἡμῶν Χριστὸς Ἰησοῦς, οὐκ ἦλθεν ἐν κόμπῳ ἀλαζονείας, οὐδὲ ὑπερηφανίας, καίπερ δυνάμενος· ἀλλὰ ταπεινοφρονῶν. See Bp. BULL, Defensio Fid. Nicæn. Sec. II. c. 3.

The sentiments here expressed by CLEMENT, are set forth with great eloquence in the *Epistle to Diognetus*, improperly ascribed to JUSTIN MARTYR. The passage is long, but so beautiful that I cannot forbear subjoining it.

The author of the Epistle, after showing the insufficiency of sacrifices and ritual observances, such as the Jews retained, proceeds thus to vindicate and explain the Christian faith. (p. 496, D.)

"The Christians are not separated from the rest of mankind by country, or by language, or by customs. They are confined to no particular cities, use no peculiarity of speech, adopt no singularity of life. Their doctrine embraces no tenet built upon the reasoning and subtilty of crafty men: neither do they, like others, uphold the opinion of any man. Dwelling in the cities, whether of Greeks or barbarians, as every man's lot is cast, following the customs of each country in dress, and diet, and manner of life, they yet display the wonderful and indeed astonishing nature of their own polity. They dwell in their own country; but as sojourners: they partake of all things, as denizens: they endure all things, as strangers. Every foreign land is their country; their own country is to each a foreign land. Like other men they marry, and have children: but their children they expose not. Their table is common, not their bed.ᵃ They are in the flesh; but they live not after flesh. They abide on earth, but they are citizens of heaven.ᵇ They obey the laws which are established; and in their own lives are superior to the laws. They love all men; and are persecuted by all. Men know them not, yet condemn them. Being slain they are made alive: being poor, they make many rich:ᶜ deprived of all things, in all things they abound. Being dishonored, they are thereby glorified: being calumniated, they are justified:

ᵃ There are here some words lost: τράπεζαν κοινὴν παρατίθενται, ἀλλ' —— κοινήν. Perhaps we should supply some such expression as ἀλλ' οὐ κοίτην κοινήν. Compare TERTULLIAN, Apol. c. xxxix. p. 439.
ᵇ Phil. iii. 20.   ᶜ 2 Cor. vi. 10.

being cursed, they bless: being reviled, they give honor. Doing good, they are punished as evil doers; when punished, they rejoice as being made alive. The Jews oppose them as a strange people; the Greeks persecute them: and they who hate them can allege no reason for their enmity.

"In a word, Christians are in the world what the soul is in the body. The soul is dispersed over all the members of the body: Christians over all the cities of the world. The soul dwells in the body, but is no part of the body: Christians dwell in the world, but are not of the world. The soul, invisible herself, is guarded in a visible body: Christians are known to be in the world, but their worship is unseen. The flesh hates the soul, which never injured it, and wars against it, because it is thereby prevented from indulging in its pleasures. The world hates Christians, who injure it not, because they are opposed to its delights. The soul loves the body and the members which hate her. Christians also love their enemies. The soul is enclosed in the body, yet she restrains the body. Christians are shut up and guarded in the world, yet they restrain the world. The soul, herself immortal, dwells in a mortal tabernacle. Christians dwell among the corruptible, looking for an incorruptible state in the heavens. The soul, straitened in meats and drinks, is thereby improved. Christians, persecuted daily, the more abound.

"In such a post hath GOD placed them, whence they must not retire. For this is no earthly invention which is committed to their trust: it is no mortal device which they guard with such jealous care; no dispensation of human mysteries which is intrusted to them. But even the Almighty, Invisible GOD, the Creator of all things, himself sent down from heaven the Truth, and the holy and incomprehensible Word, to dwell among men, and established Him in their hearts. Not, as some one might suppose, sending among men any minister, or angel, or archangel, or any of those who do his pleasure upon earth, or are intrusted with their ministry in the heavens; but [he sent] the very Framer and Maker of all things; by whom he created the heavens: by whom he shut up the sea in its own bounds: whose secret counsels all the elements faithfully obey: who taught the sun to keep the measure of his daily course: who commanded the moon to shine by night, and she obeys; whom the stars too obey, following the moon in her course: by whom all things are disposed and arranged: to whom all things are subject; the heavens and things in the heavens; the earth and things in the earth; the sea and they which are therein; fire, air, the abyss: things in the heights, things in the depths, things between. Him did he send to them [man.] But did he send him, as some men might imagine, for dominion and fear and consternation? Nay, verily: but in quietness and meekness. He sent him as a King sending his son: he sent him as GOD :* he sent him as to men. GOD, in sending him, would save mankind: he would persuade men, not compel them; for compulsion is not of GOD. In sending him, GOD would invite, not persecute; he acted as one who loved, not as a judge. For he will send *Him* to judge, and who shall abide the day of his coming?"

After discussing the impossibility that any one should know GOD but the Son of GOD, or any one please GOD by his own works, the

---

* ὡς Θεὸν ἔπεμψε.

author proceeds to speak of the love of GOD, manifested in the redemption. (p. 500, B.)

"CHRIST hated us not, nor rejected us; neither did he remember our sins, but was long-suffering, patient; as he himself declared, he bare our iniquities. GOD gave his own son a ransom for us, the holy for the unholy, the innocent for the guilty, the just for the unjust, the incorruptible for the corruptible, the immortal for the mortal. For what also was able to cover our sins but only his righteousness? How should we disobedient and impious be justified, but only in the Son of GOD? O sweet interchange! O inscrutable dispensation! O benefits surpassing all expectation! that the iniquity of many should be hidden in the Just One; and the righteousness of one justify many sinners! [GOD,] having convinced us, in the former time, how impossible it was that our nature should attain life, but now having shown us a Saviour able to save even those who could not have been saved, from both these willed us to have faith in his mercy; to conceive of him as our supporter, father, teacher, counsellor, physician, mind, light, honor, glory, strength, life."

THE EPISTLE OF POLYCARP TO THE PHILIPPIANS.

POLYCARP, and the Presbyters that are with him, to the Church of GOD which is at Philippi, mercy unto you and peace from GOD ALMIGHTY, and the Lord JESUS CHRIST our Saviour, be multiplied.

1. I rejoiced greatly with you, in our Lord JESUS CHRIST, that ye received the patterns of true love, and accompanied as it behoved you, those who were bound with chains, the fitting ornament of saints,[a] the crowns of those who are truly chosen of GOD and our LORD: and that the firm root of your faith, which was preached from ancient times, remains until now, and brings forth fruit to our Lord JESUS CHRIST, who suffered himself to be brought even to death for our sins: "whom GOD raised up, having loosed the pains of death:"[b] "in whom, having not seen him, ye believe; and believing rejoice with joy unspeakable and full of glory."[c] Into which joy many desire to enter, knowing that "by grace ye are saved, not of works,"[d] but by the will of GOD, through JESUS CHRIST.

2. "Wherefore, girding up the loins (of your minds),"[e] serve GOD in fear and truth, laying aside all empty and vain speech, and the error of many, "believing in him

---

[a] Thus IGNATIUS, in his *Epistle to the Ephesians*, c. 11. calls his chains "spiritual jewels." Compare also his *Epistle to the Smyrneans*, § 11. In like manner CYPRIAN, *Epist.* 76. (Fell.) "Dicatis DEO hominibus, et fidem suam religiosâ virtute testantibus, ornamenta sunt ista, non vincula: nec Christianorum pedes ad infamiam copulant, sed clarificant ad coronam. O pedes feliciter vincti, qui non à fabro sed DOMINO resolvuntur! O pedes feliciter vincti, qui itinere salutari ad paradisum diriguntur! O pedes in seculo ad præsens ligati, ut sint semper apud DOMINUM liberi!" Compare EUSEBIUS, *Eccles. Hist.* i. 5.
[b] Acts ii. 24. [c] 1 Pet. i. 8. [d] Eph. ii. 8, 9. [e] 1 Pet. i. 13.

that raised up our Lord JESUS CHRIST from the dead, and gave him glory," [f] and a throne at his right hand: to whom all things in heaven and earth are subject; [g] whom every living creature worships; who comes to be the judge of the quick and dead; whose blood GOD shall require of them that believe not in him. But He that raised up CHRIST from the dead, shall raise up us also, if we do his will, and walk in his commandments, and love the things which he loved; abstaining from all unrighteousness, inordinate affection, [h] love of money, evil-speaking, false-witness: not rendering evil for evil, or railing for railing, or blow for blow, or curse for curse: but remembering what the Lord taught us, saying, "Judge not, that ye be not judged: forgive, and it shall be forgiven unto you:" be merciful, that ye may obtain mercy; "for with the same measure that ye mete withal, it shall be measured to you again;" [i] and that "Blessed are the poor, and they that are persecuted for righteousness' sake: for theirs is the kingdom of GOD." [k]

3. I have not assumed to myself, brethren, the liberty of writing to you these things concerning righteousness; but you yourselves before encouraged me. For neither can I, nor any other such as I am, come up to the wisdom of the blessed and renowned Paul, who, being among you, in the presence of those who then lived, taught with exactness and soundness the word of truth; who in his absence also wrote an Epistle[l] to you, into which if you diligently look, you may be able to be edified in the faith delivered unto you, which is the mother of us all, being followed with hope, and led on by love both toward GOD and CHRIST, and toward our neighbor. For if any one hath these things, he hath fulfilled the law of righteousness: for he that hath charity is far from all sin.

---

[f] 1 Pet. i. 21.   [g] Phil. ii. 10.
[h] Eph. iv. 19.   Col. iii. 5.   1 Pet. iii. 9.
[i] Matt. vii. 1.   Luke vi. 37.   [k] Matt. v. 3—10.   Luke vi. 20.
[l] Ἔγραφεν ἐπιστολάς. The word ἐπιστολή, in the plural, is sometimes used for a single epistle, as COTELERIUS shows. POLYCARP might possibly, however, allude to the Epistles of St. Paul to the Thessalonians, or to the Corinthians, the contents of which would be communicated to the Philippians.

4. But "the love of money is the beginning of all evils."ᵐ Knowing, therefore, that "we brought nothing into the world, neither are we able to carry any thing out,"ⁿ let us arm ourselves with the armor of righteousness, and teach first ourselves to walk in the commandment of the Lord, and then your wives to walk likewise in the faith and love and purity which is given unto them, loving their own husbands in all truth, and kindly affectionate to all others equally in all temperance, and to bring up their children in the instruction and fear of God: that the widows be sober as to what concerns the faith of the Lord, praying without ceasingᵒ for all men, being far from all detraction, evil-speaking, false-witness, love of money, and all evil: knowing that they are the altars of God; and that he sees all blemishes,ᵖ and nothing is hid from him, either of words or thoughts, nor any of the secret things of the heart.

5. Knowing, therefore, that God is not mocked,ᵠ we ought to walk worthy both of his command and of his glory. In like manner the deacons must be blameless in the sight of his righteousness, as the ministers of God in Christ, and not of men: not false accusers, not double-tongued, not lovers of money, temperate in all things, compassionate, careful in walking according to the truth of the Lord, who became the servant of all; whom if we please in this present world, we shall be made partakers also of that which is to come, according as he hath promised to us that he will raise us from the dead; and that if we shall walk worthy of him, we shall also reign together with him, if we believe. In like manner the young men must be blameless in all things, above all taking care of their purity, and restraining themselves from all evil. For it is good to emergeʳ out of the lusts which are in the world: for every lust warreth against the Spirit:ˢ and "neither fornicators, nor effeminate, nor abusers of themselves with mankind, shall inherit the kingdom of God,"ᵗ neither they which

---

ᵐ 1 Tim. vi. 10. ⁿ 1 Tim. vi. 7. ᵒ 1 Thes. v. 17.
ᵖ πάντα μωροσκοπεῖται. See Clem. Rom. Sect. 41. ᵠ Gal. vi. 7.
ʳ ἀνακόπτεσθαι. This reading appears preferable to ἀνακόπτεσθαι, "to be cut off." Thus Chrysostom, *de Sacerd.* Lib. I. 1. Ὡς δὲ μικρὸν καὶ αὐτὸς ἀνέκυψα τοῦ βιωτικοῦ κλύδωνος.
ˢ 1 Pet. ii. 11. ᵗ 1 Cor. vi. 9, 10.

Vol. IV.—5

act foolishly. Wherefore it is necessary that ye abstain from all these things, being subject to the presbyters and deacons, as unto GOD and CHRIST: the virgins also should walk in a spotless and pure conscience.

6. Let the elders [u] also be compassionate, merciful to all, bringing back such as are in error,[x] seeking out all those that are weak, not neglecting the widow or the fatherless, or the poor: but providing always what is good in the sight of GOD and men;[y] abstaining from all wrath, respect of persons, and unrighteous judgment; being far from all covetousness: not ready to believe any thing against any; not severe in judgment, knowing that we are all debtors in point of sin. If therefore we pray to the LORD that he would forgive us, we ought also to forgive.[z] For we are before the eyes of our LORD and GOD, and "must all stand before the judgment seat of CHRIST,"[a] and shall every one give an account for himself. Let us therefore so serve him, with fear and all reverence, as he himself hath commanded, and as the apostles who have preached the Gospel unto us, and the prophets who have foretold the coming of our LORD, (have taught us): being zealous of what is good, abstaining from all offence, and from false brethren, and from those who bear the name of CHRIST in hypocrisy, who deceive vain men.

7. "For whosoever confesses not that JESUS CHRIST is come in the flesh, is antichrist:"[b] and whosoever confesses not his suffering upon the cross, is of the devil. And whosoever perverts the oracles of the LORD to his own lusts, and says there is neither resurrection nor judgment, he is the first-born of Satan.[c] Wherefore leaving the vanity of many, and false doctrines, let us return to the word which was delivered to us from the beginning, "watching unto prayer,"[d] and persevering in fasting; with supplication beseeching the all-seeing

---

[u] Presbyters. [x] Ezek. xxxiv. 4. [y] Rom. xii. 17. [z] Matt. vi. 12-14.
[a] Rom. xiv. 10. 2 Cor. v. 10. [b] 1 John iv. 3.
[c] Marcion is said to have once met Polycarp, and to have addressed him with the words, 'Dost thou acknowledge me?' The reply attributed to Polycarp is, 'I acknowledge thee for the first-born of Satan.' EUSEB. *Hist.* iv. 14. IREN. *Adv. Hær.* iii. 3. In the interpolated *Epistle* of IGNATIUS *to the Trallians*, Sec. 11. Simon Magus is called "the first-born of Satan," τὸν πρωτότοκον αὐτοῦ υἱόν.
[d] 1 Pet. iv. 7.

§ 8, 9, 10.]   TO THE PHILIPPIANS.   51

God, not to lead us into temptation,* as the Lord hath said, " the spirit indeed is willing, but the flesh is weak."ᶠ

8. Let us therefore without ceasing hold steadfastly to him who is our hope, and the earnest of our righteousness, even Jesus Christ, who " bare our sins in his own body on the tree;" who " did no sin, neither was guile found in his mouth:"ᵍ but endured all for our sakes, that we might live through him. Let us therefore imitate his patience; and if we suffer for his name, let us glorify him. For this example he hath given us by himself, and so we have believed.

9. I exhort you all therefore to obey the word of righteousness, and exercise all patience, which ye have seen set forth before your eyes, not only in the blessed Ignatius, and Zosimus, and Rufus, but also in others among yourselves,ʰ and in Paul himself, and the other apostles; being confident of this, that all these have not run in vain, but in faith and righteousness: and that they are gone to the place which was due to them, in the presence of the Lord, with whom also they suffered. For they loved not this present world, but him that died for us, and was raised again by God for our sake.

10. ⁱStand therefore in these things, and follow the example of the Lord, being firm and immutable in the faith, lovers of the brotherhood, lovers of one another, companions together in the truth, being kind and gentle toward each other, despising none. When it is in your power to do good, defer it not, for " charity delivereth from death."ᵏ " Be all of you subject one to another, having your conversation honest among the Gentiles,"ˡ that by your good works both ye yourselves may receive praise, and the Lord may not be blasphemed through you.ᵐ But wo to him by whom the name of the Lord is blasphemed. Wherefore

---

* Matt. vi. 13.   ᶠ Matt. xxvi. 41.   ᵍ 1 Pet. ii. 22–24.

ʰ ὑμῶν—Dodwell, in his *Dissertationes Cyprianicæ*, Diss. xi. 27. supposes ἡμῶν to be the correct reading: and imagines that Polycarp is speaking of a persecution which took place in his own time, either in the Church of Smyrna or in that of Philippi.

ⁱ Sections 10, 11, 12 are lost in the Greek. The loss is supplied by the old Latin version.

ᵏ Tobit xii. 9.   ˡ 1 Pet. ii. 12.   ᵐ Rom. ii. 24. Tit. ii. 5.

teach all men sobriety, in which do ye also exercise yourselves.

11. I am greatly afflicted for Valens, who was once made a Presbyter among you; that he should so little understand the place that was given unto him. Wherefore I admonish you that ye abstain from concupiscence;ⁿ and that ye be chaste and true of speech. Keep yourselves from all evil.º For he that in these things cannot govern himself, how shall he be able to prescribe them to another? If a man doth not keep himself from concupiscence, he shall be polluted with idolatry,ᵖ and he shall be judged as if he were a Gentile. But who of you are ignorant of the judgment of GOD? "Do ye not know that the saints shall judge the world,"ᑫ as Paul teaches? But I have neither perceived nor heard any thing of the kind in you, among whom the blessed Paul labored; and who are named in the beginning of his epistle.ʳ For he glories of you in all the churches which alone had then known GOD: for we had not yet known him. Wherefore, brethren, I am exceedingly sorry both for him, and for his wife: may GOD grant them true repentance. And be ye also moderate on this occasion; and consider not such as enemies, but call them back, as suffering and erring members, that ye may save your whole body. For by so doing ye edify yourselves.

12. For I trust that ye are well exercised in the holy Scriptures, and that nothing is hid from you. But at present it is not granted unto me to practise that which is written, "Be ye angry and sin not," and "Let not the sun go down upon your wrath."ˢ Blessed is he that believeth and remembereth these things; which also I trust ye do. Now the GOD and Father of our Lord JESUS CHRIST, and he himself who is our everlasting High Priest, the Son of GOD, even JESUS CHRIST,

---

ⁿ The old Latin translation has *avaritia:* the Greek probably had πλεονεξία. That this word should, in many places, be rendered in the sense here given, is fully shown by SUICER on the words πλεονεκτέω and πλεονεξία, and by HAMMOND on Rom. i. 29. and 1 Cor. v. 10. See also PALEY, *Sermon* xlii. edit. 1825.

It appears from what follows, that both Valens and his wife had fallen into adultery.

º 1 Thes. v. 22.   ᵖ Col. iii. 5. Eph. v. 5.   ᑫ 1 Cor. vi. 2.
ʳ Phil. i.   ˢ Ps. iv. 4. Eph. iv. 26.

build you up in faith and truth, and in all meekness and lenity, and in patience and long-suffering, and forbearance and chastity: and grant unto you a lot and portion among his saints, and unto us with you, and unto all that are under heaven, who shall believe in our Lord JESUS CHRIST, and in his Father who raised him from the dead.[t] Pray for all the saints. Pray also for kings, and authorities, and princes, and for those who persecute you and hate you, and for the enemies of the cross: that your fruit may be manifest in all, and that ye may be perfect in CHRIST.

13. Both ye and Ignatius wrote to me,[u] that if any one went (hence) into Syria, he should also bring back your letters with him; which also I will do, if I have a convenient opportunity, either by myself, or by him whom I shall send upon your account. The Epistles of Ignatius which he wrote unto us,[x] and others as many as we have with us, we have sent to you, according to your order; which are subjoined to this Epistle; from which ye may be greatly profited. For they treat of faith and patience, and of all things which pertain to edification in our LORD.

14. What ye know certainly of Ignatius, and those that are with him, signify unto us.

These things have I written unto you by Crescens, whom by this present Epistle I have recommended to you, and do now again commend. For he hath had his conversation without blame among us, and I trust in like manner also with you. You will also have regard unto his sister when she shall come unto you. Be ye safe in the Lord JESUS CHRIST; and his grace be with you all. Amen.

---

[t] Gal. i. 1.
[u] See IGNATIUS' *Epistle to the Smyrneans*, Sect. 11.
[x] The two Epistles which IGNATIUS wrote, one to Polycarp, the other to the Church of the Smyrneans.

THE EPISTLE OF IGNATIUS TO THE EPHESIANS.

IGNATIUS, who is also called Theophorus,[a] to the Church which is at Ephesus in Asia, deservedly happy, being blessed through the greatness and fulness[b] of GOD the Father, and predestinated before the world began that it should be always unto an enduring and unchangeable glory; being united and chosen through

---

[a] Theophorus. All Christians were denominated *Theophori*, (Θεοφόροι) 'Temples of GOD,' and sometimes *Christophori*, (EUSEB. *Hist. Eccles.* viii. 10. IGNAT. *Ep. to Ephes.* § 9. Compare *Ep. to Magnes.* § 12.) 'Temples of CHRIST.' The reason of the appellation, which was constantly applied to Ignatius, both by himself and others, is given in the *History of his Martyrdom*, Sect. 2. "As soon then as he stood in the presence of the Emperor Trajan, the Emperor demanded of him, 'Who art thou, unhappy and deluded man, who art so active in transgressing our commands, and, besides, persuadest others to their own destruction?'" Ignatius replied, "No one ought to call (one who is properly styled) Theophorus, unhappy and deluded: for the evil spirits (which delude men) are departed far from the servants of GOD. But if you so call me because I am a trouble to those evil spirits, and an enemy to their delusions, I confess the justice of the appellation. For having (within me) CHRIST the heavenly King, I loosen all their snares." Trajan replied, "And who is Theophorus?" Ignatius answered, "He that hath CHRIST in his heart." Then answered Trajan, "Carriest thou, then, within thee him who was crucified?" "Yea," replied Ignatius, "for it is written, 'I will dwell in them and walk in them.'" (2 Cor. vi. 16.)
The notion of the later Greeks, that Ignatius was called *Theophorus* (Θεόφορος, borne by GOD) because he was the child whom CHRIST took up in his arms, (Matt. xviii. 2. Mark ix. 36.) although adopted by several writers, is a mere fancy. Had such a tradition existed even in the time of CHRYSOSTOM, he would surely have known it, and was not of a disposition to have omitted it, in the Homily which he composed on the Martyrdom of Ignatius: whereas he there expressly states, that Ignatius never saw JESUS, nor had any intercourse with him. (*Homil.* on Ignatius, Vol. V. p. 503. 37 ed. Savile.)

[b] Eph. iii. 19.

actual suffering,[c] according to the will of the Father, and JESUS CHRIST our GOD all happiness, by JESUS CHRIST, and his undefiled grace.

1. I have heard of your name which is much beloved in GOD, that which ye have attained by a habit of righteousness, according to the faith and love which is in JESUS CHRIST our Saviour; that being followers of GOD, and stirring up ourselves by the blood of GOD,[d] ye have perfectly accomplished the work which was agreeable to your nature. For hearing that I came bound from Syria, for the name and hope that are common to us all, trusting through your prayers to fight with beasts at Rome, that so by suffering martyrdom I may become indeed the disciple of him, who gave himself to GOD, an offering and sacrifice for us,[e] (ye hastened to see me). I receive therefore in the name of GOD your whole multitude in (the person of) Onesimus,[f] who for his love hath no word by which he can be described, but according to the flesh is your bishop: whom I beseech you in JESUS CHRIST to love, and that ye would all strive to be like unto him. And blessed be GOD, who hath granted unto you, who are so worthy of him, to possess such a bishop.

2. But with regard to my fellow-servant Burrhus, your deacon, in the service of GOD, blessed in all things, I entreat you that he may remain to the honor both of you and of your bishop. And Crocus also, worthy both of GOD and of you, whom I have received as a pattern of your love, hath in all things refreshed[g] me, as (I

---

[c] ἐν πάθει ἀληθινῷ. Archbishop WAKE follows the interpretation proposed by SMITH, "chosen through (his) true passion," through the meritorious sufferings of CHRIST, which he truly underwent. Compare *Epist. to the Trallians*, § 9, 10.

[d] Compare Acts xx. 28. "Feed the Church of GOD, which he hath purchased with his own blood."   [e] Eph. v. 2.

[f] Compare the *Epistle to the Magnesians*, Sect. 6. Some suppose this Onesimus to be the servant of Philemon, who is mentioned as the first Bishop of Beroea, in the *Apostolical Constitutions*, Book vii. 46. Although that book is not genuine, it may yet have preserved the tradition of such a fact, and he might have been removed to Ephesus. The name of Onesimus was, however, by no means uncommon at that time.

[g] πολλάκις με ἀνέπαυσεν, ὡς καὶ αὐτὸν ὁ πατὴρ Ἰησοῦ Χριστοῦ ἀναψύξαι.— See 1 Cor. xvi. 18. 2 Cor. vii. 13. and 2 Tim. i. 16.

pray) the Father of our Lord JESUS CHRIST may refresh him, together with Onesimus, and Burrhus, and Euplus, and Fronto, in whom I have, as to your charity, seen you all. May I always have joy of you,[h] if I shall be worthy of it. It is therefore fitting that ye should by all means glorify JESUS CHRIST, who hath glorified you: that by a uniform obedience ye may be perfectly joined together in the same mind, and in the same judgment, and may all speak alike concerning every thing;[i] and that being subject to the Bishop and the Presbytery ye may be altogether sanctified.

3. These things I command you not, as if I were any one.[k] For although I am even bound for his name, I am not yet perfect in JESUS CHRIST. But now I begin to learn; and I speak to you as my fellow disciples. For I ought to have been stirred up by you, in faith, in admonition, in patience, in long-suffering. But forasmuch as charity suffers me not to be silent toward you, I have therefore first taken upon me to exhort you, that ye would all run together according to the will of GOD. For JESUS CHRIST, our inseparable life, he is by the will of the Father:[l] as also the bishops, appointed unto the utmost bounds of the earth, are by the will of JESUS CHRIST.

4. Wherefore it becomes you to run together according to the will of your bishop, even as also ye do. For your renowned Presbytery, worthy of GOD, is fitted as exactly to the Bishop, as the strings are to a harp.[m] Wherefore, in your concord and harmonious love, JESUS CHRIST is sung. And every single person among you makes up the chorus; that all being harmonious in concord, taking up the song of GOD, in perfect unity, ye may sing with one voice to the Father, through JESUS CHRIST; to the end that he may both hear you, and perceive by your works, that ye are members of his SON. Wherefore it is profitable for you to live in an unblameable unity, that ye may always have fellowship with GOD.

---

[h] Philemon 20.   [i] 1 Cor. i. 10.   [k] Comp. Acts v. 36.
[l] Ἰησοῦς Χριστός—τοῦ πατρὸς ἡ γνώμη. "JESUS CHRIST—is the Will of the Father." SMITH proposes to read τῇ γνώμῃ, which is adopted in the text.
[m] See the *Epistle to the Philadelphians*, Sect. 1.

5. But if I, in this little time, have had such a familiarity with your bishop, (whom I have known) not in the flesh but in the spirit, how much more must I think you happy, who are so joined to him as the Church is to JESUS CHRIST, and JESUS CHRIST to the Father, that all things may agree together in unity. Let no man deceive himself. Except a man be within the altar, he is deprived of the bread of GOD. For if the prayer of one or two be of such avail,[n] how much more shall that of the Bishop and the whole Church be? He therefore that comes not together into the same place with it, he is proud already, and hath condemned himself.[o] For it is written,[p] "GOD resisteth the proud." Let us take heed, therefore, that we set not ourselves against the Bishop, that we may be subject to GOD.

6. The more any one sees his bishop silent, the more let him revere him. For whomsoever the master of the house sends, to be over his own household, we ought to receive him, even as we would him that sent him. It is evident, therefore, that we ought to respect the bishop, even as the LORD himself. And indeed Onesimus himself greatly commends your good order in GOD; in that ye all live according to the truth, and no heresy dwells among you. For neither do ye hearken to any one more than to JESUS CHRIST, speaking to you in truth.

7. For some there are who are wont to carry about the name (of CHRIST) in deceitfulness, but do things unworthy of GOD; whom ye must avoid, as ye would wild beasts. For they are ravening dogs, which bite secretly; of whom ye must beware, as of men hardly to be cured. There is one physician, both carnal and spiritual; create and uncreate;[q] GOD, manifest in the

---

[n] Jas. v. 16. Matt. xviii. 19. [o] Compare John iii. 18. [p] Jas. iv. 6.
[q] γενητὸς καὶ ἀγένητος. This is the reading adopted by SMITH. The other editions have γεννητὸς καὶ ἀγέννητος, "begotten and unbegotten." BULL, (*Defensio Fid. Nic.* Cap. ii. 2. s. 6.) although he reads γεννητὸς καὶ ἀγέννητος, translates the words "create and uncreate," following the old Latin version, and ATHANASIUS *de Synodis Arim. et Seleuc.* Tom. I. 922.

Πεισόμεθα ὅτι καὶ ὁ μακάριος Ἰγνάτιος ὀρθῶς ἔγραψε, γενητὸν αὐτὸν λέγων διὰ τὴν σάρκα· ὁ γὰρ Χριστὸς σὰρξ ἐγένετο· ἀγένητον δέ, ὅτι μὴ τῶν ποιημάτων καὶ γενητῶν ἐστιν, ἀλλ' υἱὸς ἐκ πατρός.

"We are persuaded, that the blessed Ignatius also did well declare

flesh; true life, in death; both of Mary, and of God: first capable of suffering, and then liable to suffer no more, (even Jesus Christ our Lord).

8. Wherefore let no man deceive you: as indeed ye are not deceived, being wholly (the servants) of God. For inasmuch as there is no contention nor strife among you, which can trouble you, doubtless ye live according to God's will. May my soul be for yours; and I myself be the expiatory offering for your Church of Ephesus, so famous to all ages. They that are of the flesh cannot do the works of the Spirit; neither they that are of the Spirit the works of the flesh. As also faith cannot do the works of unfaithfulness, nor unfaithfulness the works of faith. But even those things which ye do according to the flesh are spiritual; for ye do all things in Jesus Christ.

9. Nevertheless, I have heard of some who have passed by you, having perverse doctrine; whom ye did not suffer to sow among you; but stopped your ears that

---

in his writings, respecting Christ, that he was made according to the flesh, for Christ was made flesh: and that he was uncreate, because he is not among those things which were created and formed, but the Son proceeding of the Father."

Cotelerius shews that γενητός and γεννητός, ἀγένητος and ἀγέννητος, have been not unfrequently confounded. This confusion may have sometimes arisen from the errors of transcribers; but, before the council of Nice the distinction between the words was not so scrupulously observed as it was afterward. Origen was censured for calling the Son γενητὸς Θεός· although in another part of his works (Contra Celsum vi. 17,) he expressly calls him ἀγένητος. See Burton, Testimonies of the Antenicene Fathers, No. 12. Suicer, Thesaurus, on the words ἀγένητος and γενητός. Theodoret reads γεννητὸς ἐξ ἀγεννήτου, "begotten of him who is unbegotten."

Tertullian (De Carne Christi, Cap. 5.) has a plain reference to this passage of Ignatius: "Ita utriusque substantiæ census hominem et Deum exhibuit: hinc natum, inde non natum; hinc carneum, inde spiritalem; hinc infirmum, inde præfortem: hinc morientem, inde viventem. Quæ proprietas conditionum, divinæ et humanæ, æquâ utique naturæ utriusque veritate dispuncta est, eâdem fide et spiritûs et carnis."

ἐν θανάτῳ ζωὴ ἀληθινή. This seems to be the true reading, instead of ἐν ἀθανάτῳ ζωῇ ἀληθινῇ, words which convey no distinct meaning.

These words are added in the old Latin version, and in the passage as quoted in the fifth Century by Theodoret, Epist. ad Monachos Constantinopolitanos, and Gelasius, at the end of his work De duabus Naturis Christi.

Gal. v. 17.

ye might not receive those things which were sown by them as being the stones" of the temple of the Father, prepared for the building of GOD the Father, raised up on high by the engine of JESUS CHRIST, which is the cross; and using the HOLY GHOST as the rope. And your faith is your support:˟ and your charity the way which leads to GOD. Ye are, therefore, and all your companions, full of GOD, his (spiritual) temples, full of CHRIST, full of holiness : adorned in all things with the commands of CHRIST : in whom also I rejoice that I have been thought worthy by this present epistle to converse, and joy together with you; that with respect to the other life, ye love nothing but GOD only.

10. Pray also without ceasing ʸ for other men. For there is hope of repentance in them, that they may attain unto GOD. Suffer them, therefore, to receive instruction of you if it be only from your works. To their anger, be ye meek; to their boastings, be ye humble; to their blasphemies (return) your prayer; to their error (oppose) your firmness in the faith ; to their cruelty, be ye gentle; not studying in return to imitate them. Let us be found their brethren in moderation, and study to be followers of the LORD : for who was ever more unjustly used, more destitute, more despised ? that no herb ᶻ of the devil may be found in you ; but ye

---

ᵘ Eph. ii. 20, 21, 22. 1 Pet. ii. 5.

˟ ἀναγωγεύς. VOSSIUS thinks this word here signifies a pulley. ἀγωγεύς is sometimes used for the rein with which a horse is guided. Ignatius probably alludes to the metaphor used by St. Paul in writing to the same Ephesians, Eph. ii. 20. &c. He compares the faithful to the stones composing the Temple of the FATHER, JESUS CHRIST to an engine by which they are raised on high, the HOLY SPIRIT to the rope by which they are drawn, faith to the pulley or windlass, and charity to the levelled road along which the stones are drawn from the quarry. Comparisons of this kind, carried even to a greater degree of minuteness, are common in the early Christian writers. Those who object to them, as opposed to our present notions of taste, must remember that refinement upon such points formed no part of the habits of those who were addressed : and that the writings of St. Paul, as for instance Eph. vi. 14–18, owe much beautiful and forcible illustration to comparisons of a similar nature.

ʸ 1 Thes. v. 17.

ᶻ This is a favorite metaphor with Ignatius, to signify false doctrine; compare his *Epistle to the Philadelphians*, Sect. 3. and *Epistle to the Trallians*, Sect. 6.

may remain in all holiness and sobriety in CHRIST JESUS, both bodily and spiritually.[a]

11. The last times are at hand. Let us reverence, let us fear the long-suffering of GOD, that it be not to us unto condemnation. For let us either fear the wrath to come, or love the grace that we at present enjoy; one of the two: only that we be found in CHRIST JESUS unto true life. Let nothing become you, beside him; for whom also I bear about these bonds, these spiritual jewels,[b] in which I would to GOD that I might arise, through your prayers; of which I entreat you to make me always partaker, that I may be found in the lot of the Christians of Ephesus, who have always agreed with the apostles, through the power of JESUS CHRIST.

12. I know who I am; and to whom I write. I, a person condemned; ye, such as have obtained mercy; I, exposed to danger; ye, established. Ye are the passage of those that are killed for GOD; who have been instructed in the mysteries of the Gospel[c] with Paul, who was sanctified, and bore testimony even unto death, and is deservedly most happy; at whose feet I would that I might be found, when I shall have attained unto GOD; who throughout all his Epistle makes mention of you in JESUS CHRIST.

13. Let it be your care, therefore, to come more frequently together to the praise[d] and glory of GOD. For when ye frequently meet together in the same

---

[a] 1 Cor. vii. 34.

[b] See the *Epistle of* POLYCARP, Sect. 1.

[c] συμμύσται. Baptized Christians were denominated μύσται and οἱ μεμυημένοι, *the initiated*, while the Catechumens were called ἄμυστοι, ἀμύητοι, and ἀμυσταγώγητοι, *uninitiated*, as not yet admitted to the use of the sacred offices, and knowledge of the mysteries of the Christian religion. Hence the phrase ἴσασιν οἱ μεμυημένοι, *the initiated know what is said*, so constantly used in the early homilies and addresses to the people, when any reference is made to the higher doctrines of Christianity. CASAUBON observes that this phrase occurs fifty times in the writings of CHRYSOSTOM and AUSTIN. See CAVE's *Primitive Christianity*, Part I. ch. 8. BINGHAM's *Antiquities of the Christian Church*, Book I. ch. IV. 2.

[d] εἰς εὐχαριστίαν Θεοῦ καὶ εἰς δόξαν. He exhorts them to frequently gathering themselves together, for public worship, and especially to the celebration of the Eucharist, in which an offering of praise and thanksgiving is made to GOD. Compare 1 Cor. xi. 18–20.

place, the powers of Satan are destroyed, and his mischief is dissolved by the unity of your faith. Nothing is better than peace; by which all war is abolished, whether of heavenly or of earthly things.

'14. Of all which nothing is hid from you, if ye have perfect faith and charity in CHRIST JESUS, which are the beginning and end of life: the beginning, faith; the end, charity. And these two, being in unity, are of GOD. And all other things which concern a holy life are the consequence of these. No man, who professes the true faith, sins: neither doth he, who hath charity, hate. The tree is made manifest by its fruit.* So they who profess themselves to be Christians, shall be made known by their deeds. For now (Christianity) is not the work of an outward profession, but (shows itself) in the power of faith, if a man be found (faithful) unto the end.

15. It is better to be silent, and to be; than to say (a man is a Christian) and not to be. It is good to teach, if he who speaks, acts. He therefore is the only Master, who spake, and it was done.' And even those things, which he did in silence,ᵍ are worthy of the FATHER. He that possesses the word of JESUS is truly able to hear even his silence, that he may be perfect: and may both do according to what he speaks, and be known by those things of which he is silent. There is nothing hid from GOD: but even our secret things are nigh unto him. Let us therefore do all things as becomes those who have GOD dwelling in them; that we may be his temple; and he may be one GOD within us; as also he is, and will manifest himself before our faces, by those things for which we justly love him.

16. Be not deceived, my brethren. Those who corrupt houses (by adultery) shall not inherit the kingdom of GOD.ʰ If therefore they who do this according to the flesh, have suffered death;ⁱ how much more shall he die, who by his wicked doctrine corrupts the faith of GOD, for which CHRIST was crucified? He that is thus defiled, shall depart into unquenchable fire; and in like manner he that hearkens to him.

---

* Matt. xii. 33.   ᶠ Ps. xxxiii. 9.
ᵍ Those actions which CHRIST performed in all humility.
ʰ 1 Cor. vi. 9, 10.   ⁱ 1 Cor. x. 8.

§ 17, 18, 19.]   TO THE EPHESIANS.   63

17. For this cause did the Lord receive ointment upon his head,[k] that he might breathe (the breath of) immortality into his Church.[l] Be not ye therefore anointed with the evil savor of the doctrine of the Prince of this world. Let him not take you captive from the life that is set before you. And why are ye not all wise, seeing ye have received the knowledge of God, which is Jesus Christ. Why do we perish in our folly, ignorant of the gift which the Lord hath truly sent us?

18. Let my life be sacrificed for the doctrine of the cross, which is a stumbling-block to them that believe not, but to us is salvation and life everlasting.[m] Where is the wise? Where is the disputer?[n] Where is the boasting of those who are called men of understanding? For our God Jesus Christ was borne in the womb of Mary, according to the dispensation of God, of the seed of David, yet by the Holy Ghost. He was born, and was baptized, that through his passion, he might purify water (to the washing away of sin).

19. And the Prince of this world knew not the virginity of Mary,[o] and him who was born of her, and the

---

[k] Ps. xlv. 7. cxxxiii. 2.   [l] Compare John xx. 22.
[m] 1 Cor. i. 18–23, 24.   [n] 1 Cor. i. 20.

[o] It was a favorite notion with the early Christian writers, that Mary was espoused to Joseph before the birth of Jesus, that his being born of a virgin might escape the knowledge of Satan. Thus Theophilus, the sixth bishop of Antioch, in the Latin version of his *Commentary on St. Matthew's Gospel*, i. 18. has this observation. "Quare non ex simplici virgine, sed ex desponsatâ concipitur Christus? Primò, ut per generationem Josephi origo Mariæ monstraretur: secundò, ne lapidaretur à Judæis ut adultera: tertiò, ut in Ægyptum haberet solatium viri: quartò, ut partus ejus falleret diabolum, putantem Jesum de uxoratâ, non de Virgine natum." [Why was Christ conceived not of a mere virgin, but of one betrothed? First, that the origin of Mary might be shown by the genealogy of Joseph: secondly, lest she should be stoned by the Jews for an adultress: thirdly, that in Egypt she might have the comfort of her husband's company: fourthly, that her delivery might deceive the devil, causing him to think Jesus the son of a married woman, not of a virgin."] Jerome ascribes this very reason to Ignatius, "Martyr Ignatius etiam quartam addit causam cur à desponsatâ conceptus sit, ut partus, inquiens, ejus celaretur à diabolo, dum eum putat non de virgine sed de uxore generatum." [The Martyr Ignatius adds also a fourth reason why he was conceived of one betrothed, saying that it was that her delivery might be concealed from the devil, he being led to think her child the offspring not of a virgin but of a wife.] Basil, in his *Sermon on the Nativity of Christ*,

death of the Lord: three mysteries every where noised abroad, yet done by God in silence. How then was he manifested to the world? A star shone in heaven above all other stars; and its light was inexpressible; and its novelty struck terror. All the rest of the stars, with the sun and moon, were the chorus to this star; and that sent forth its light above all. And there was trouble, whence this novelty came, so unlike to all the others. Hence all (the power of) magic was dissolved; and every bond of wickedness was destroyed: ignorance was taken away; the old kingdom was abolished; God being made manifest in the form of a man, for the renewal of eternal life. Thence began what God had prepared. From thenceforth all things were disturbed, forasmuch as he designed to abolish death.

20. But if Jesus Christ shall give me grace through your prayers, and it be his will, I purpose in a second Epistle, which I am about to write to you, to declare more fully to you the dispensation of which I have now begun to speak, unto the new man, which is Jesus Christ: both in his faith and charity; in his suffering, and in his resurrection, especially if the Lord shall make it known unto me by revelation:[p] since ye all individually come together in common in one faith, and in one Jesus Christ, who was of the race of David according to the flesh, the Son of man, and the Son of God: obeying your Bishop and the Presbytery with an entire affection: breaking one bread, which is the medicine of immortality; our antidote, that we should not die, but live for ever in Jesus Christ.

21. My soul be for yours, and for those whom ye have sent, for the glory of God, to Smyrna, whence also I write unto you, giving thanks unto the Lord;

---

quotes the same opinion. These passages appear to be allusions to this Epistle of Ignatius. 'Origen, in his sixth *Homily on St. Luke*, translated by Jerome, says, "Eleganter in cujusdam Martyris Epistolâ scriptum reperi, Ignatium dico, Episcopum Antiochiæ post Petrum secundum, qui in persecutione Romæ pugnavit ad bestias, Principem sæculi hujus latuit virginitas Mariæ." [I have found it elegantly written in the epistle of a certain martyr, (I mean Ignatius, the second bishop of Antioch after Peter, who in the persecution fought with beasts at Rome,) that the virginity of Mary was hidden from the prince of this world.]—Pearson *Vindiciæ Ignatianæ*, Par. I. cap. 2.

[p] Compare 1 Cor. xiv. 36.

and loving Polycarp, even as I do you. Remember me, even as JESUS CHRIST doth remember you. Pray for the Church which is in Syria, whence I am being carried bound^q to Rome, being the least of all the faithful that are there, as I have been deemed worthy to be found to the glory of GOD. Farewell in GOD the Father, and in JESUS CHRIST, our common hope.

---

^q Ignatius was bound in chains, at Antioch in Syria, and there delivered to the soldiers, to be carried to Rome, as he expresses in his Epistle to the Romans.

THE EPISTLE OF IGNATIUS TO THE MAGNESIANS.

Ignatius, who is also called Theophorus to the (Church) blessed by the grace of God the Father, in Jesus Christ our Saviour; in whom I salute the Church which is at Magnesia, near the Mæander; and wish it all joy, in God the Father, and in Jesus Christ.

1. Having heard of your well ordered love and charity in God, I determined, with much joy, to speak unto you in the faith of Jesus Christ. For having been thought worthy to obtain a most excellent name, in the bonds which I carry about, I salute the Churches, wishing in them a union both of the body and spirit of Jesus Christ, our eternal life; (as also) of faith and charity, to which nothing is to be preferred; but especially of Jesus and the Father, in whom if we undergo all the injuries of the prince of this world, and escape, we shall enjoy God.

2. Seeing then that I have been thought worthy to see you, by Damas[*] your godly and excellent Bishop, and by your worthy Presbyters, Bassus and Apollonius; and by my fellow servant Sotio the Deacon, in whom I rejoice, forasmuch as he is subject unto his Bishop as unto the grace of God, and to the Presbytery, as unto the law of Jesus Christ, (I determined to write unto you.)

3. It is your duty also not to despise the youth of your Bishop, but to yield all reverence to him, according to the power of God the Father. As also I perceive your holy Presbyters do, not considering his youthful

---

[*] Compare Ignatius' *Epist. to Ephes.* Sect. 1. Eusebius, *Eccles. Hist.* iii. 36. says that 'Ignatius wrote an Epistle to the Church in Magnesia near the Mæander, in which he makes mention of their Bishop Damas.'

appearance,[b] but as men prudent in God, submitting to him; and not to him (indeed), but to the Father of our Lord Jesus Christ, the Bishop of us all. It becomes you therefore to be obedient with all sincerity, in honor of him whose pleasure it is (that ye should do so). For, otherwise, a man deceives not this Bishop whom he sees, but affronts him who is invisible. For whatsoever of this kind is done, it reflects not upon men, but upon God, who knows the secrets of our hearts.

4. It is therefore fitting that we should not only be called Christians, but be so: as some call a Bishop by the name (of his office), but do all things without him. But such men appear to me void of a good conscience, since they are not gathered together firmly, according to God's commandment.

5. Seeing then all things have an end, there are set before us at once these two things, death and life: and every one shall depart into his proper place. For as there are two sorts of coins, the one of God, the other of the world, each having its own stamp impressed upon it,[c] so the unfaithful bear the mark of this world, and the faithful in charity that of God the Father through Jesus Christ, through whom unless we hold ourselves in readiness to die, after the likeness of his passion, his life is not in us.

6. Forasmuch, then, as I have seen in faith and love your whole multitude, in the persons of whom I have before written, I exhort you that ye study to do all things in a divine concord; your Bishop presiding in the place of God, and your Presbyters in the place of the council of the Apostles, and your Deacons, most dear to me, being intrusted with the ministry of Jesus Christ, who was with the Father before all ages, and in the end hath appeared.[d] Do ye all, therefore, be in subjection one to another,[e] following the same holy course. And let no man look upon his neighbor after the flesh, but in all things love ye one another in Jesus Christ. Let there be nothing among you which can cause a division; but be ye united to your Bishop, and

---

[b] τὴν φαινομένην νεωτερικὴν τάξιν—This may refer either to his youth, or to his recent ordination.
[c] Compare Rev. xiii. 16. [d] Heb. i. 2. ix. 26.
[e] Eph. v. 21.

to those who preside over you, to be your pattern and direction᷃ unto immortality.

7. As therefore the Lord did nothing without the Father,ᵍ being united to Him; neither by himself nor yet by his Apostles, in like manner do ye nothing without the Bishop and the Presbyters. Neither endeavor that any thing may appear reasonable unto yourselves privately; but being come together into one place, have one prayer, one supplication, one mind, one hope, in love and in joy undefiled.ʰ There is one (Lord) Jesus Christ, than whom nothing is better. Wherefore come ye all together, as unto one temple of God, as unto one altar, as unto one Jesus Christ, who proceeded from one Father, and exists in One, and is returned (to One).ⁱ

8. Be not deceived with strange doctrines, nor with old fables which are unprofitable.ᵏ For if we still continue to live according to the Jewish law, we acknowledge that we have not received grace.ˡ For even the most holy prophets lived according to Christ Jesus. For this cause they were persecuted also, being inspired by his grace, fully to convince the unbelievers that there is One God, who hath manifested himself by Jesus Christ his Son; who is his eternal word,ᵐ not coming forth from silence,ⁿ who in all things was well-pleasing to him that sent him.

9. If, therefore, they who were brought up in these ancient laws, have come to the newness of hope, no longer observing sabbaths, but keeping the Lord's day,*

ᶠ Compare Rom. vi. 17. Phil. iii. 17.
ᵍ John x. 30. xiv. 11, 12. xvii. 21, 22.   ʰ Eph. iv. 3–6.
ⁱ John xvi. 28.   ᵏ Tit. iii. 9.   ˡ Gal. v. 4.   ᵐ John i. 1.
ⁿ See note (C) at the end of the volume.

* The error here pointed out is that of observing the Jewish Sabbath, to the neglect of the Lord's day. That the first day of the week was constantly observed by the early Christians is plain, as well from instances in the New Testament, in which the habitual assembling of Christians, and their celebration of the holy sacrament, on that day, are distinctly ascertained, (Acts xx. 7. 1 Cor. xvi. 2. compared with 1 Cor. xi. 20.) as from the testimony of Justin Martyr, (*Apology*, Sect. 89.) Tertullian, (*Apology*, c. 16.) and others. It was kept so strictly as a festival, that fasting was forbidden on that day. "Die Dominico jejunium nefas ducimus." Tertullian *De Corona Militis*, cap. 3.

The seventh day of the week, which is always designated by the

in which also our life is sprung up by him, and through his death which (yet) some deny:—By which mystery we have been brought to believe, and therefore wait, that we may be found the disciples of JESUS CHRIST our only teacher:—How shall we be able to live without him, whose disciples the very prophets were, and whom by the Spirit they expected as their teacher? And therefore he, whom they righteously waited for, being come, raised them up from the dead.

10. Let us then not be insensible of his goodness. For if he had dealt with us according to our works, we should not now have had a being. Wherefore being become his disciples, let us learn to live a Christian life. For whosoever is called by any other name beside this, is not of GOD. Lay aside therefore the evil leaven, which is grown old and sour; and be changed into the new leaven, which is JESUS CHRIST. Be ye salted in him, lest any of you should be corrupted, for by your savor ye shall be judged. It is absurd to name CHRIST JESUS, and to be still a Jew. For Christianity embraced not the Jewish religion, but the Jewish the Christian: that so every tongue that believed might be gathered together unto GOD.

---

word *Sabbatum* in the early Christian writers, was also observed as a religious festival. Even the Montanists, although very anxious to introduce severe discipline in the observance of fasts, abstained from fasting on Saturday and Sunday, when they kept their two weeks of *Xerophagiæ*. "Duas in anno hebdomadas Xerophagiarum, nec totas, exceptis scilicet Sabbatis et Dominicis, offerimus Deo." (TERTULLIAN *de Jejuniis*, c. 15.) The Saturday before Easter day was, however, observed as a fast. In the *Apostolical Constitutions*, which may be taken to represent the usage of the Church in the fourth century, sentence of suspension is denounced against any of the clergy who should fast on Saturday or Sunday. (Canon 64.) This observance, which probably arose from a desire of conciliating the Jewish converts, continued in the Eastern Church for many centuries. In the Western Church, Saturday was usually observed as a fast. The custom, however, was not general even in Italy. Ambrose, bishop of Milan, in the fourth century, when he was at Rome, observed the day as a fast, but at Milan made no distinction between Saturday and the rest of the week. His answer to Augustine, who consulted him upon the point, has become almost proverbial. "When I come to Rome, I fast on Saturday, as they do at Rome; when I am here I observe no fast. In like manner my advice is that you observe the custom of every Church, where you happen to be." (AUGUSTINI *ad Januar. Epist.* 118. CAVE's *Primitive Christianity*, Part. I. ch. 7. Bp. KAYE's *Tertullian*, chap. vi. p. 409. 1st edit.)

11. These things, my beloved, (I write unto you,) not that I know of any among you who are thus disposed, but, as one less than yourselves, I would warn you, not to fall into the snares of vain-glory, but to be fully instructed in the birth, and sufferings, and resurrection (of CHRIST), which was accomplished in the time of the government of Pontius Pilate; all which was truly and surely performed by JESUS CHRIST, our hope, from which GOD forbid that any of you should ever be turned aside.

12. May I have joy of you in all things, if I shall be worthy of it. For although I am bound, I am not worthy to be compared to one of you who are at liberty. I know that ye are not puffed up. For ye have JESUS CHRIST in your hearts. And the rather when I commend you, I know that ye are ashamed, as it is written, The just man condemneth himself.[p]

13. Give diligence, therefore, to be established in the doctrines of our LORD and the Apostles, that so whatsoever ye do, ye may prosper both in body and spirit: in faith and charity, in the Son and in the Father, and in the Spirit, in the Beginning and in the End;[q] together with your most worthy Bishop, and the well-woven spiritual crown of your Presbytery, and your godly Deacons. Be subject to your Bishop, and to one another, as JESUS CHRIST to the Father, according to the flesh; and the Apostles to CHRIST and to the Father, and to the Spirit; that so there may be (among you) an union both in body and spirit.[r]

14. Knowing you to be full of GOD, I have the more briefly exhorted you. Remember me in your prayers, that I may attain unto GOD; as also the Church which is in Syria, whence I am not worthy to be called. For I stand in need of your joint prayers in GOD, and of your charity, that the Church, which is in Syria, may be thought worthy to be nourished[s] by your Church.

15. The Ephesians from Smyrna, whence also I write, salute you; being present here to the glory of

---

[p] Prov. xviii. 17. Septuagint.
[q] Rev. i. 8.   [r] Eph. iv. 4.
[s] δροσισθῆναι, to be bedewed. Compare Hos. xiv. 5.

God, in like manner as ye are, who have in all things refreshed me, together with Polycarp, the Bishop of the Smyrneans. The rest of the Churches, in the honor of Jesus Christ, salute you. Fare ye well in the concord of God, possessing his inseparable Spirit, which is Jesus Christ.

THE
EPISTLE OF IGNATIUS
TO THE
TRALLIANS.

IGNATIUS, who is also called Theophorus, to the holy Church which is at Tralles in Asia, beloved of GOD the Father of JESUS CHRIST, elect and worthy of GOD, having peace through the flesh, and blood, and passion of JESUS CHRIST, our hope, in the resurrection unto him; whom also I salute in its fulness, (continuing) in the apostolic character, wishing it all joy and happiness.

1. I have heard of your blameless and constant disposition through patience, which not only appears in your outward conversation, but is naturally rooted and grounded in you; even as Polybius[a] your bishop hath declared unto me; who came to me at Smyrna, by the will of GOD and JESUS CHRIST, and so rejoiced with me in my bonds for JESUS CHRIST, that I saw your whole assembly in him. Having therefore received by him the testimony of your good will toward me for GOD's sake, I seemed to find you, as I knew ye were, the followers of GOD.

2. For inasmuch as ye are subject to your Bishop as to JESUS CHRIST, ye appear to me to live not after the manner of men, but according to JESUS CHRIST, who died for us, in order that, believing in his death, ye may escape death. It is therefore necessary that ye do nothing without your Bishop, even as ye are wont: and that ye be also subject to the Presbytery as to the Apostles of JESUS CHRIST, our hope, in whom if we walk, we shall be found (in him).[b] The Deacons also,

---

[a] EUSEBIUS mentions this Polybius, in his account of this Epistle. *Hist. Eccles.* iii. 36.
[b] Compare Phil. iii. 9.

[§ 3, 4, 5.] TO THE TRALLIANS.

as being the (ministers) of the mysteries of JESUS CHRIST, must by all means please all. For they are not the ministers of meat and drink, but of the Church of GOD. Wherefore they must avoid all offences, as (they would avoid) fire.

3. In like manner, let all reverence the Deacons as JESUS CHRIST, and the Bishop as the Father: and the Presbyters as the council of GOD, and the assembly of the Apostles. Without these there is no Church. Concerning all which I am persuaded that ye think after the very same manner. For I have received, and even now have with me, the pattern of your love in your Bishop: whose very look is much instruction, and his mildness, power: whom I am persuaded that even the ungodly reverence. But[c] because I have a love toward you, I will not write any more sharply unto you about this matter, although I very well might; I have even taken so much upon myself, who am but a condemned (captive), as to command you as if I were an apostle.

4. I know many things in GOD; but I refrain myself, lest I should perish in my boasting. For now I ought the more to fear, and not hearken to those that would puff me up. For they, who (so) speak to me, chasten me. I love to suffer, but I know not if I be worthy. And this desire, though to others it doth not appear, yet to myself is (on that account) the more violent. I have, therefore, need of moderation, by which the Prince of this world is destroyed.

5. Am I not able to write to you of heavenly things? But I fear lest I should harm you who are babes in CHRIST: excuse me (this care): lest, not being able to receive them, ye should be choked with them. For even I myself, although I am in bonds, yet am not therefore able to understand heavenly things, as the

---

[c] ὃν λογίζομαι καὶ τοὺς ἀθέους ἐντρέπεσθαι. ἀγαπῶντας ὡς οὐ φείδομαι ἑαυτὸν πότερον, δυνάμενος γράφειν ὑπὲρ τούτου εἰς τοῦτο ᾠήθην, ἵνα ὢν κατάκριτος ὡς ἀπόστολος ὑμῖν διατάσσωμαι. This passage is evidently corrupted, and was so, before the old Latin Version was made, which is here only a verbal translation of the separate Greek words. SALMASIUS, PEARSON, and SMITH all endeavor to explain the passage, without success. The translation in the text is that of Archbishop WAKE. It is founded upon the reading suggested by the corresponding passage in the interpolated Epistle: Ἀγαπῶν ὑμᾶς φείδομαι συντονώτερον ἐπιστεῖλαι κ. τ. λ.

orders of the angels, and the several companies of them under their respective princes, things visible and invisible: but in these I am yet a learner. For many things are wanting to us, that we come not short of GOD.

6. I exhort you therefore (or rather) not I, but the love of JESUS CHRIST, that ye use none but Christian nourishment; abstaining from all strange pasture,[d] which is heresy. For such confound JESUS CHRIST with their own poison,[e] while they seem worthy of belief. As men give a deadly potion mixed with sweet wine; which he who is ignorant of doth with the treacherous pleasure sweetly drink in his own death.[f]

---

[d] βοτάνη—Compare *Epist. to Ephes.* § 10; *Epist. to Philadelph.* § 3.

[e] οἱ καιροὶ παρεμπλέκουσιν Ἰησοῦν Χριστόν—VOSSIUS' conjecture, οἱ καὶ τοῖς, founded upon the old Latin Version and the reading of the interpolated Epistle, appears highly probable, and is here followed.

[f] Compare *Epist. to Philadelph.* § 2. A similar comparison, but more poetical, is used by CHRYSOSTOM, *Contra Judæos* iii. (Tom. VI. p. 344. 24 Savile.) Καθάπερ οἱ τὰ δηλητήρια κεράννυντες φάρμακα, μέλιτι τὸ στόμα τῆς κύλικος περιχρίοντες, εὐπαράδεκτον ποιοῦσι τὴν βλάβην. Although CHRYSOSTOM's application is the same as that of IGNATIUS, it might almost be supposed that he was acquainted with the beautiful passage of LUCRETIUS, as beautifully imitated by TASSO, in which the application is different.

> Nam veluti pueris absinthia tetra medentes
> Quum dare conantur, prius oras pocula circum
> Contingunt mellis dulci flavoque liquore,
> Ut puerorum ætas improvida ludificetur
> Labrorum tenus, interea perpotet amarum
> Absinthi laticem, deceptaque non capiatur,
> Sed potius tali tactu recreata valescat.
>   LUCRET. IV. 11.

> [——For, as oft, benign,
> The sapient nurse, when anxious to enforce
> On the pale boy the wormwood's bitter draught,
> With luscious honey tints the goblet's edge,
> Deceiving thus, while yet unused to guile,
> His unsuspecting lip, till deep he drinks;
> And gathers vigor from the venial cheat;—
>   GOOD's *Lucretius*, IV. 10 ss.]

> Cosi all' egro fanciul porgiamo aspersi
> Di soave licor gli orli del vaso:
> Succhi amari ingannato intanto ei beve,
> E dall' inganno suo vita riceve.
>   TASSO *Ger. Lib.* 1. 3.

> [Thus the sick infant's taste disguised to meet,
> We tinge the vessel's brim with juices sweet;
> The bitter draught his willing lip receives;
> He drinks deceived, and so deceived he lives.
>   HOOLE's *Tasso*, 1. 21 ss.]

7. Wherefore, guard yourselves against such persons. And that ye will do, if ye are not puffed up, but continue inseparable from JESUS CHRIST our GOD, and from your Bishop, and from the commands of the Apostles. He that is within the altar is pure. But he that is without is not pure. That is, he that doeth any thing without the Bishop and the Presbyters, and the Deacons, is not pure in his conscience.

8. Not that I know there is any thing of this nature among you; but I forewarn you, as greatly beloved of me, foreseeing the snares of the devil. Wherefore putting on meekness, renew yourselves in faith, that is the flesh of the LORD, and in charity, that is the blood of JESUS CHRIST. Let no one of you bear a grudge against his neighbor. Give no occasion to the Gentiles, lest by means of a few foolish men, the whole congregation of GOD be evil spoken of. For wo to that man through whose vanity my name is blasphemed by any.[e]

9. Stop your ears, therefore, when any one speaks to you against JESUS CHRIST, who was of the race of David, of the Virgin Mary: who was truly born, and did eat and drink, was truly persecuted under Pontius Pilate, was truly crucified, and died, in the sight of those in heaven, and of those on earth, and of those under the earth. Who also was truly raised from the dead, by his Father; after the same manner as he will also raise up us who believe in him, by CHRIST JESUS, without whom we have no true life.

10. But if, as some who are Atheists,[h] that is to say, unbelievers, pretend, he suffered only in appearance—they themselves living only in appearance—why then am I bound? Why do I desire to fight with beasts? Then do I die in vain. Verily I lie not against the LORD.

---

[e] Isa. liii. 5.

[h] This is a plain allusion to the heresy of the Docetæ, to which St. John probably refers in 1 John iv. 3. "Every spirit that confesseth not that JESUS CHRIST is come in the flesh, is not of GOD." They imagined that the body of our LORD was no real substance, but an unsubstantial phantom. Simon Magus is said to have been the author of this heresy. Menander, his disciple, was a contemporary of Ignatius, and is said by JUSTIN MARTYR, *Apol.* c. 34. to have deceived many in Antioch. Compare IGNATIUS' *Epistle to the Smyrneans*, Sect. 1, 2.

11. Flee, therefore, these evil scions, which bring forth deadly fruit; of which if any one taste he shall presently die. For these are not plants of the Father. For if they were, they would appear to be branches of the cross, and their fruit would be incorruptible; by which he invites you through his passion, who are members of him. For the head cannot be without its members, GOD having promised a union, which is himself.

12. I salute you from Smyrna, together with the Churches of GOD, which are present with me, who have refreshed me in all things, both in body and in spirit. My bonds, which I carry about me, for the sake of CHRIST, beseeching him that I may attain unto GOD, exhort you. Continue in concord among yourselves, and in prayer one with another. For it becomes every one of you, especially the Presbyters, to refresh the Bishop, to the honor of the Father, of JESUS CHRIST, and of the Apostles. I beseech you that you hearken to me, in love, that I may not, by those things which I write, rise up in witness against you. Pray also for me, who stand in need of your love, through the mercy of GOD, that I may be worthy of the portion which I am about to obtain, that I be not found a cast-away.[k]

13. The love of those who are at Smyrna and Ephesus salutes you. Remember ye in your prayers the Church of Syria, from which I am not worthy to be called, being one of the least of it. Fare ye well[l] in JESUS CHRIST, being subject unto your Bishop, as to the command (of GOD), and in like manner to the Presbytery. Love every one his brother in simplicity of heart. May my soul be your expiation,[m] not only now, but when I shall have attained unto GOD. For I am yet under danger. But the Father is faithful in JESUS CHRIST, to fulfil both my petition and yours: in whom may ye be found unblameable.

---

[j] Matt. xv. 13. [k] 1 Cor. ix. 27. [l] ἔῤῥωσθε—Be strong.
[m] The Greek text here has ἁγνίζετε ὑμῶν τὸ ἐμὸν πνεῦμα. VOSSIUS proposes to read ἅγνισμα ὑμῶν, and COTELERIUS ἁγνίζηται.

THE EPISTLE OF IGNATIUS TO THE ROMANS.

IGNATIUS, who is also called Theophorus, to the Church which hath obtained mercy in the Majesty of the most high Father, and his only Son JESUS CHRIST, beloved and illuminated through the will of Him who willeth all things, which are according to the love of JESUS CHRIST, our GOD; (to the Church) which presides also in the place of the region of the Romans, worthy of GOD, and of all honor and blessing and praise; worthy to receive that which she wishes, chaste, and pre-eminent in charity, bearing the name of CHRIST and of the Father, which I salute in the name of JESUS CHRIST, the Son of the Father: to those who are united both in flesh and spirit to all his commands, and wholly filled with the grace of GOD, and entirely cleansed from the stain of any other doctrine, be all undefiled joy in JESUS CHRIST our GOD.

1. Forasmuch as, through my prayers to GOD, I have obtained to see your faces worthy of GOD,[*] which I much desired to do, being bound in CHRIST JESUS I hope to salute you, if it shall be the will of GOD that I shall be thought worthy to attain unto the end. For the beginning is well disposed, if I shall but have grace, without hinderance to take upon me my lot. But I fear your love, lest it injure me. For to you it is easy to do as ye will: but to me it is difficult to attain unto GOD, if ye be (too) indulgent to me.

2. For I would not have you please men, but GOD; even as also ye do. For I shall never have such an opportunity of attaining unto GOD; nor will your

[*] This Epistle was written from Smyrna. But Ignatius, having set out to be brought to Rome, speaks in anticipation of his arrival.

names ever be inscribed upon a better work, if ye only keep silence. For if ye are silent with respect to me, I shall be made partaker of GOD: but if ye shall love my flesh, I shall again have my course to run. Ye can do me no greater favor, than to suffer me to be offered up to GOD, now that the altar is prepared; that when ye are gathered together in love, ye may sing praises to the Father, in CHRIST JESUS, that he hath vouchsafed that a Bishop of Syria [b] should be found, and to call him from the east unto the west. It is truly good for me to set from the world, unto GOD, that I may rise again unto him.

3. Ye have never envied any one; ye have taught others.[c] I would therefore that those things, which ye have commanded others in your teaching, be now established among yourselves. Only pray for me, that GOD would give me both inward and outward strength, that I may not only say, but will: in order that I may not only be called a Christian, but be found one. For if I be so found, I may deservedly be called a Christian; and be faithful then, when I shall no longer appear to the world. Nothing that is seen is eternal; "for the things which are seen are temporal, but the things which are not seen are eternal."[d] For even our GOD, JESUS CHRIST, now that he is in the Father, doth the more appear.[e] A Christian is not made so by the mere power of persuasion, but by greatness of mind: especially when he is hated of the world.[f]

4. I write to all the Churches, and signify to them all, that I am willing to die for GOD, unless you hinder

[b] Ignatius, as the Bishop of Antioch, the chief city of Syria, styles himself Bishop of Syria. Compare Sect. 9. where he refers to himself, as 'the shepherd of Syria.'

[c] Ye have never envied any other the glory of becoming a martyr for the name of CHRIST; nay, ye have encouraged them by your exhortations to remain faithful unto death.

[d] 2 Cor. iv. 18.

[e] By the power which he infuses into his servants, enabling them to undergo all sufferings for his sake.

[f] The Greek text has, οὐ σιωπῆς μόνον τὸ ἔργον, ἀλλὰ μεγέθους ἐστὶν ὁ Χριστιανισμός. "The Christian religion is not to be silently nourished, but magnanimously professed." The reading followed in the text is that of VOSSIUS, suggested by the old Latin version, "οὐ πεισμονῆς τὸ ἔργον, ἀλλὰ μεγέθους ἐστὶν ὁ Χριστιανός, μάλιστα ὅταν μισῆται ὑπὸ κόσμου."

§ 5.] TO THE ROMANS. 79

me. I beseech you that ye show not an unseasonable good-will toward me. Suffer me to be the food of wild beasts, by which I may attain unto GOD. I am the wheat of GOD :[g] and by the teeth of wild beasts I shall be ground, that I may be found the pure bread of CHRIST. Rather encourage the wild beasts, that they may become my sepulchre, and may leave nothing of my body; that when I sleep I may be burdensome to no one. Then shall I truly be a disciple of CHRIST, when the world shall not see so much as my body. Pray to CHRIST for me, that by these instruments I may be made a sacrifice (of GOD). I command you not, as Peter and Paul did: they were apostles, I a condemned man: they were free, but I hitherto a servant: but if I shall suffer, I shall then become the free-man of JESUS (CHRIST), and shall rise free in him. And now, being in bonds, I learn to desire no worldly or vain thing.

5. From Syria even to Rome I fight with beasts both by sea and land, by night and day; being bound to ten leopards, that is to say, a band of soldiers, who even when kindly treated become the worse.[h] But by their unjust treatment I am the more instructed: yet am I not thereby justified.[i] May I enjoy the wild beasts which are prepared for me;[k] and pray that they may

---

[g] These remarkable words are quoted by IRENÆUS, *Adv. Hæres.* v. 28. EUSEBIUS, *Hist. Eccles.* iii. 36. JEROME, in his *Catalogue of Ecclesiastical Writers*, the *Menologia Græca*, and others, say that Ignatius addressed to the people expressions of the same nature, when he was brought out before the wild beasts. "O Romans, the spectators of this contest, I am not thus condemned for any evil deed, but for the sake of my religion. For I am the wheat of GOD, and by the teeth of wild beasts I shall be ground, that I may be the pure bread (of CHRIST)."

[h] This passage also is quoted by EUSEBIUS, *Hist. Eccles.* iii. 36. Ignatius compares the ill usage which he experienced from the soldiers to the violence with which the beasts, to which he was condemned, would treat him. "My contest with wild beasts is already begun, and continues all the way from Syria even to Rome. Rather than endure the insults, could I rejoice in the wild beasts which are prepared for me."

[i] 1 Cor. iv. 4.

[k] CHRYSOSTOM quotes this expression in his *Homily on the Martyrdom of Ignatius*. The annals of the primitive martyrs present many instances, in which those who were exposed to wild beasts or subjected to other punishment, used means to accelerate their own

be found ready for me: which I will even encourage to devour me all at once, and not fear to touch me, as they have some others. And even if they refuse, and will not, I will compel them. Bear with me (in this): I know what is profitable for me; now I begin to be a disciple.[l] Let nothing, of things either visible or invisible, deprive me of attaining unto JESUS CHRIST. Let fire and the cross, and the companies of wild beasts, let tearings and rendings, let breakings of bones, and the cutting off of limbs, let the shatterings of the whole body, and all the evil torments of the devil come upon me: only let me attain unto JESUS CHRIST.

6. All the pleasures of the world and the kingdoms of this life will avail me nothing. Better is it for me to die for CHRIST JESUS than to reign over the ends of the earth. "For what is a man profited, if he shall gain the whole world, and lose his own soul?"[m] Him I seek, who died for us: him I desire, who rose again for us. This is the gain that is laid up for me.[n] Pardon me, brethren: hinder me not from living, let me not die,[o] who am willing to be GOD's. Rejoice not in the world; suffer me to enter into pure light: when I shall be there, I shall be a man of GOD. Suffer me to imitate the sufferings of my GOD. If any one hath Him within himself, let him consider what I desire, and sympathize with me, knowing how I am straitened.

7. The Prince of this world would fain carry me away, and corrupt my resolution toward my GOD. Let none of you therefore assist him: rather join yourselves to me, that is to GOD. Do not speak of JESUS CHRIST, and yet covet the world. Let not envy dwell in you: obey not even me, if, when I shall be present with you, I should exhort you (to the contrary): but rather obey these commands which I write unto you. I write to you desiring to die, though I live. My love is crucified:[p] and in me, who love (a heavenly object), there

---

death. See the *Circular Epistle of the Church of Smyrna* on the martyrdom of Polycarp, c. 3.

[l] Luke xiv. 27.   [m] Matt. xvi. 26.   [n] Phil. i. 21.

[o] Hinder me not from attaining immortal life, let me not die eternally, by refusing to suffer for CHRIST's sake.

[p] The Greek here has, ὁ ἐμὸς ἔρως ἐσταύρωται, καὶ οὐκ ἔστιν ἐν ἐμοὶ πῦρ φιλόϋλον· ὕδωρ δὲ ζῶν, κ. τ. λ. "There is in me no fire delighting

is no (earthly) fire; but living water, springing up in me, saying with me, Come unto the Father.⁹ I delight not in the food of corruption, nor in the pleasures of this life; I desire the bread of GOD; the heavenly bread, the bread of life, which is the flesh of JESUS CHRIST the Son of GOD, who was born, in these last days, of the seed of David and Abraham: and the drink of GOD which I desire is his blood, which is incorruptible love and eternal life.

8. I have no desire to live any longer after the manner of men; neither shall I, if ye consent. Consent therefore, that (GOD) may also consent unto you. I exhort you in few words; believe me. And JESUS CHRIST will show you that I speak truth, he who is the mouth of the Father, without deceit, in whom the Father speaks truly. Pray for me, that I may attain. I have not written unto you after the flesh, but according to the will of GOD. If I shall suffer, ye have consented to my wishes; if I shall be rejected, ye have hated me.

9. Remember in your prayers the Church of Syria, which now enjoys GOD for its shepherd, instead of me. JESUS CHRIST alone shall supply the place of its Bishop,

---

in matter, &c." SIMEON METAPHRASTES has also φιλόυλον. The old Latin Version, which is usually a strictly verbal translation, has "et non est in me ignis amans aliquam aquam; sed vivens et loquens est in me, &c." The interpolated Epistle has the same reading as the old Latin Version οὐκ ἔστιν ἐν ἐμοὶ πῦρ φιλοῦντι. The sense of the passage being to this effect: "While I contemplate JESUS, whose love dwells in me, crucified for me, the fire which the vain desires of the world kindle, is extinguished within me. I perceive my whole heart bedewed with the effusion of the HØLY SPIRIT, as by a copious and perpetual stream of living water, springing up unto everlasting life. And thence I hear as it were a heavenly voice, calling unto me, and saying, Come unto the Father."

ORIGEN, in the introduction to his *Commentary on the Book of Canticles*; the book *De Divinis Nominibus*, ascribed to DIONYSIUS THE AREOPAGITE, Cap. 4; the *Menologia Græca*, on the 20th of December; and many modern writers, agree in considering the terms "my love is crucified," as expressing the love of Ignatius to his Saviour who was crucified for him. This seems the most natural meaning of the expression.

CAVE, in his *Life of Ignatius*, Ch. xi., follows the opinion of those who refer the words to the disposition of Ignatius himself, who had "crucified the flesh with the affections and lusts."

⁹ John iv. 14.

together with your love. But I am ashamed even to be reckoned as one of them. For neither am I worthy, being the least among them, and as one born out of due time.[r] But through mercy I have obtained to be somebody, if I shall attain unto GOD. My spirit salutes you: and the charity of the Churches which have received me in the name of JESUS CHRIST, not simply as a passenger. For even those which belonged not at all to me, have brought me on my journey from city to city, in my way according to the flesh.

10. These things I write to you from Smyrna, by the most worthy of the Church of Ephesus. There is now with me, together with many others, Crocus, most beloved of me. I doubt not that ye have known of those who are gone before me out of Syria to Rome, to the glory of GOD: to whom signify also that I am near at hand: for they are all worthy both of GOD and of you, whom it is fit that ye refresh in all things.

This have I written to you, on the twenty-fourth day of August. Be strong unto the end, in the patience of JESUS CHRIST.

---

[r] 1 Cor. xv. 8. Compare *Epist. to the Smyrnæans*, Sect. 11.

THE EPISTLE OF IGNATIUS TO THE PHILADEPHIANS.

IGNATIUS, who is also called Theophorus, to the Church of GOD the Father, and our Lord JESUS CHRIST, which is at Philadelphia in Asia, which hath obtained mercy and is fixed in the unity of GOD, and rejoices evermore in the passion of our LORD, and is fulfilled in all mercy through his resurrection: which also I salute in the blood of JESUS CHRIST, which is our eternal and abiding joy, especially if they be at unity with the Bishop and the Presbyters and Deacons with him, appointed according to the will of JESUS CHRIST whom he hath settled according to his own will, in all firmness by the HOLY SPIRIT.

1. Which Bishop I know obtained that ministry which appertains to the public good, neither of himself nor by men, nor through vain glory, but in the love of GOD the Father and our Lord JESUS CHRIST; whose moderation I admire; who by his silence prevails more than the vain speech of others. For (his mind) is aptly fitted to the commandments, as a harp to its strings.[a] Wherefore my soul esteems his mind toward GOD most happy, knowing it to be fruitful in all virtue, and perfect, full of constancy, free from passion, and according to all the moderation of the living GOD.

2. Wherefore, as becomes children of light and of truth, flee divisions and false doctrines: for where the shepherd is, there do ye, as sheep, follow after. For many wolves,[b] which appear worthy of belief, do through the allurements of evil pleasure lead captive

---

[a] See IGNATIUS' *Epistle to the Ephesians*, Sect. 4.
[b] Acts xx. 29.

those that run in the course of God. But in your concord they shall find no place.

3. Abstain from those evil herbs,* which Jesus Christ cultivates not, since they are not planted by the Father. Not that I have found any division among you, but purity from all defilement.[d] For as many as are of God, and of Jesus Christ, are also with their Bishop. And as many as shall with repentance return into the unity of the Church, even these shall also be the servants of God, that they may live according to Jesus Christ. Be not deceived, my brethren: if any one follows him that makes a schism (in the Church), he shall not inherit the kingdom of God. If any one walks after any other opinion, he agrees not with the passion (of Christ).

4. Give diligence, therefore, to partake all of the same Eucharist. For there is but one flesh of our Lord Jesus Christ, and one cup, in the unity of his blood: one altar, as there is also one Bishop, together with the Presbytery, and the Deacons, my fellow-servants. That so, whatsoever ye do, ye may do it according to the will of God.

5. My brethren, I am greatly enlarged in my love toward you; and in my great joy I would establish you: yet not I, but Jesus Christ, in whom being bound I fear the more, as yet being imperfect.[e] But your prayer to God shall make me perfect, that I may attain that portion, which by God's mercy, is allotted unto me: fleeing to the Gospel,[f] as to the flesh of Christ, and to the Apostles, as unto the Presbytery of the Church. Let us also love the prophets, forasmuch as they also proclaimed the coming of the Gospel, and hoped in Christ, and waited for him: in whom believing

---

* Compare the *Epistle to the Trallians*, Sect. 6.

[d] ἀποδιϋλισμόν, the clearness which is produced by filtering or straining a liquid, so as to separate from it all extraneous substances.

[e] Compare Ignatius' *Epistle to the Ephesians*, Sect. 3.

[f] Having recourse to the Gospel, as if it were to Jesus Christ himself, and to the writings of the Apostles, who are the council of the Church.—Le Clerc well observes that Ignatius here specifies, in the first place, the Scriptures of the New Testament, as his refuge: and, in the second place, those of the Old Testament, as confirmatory of the New.

He ascribes also the salvation of the prophets to their faith.

also they were saved, in the unity of JESUS CHRIST, being holy men worthy of all love and admiration, who have received testimony from JESUS CHRIST, and are numbered in the Gospel of our common hope.

6. But if any one shall teach you the Jewish law, hear him not. For better is it to receive the law of CHRIST from one that is circumcised, than the law of the Jews from one that is uncircumised.[g] But if either the one or the other do not speak concerning CHRIST JESUS, they seem to me but as monuments and sepulchres of the dead, upon which are written only the names of men. Flee, therefore, the wicked arts and snares of the prince of this world, lest at any time being oppressed by his craftiness ye grow weak in charity. But come all together into the same place with an undivided heart. And I bless my GOD that I have a good conscience toward you, and that no one among you hath to boast, either openly or privately, that I have been burdensome to any either in much or little.[h] And I pray that this be not for a testimony to all among whom I have conversed.

7. For although some would have deceived me according to the flesh, yet the Spirit is not deceived, being from GOD. For it knows both whence it comes, and whither it goes,[i] and reproves the secrets (of the heart).[k] I cried, whilst I was among you, I spake with a loud voice, Give ear to the Bishop, and to the Presbytery, and to the Deacons. And some suppose that I spake this, as knowing before the separation of some. But He is my witness, for whose sake I am in bonds, that I know nothing from any man. But the Spirit spake, saying on this wise; do nothing without the Bishop: keep your bodies as the temples of GOD: love unity: flee divisions: be the followers of CHRIST, as he was of his Father.

8. I therefore performed my part, as a man anxious for unity. For where there is division and strife, GOD dwells not. But GOD forgives all that repent, if they return to the unity of GOD, and to the council of the Bishop. For I trust in the grace of JESUS CHRIST, that

---

[g] See note on IGNATIUS' *Epistle to the Magnesians*, § 8.
[h] 2 Cor. xi. 9.   [i] John iii. 8.   [k] Heb. iv. 12.

he will free you from every bond. Nevertheless, I exhort you that ye do nothing out of strife, but according to the instruction of CHRIST.[1] Because I have heard some say, Unless I find it in the ancient writings, I will not believe in the Gospel. And when I said to them, It is written (in the Gospel), they answered me, It is found written before (in the Law). But to me the most ancient records are JESUS CHRIST; the most uncorrupted records, his cross, and death, and rising again, and faith in him, by which I desire, through your prayers, to be justified.

9. The priests themselves are good. But much better is the High Priest, to whom only hath been committed the Holy of Holies, to whom alone have been intrusted the secret things of GOD. He is the door of the Father, by which enter in Abraham and Isaac, and Jacob, and the Prophets, and the Apostles, and the Church. All these things are for the unity of GOD. Howbeit the Gospel hath somewhat in it far above, the appearance of our Lord JESUS CHRIST, his passion, and resurrection. For the beloved prophets referred to him; but the Gospel is the perfection of incorruption. All, therefore, together are good, if ye believe with charity.

10. Forasmuch as I am told, that, through your prayers and the bowels which ye have in CHRIST JESUS, the Church, which is in Antioch in Syria, is at peace,[m] it will become you, as the Church of GOD, to appoint a Deacon to go to them thither as the ambassador of GOD, that he may rejoice with them when they meet together, and glorify the name of GOD.

---

[1] This seems to be a caution against the early heretics, such as the Cerinthians and Ebionites, who would not admit any doctrine of the Gospel, except such as could be proved by the writings of the Old Testament. LARDNER, (*Credibility*, Part II. c. 17, p. 323,) agrees with LE CLERC, in supposing that a reference is here made to those who appealed, on all controverted points, to the original autographs of the Gospels. The whole tenor of the passage, however, from Sect. 6. to Sect. 9. appears to relate to the Jewish law, compared with the Gospel.

[m] Compare IGNATIUS' *Epist. to the Smyrneans*, § 11. and *to Polycarp*, § 7. Archbishop USHER is of opinion that this peace to the Church of Antioch arose from the Edict of Trajan, that the Christians should no longer be sought out for punishment.

Blessed be that man in CHRIST JESUS, who shall be found worthy of such a ministry; and ye yourselves also shall be glorified. If, now, ye be willing, it is not impossible for you, (to do this) for the sake of GOD, as also the other neighboring churches have sent them, some Bishops, and other Priests and Deacons.

11. As concerning Philo the Deacon of Cilicia, a man of honest report,[a] who now also ministers unto me in the word of GOD, with Rheus Agathopus,[o] a chosen man, who is also following me from Syria, not regarding his life, these also bear witness of you. And I myself give thanks to GOD for you, that ye have received them, even as the LORD hath received us. And for those who dishonored them, may they be forgiven through the grace of JESUS CHRIST. The love of the brethren that are at Troas salutes you; whence also I now write by Burrhus, who was sent together with me by those of Ephesus and Smyrna, for respect sake. May our Lord JESUS CHRIST honor them; in whom they hope, both in body, and soul, and spirit,[p] in faith, and love, and unity. Fare ye well in CHRIST JESUS, our common hope.

---

[a] Acts vi. 3.   [o] See *Epist. to the Smyrneans,* § 10.
[p] 1 Thes. v. 23.

THE
EPISTLE OF IGNATIUS
TO THE
SMYRNEANS.

IGNATIUS, who is also called Theophorus, to the Church of GOD the Father, and of the beloved JESUS CHRIST, which is at Smyrna, in Asia, (a Church, which is mercifully blessed with every good gift,[a] being filled with faith and charity, so that it is wanting in no good gift, most godly, and fruitful in saints,) all joy through the immaculate spirit and the word of GOD.

1. I glorify GOD, even JESUS CHRIST, who hath given you such wisdom. For I have observed that you are settled in an immoveable faith, nailed, as it were to the cross of the Lord JESUS CHRIST, both in the flesh, and in the spirit, and are confirmed in love through the blood of CHRIST, being fully persuaded of those things which relate unto our LORD, who was truly[b] of the race of David according to the flesh, (but) the SON of GOD, according to the will and power of GOD, truly born of a virgin, and baptized by John, that so all righteousness might be fulfilled in him,[c] truly crucified for us in the flesh under Pontius Pilate and Herod the Tetrarch. By the fruits of which, by his most blessed passion, we are: that he might set up a token[d] for all ages through his resurrection, to all his holy and faithful servants, whether they be Jews or Gentiles, in one body of his Church.

2. Now all these things he suffered for us, that we might be saved. And he suffered truly, as he also

---

[a] 1 Cor. vii. 25.
[b] These observations are directed against the Docetæ, who denied CHRIST had a real body. Compare Sect. 4. and *Epist. to Trallians*, § 10.
[c] Matt. iii. 15.   [d] Isa. v. 26. xlix. 22. lxii. 10.

§ 3.]   IGNATIUS TO THE SMYRNEANS.   89

truly raised up himself. And not, as some unbelievers say that he only seemed to suffer, they themselves seeming only to be (Christians).[e] And as they believe so shall it happen unto them, when they are divested of the body, and shall become mere spirits.

3. For I know that even after the resurrection he was in the flesh, and believe that he is still so. And when he came to those who were with Peter, he said unto them, Take, handle me, and see that I am not an incorporeal demon.[f] And straightway they touched him and believed, being convinced both by his flesh and by his spirit. For this cause they despised death, and were found above it. But after the resurrection, he did

---

[e] Compare *Epist. to Trallians*, § 10. Thus Tertullian, *Adv. Valentinianos*, c. 27. "Ita omnia in imagines urgent, planè et ipsi imaginarii Christiani."

[f] λάβετε, ψηλαφήσατε με, καὶ ἴδετε, ὅτι οὐκ εἰμὶ δαιμόνιον ἀσώματον.
These words are in all probability, a loose quotation from the Gospel of St. Luke xxiv. 39. ψηλαφήσατε με, καὶ ἴδετε· ὅτι πνεῦμα σάρκα καὶ ὀστέα οὐκ ἔχει καθὼς ἐμὲ θεωρεῖτε ἔχοντα. "Handle me, and see; for a spirit hath not flesh and bones as ye see me have." Ignatius evidently here uses the word *demon* to mean no more than "spirit." It is so much the custom for the early Christian writers to quote the substance, and not the very words of Scripture; and Ignatius, when he wrote this Epistle, was so likely to quote from memory; that probably the allusion, in this case, would scarcely have been questioned, had not Eusebius (*Eccles. Hist.* iii. 36.) expressed his ignorance of the place whence the quotation was taken: and Jerome on two occasions (*De Scriptoribus Ecclesiasticis*, and in his *Commentary on Isaiah*, lib. 18.) stated that Ignatius quotes the passage from the *Gospel according to the Hebrews*. In another place (*Adversus Pelagianos*, lib. 3.) Jerome describes this Gospel as being "written in the Chaldean or Syrian language, but in Hebrew characters;" and says that in his time, the early part of the fifth century, it was in use among the Nazarenes, and called the Gospel according to the Apostles, or more generally "the Gospel according to Matthew."
Origen, (περὶ ἀρχῶν, lib. 1.) says that in the book which is called "the Doctrine of Peter," the Saviour appears to say to his disciples, that he is not an incorporeal demon.
The testimony of Jerome leaves no doubt that these words were found in the *Gospel according to the Hebrews*: but it certainly does not appear that Ignatius quoted from that Gospel. Le Clerc, in his third Dissertation, at the end of his *Harmonia Evangelica*, and Lardner, (*Credibility of the Gospel History*, Part ii. c. 5. 55.) are of opinion that Ignatius here merely alludes to St. Luke. Bp. Pearson, (*Vindiciæ Ignatianæ*, Part ii. c. 9. p. 103.) agrees with Isaac Casaubon in supposing that Ignatius refers to some verbal tradition, which might afterward be inserted in the Gospel according to the Hebrews, ascribed to St. Matthew.

8*

eat and drink with them, although as to his spirit he was united to the Father.

4. Now of these things I remind you brethren, not questioning but that ye yourselves also believe that they are so. But I forewarn you to beware of certain beasts in the shape of men, whom ye must not only not receive, but, if possible, not even meet with. Only ye must pray for them,[g] that if it be the will of GOD they may repent, which yet will be very hard. But of this JESUS CHRIST hath the power, who is our true life. For if all these things were done by our LORD in appearance only,[h] then I am bound in appearance only. Wherefore then have I given myself over unto death, to fire, to sword, to wild beasts? But now the nearer I am to the sword, the nearer to GOD; when I am among the wild beasts, I am with GOD. Only in the name of JESUS CHRIST, I undergo all, to suffer together with him; since he, who was made perfect man, strengthens me.

5. Whom some, not knowing, do deny: or rather have been denied by him, being the advocates of death, rather than of the truth. Neither the prophets, nor the law of Moses, nor even the Gospel itself, even to this day, nor the sufferings of every one of us, have persuaded these men. For they think also the same things of us. For what doth any one profit me, if he shall praise me, and blaspheme my LORD, confessing not that he was truly made flesh? Now he that doth not say this, doth in effect deny him, and is in death.[i] But

---

[g] This is an early instance of distinct prayer for the conversion of heretics; as in IRENÆUS, (*Adv. Hæres.* iii. 46.) "Nos autem precamur non perseverare illos in foveâ quam ipsi foderunt, sed segregari— et legitimè eos generari, conversus ad ecclesiam Dei. Hæc precamur de illis, utiliùs eos diligentes quàm ipsi semet ipsos putant diligere."
Our own Church, in the third Collect for Good Friday, expressly follows the example thus set, and continued in the Christian Church. See PALMER's *Antiquities of the English Liturgy*, ch. 14. Vol. I. p. 333.

[h] Compare *Epistle to the Trallians*, Sect. 10.

[i] There is here a correspondence in terms, which cannot be expressed in a translation. He who doth not confess that JESUS CHRIST truly *bore* our flesh (σαρκοφόρος) is himself (νεκροφόρος) *a bearer* of the dead, who carries about his own body, "dead while he liveth." CYPRIAN expresses the same sentiment in his treatise *De Lapsis* (p. 135. Fell.) "Animam tuam misera perdidisti: spiritualiter

for the names of such persons, thus being unbelievers, I thought it not fitting to write them unto you. Yea, GOD forbid that I should make any mention of them, till they shall repent to a true belief of CHRIST's passion, which is our resurrection.[k]

6. Let no man deceive himself. Both the things which are in heaven, and the glory of angels, and princes whether visible or invisible, unless they believe in the blood of CHRIST, even they shall receive condemnation.[l] He that is able to receive this, let him receive it.[m] Let no man's place puff him up. For that which is worth all is faith and charity, to which nothing is to be preferred. But consider those who are of a different opinion with respect to the grace of JESUS CHRIST which is come unto us, how contrary they are to the design of GOD. They have no regard to charity, (no care) of the widow, the fatherless, and the oppressed, of the bound or free, of the hungry or thirsty.

---

mortua supervivere hic tibi, et ipsa ambulans *funus tuum portare coepisti*; et non acriter plangis, non jugiter ingemiscis?" [Miserable woman, thou hast lost thy soul: spiritually dead, thou hast begun here to survive thyself, and in walking to *carry thine own corpse;* and dost thou not bitterly complain, dost thou not incessantly bewail thyself?] And JEROME, (*Ep.* xiii.) "Quanti hodie diu vivendo *portant funera sua.*" [How many at this day *carry their own corpses* through a long life?]

[k] Until they shall renounce their heretical opinions respecting his passion, which they hold to have been merely imaginary, and acknowledge that his sufferings were real, by virtue of which alone we look for our own resurrection.

[l] IGNATIUS is not the only early Christian writer, who held that the death of CHRIST was influential in the salvation of orders of beings superior to man. JEROME, in his *Commentary on the Epistle to the Ephesians,* lib. ii. says, "Descendit ergo in inferiora terræ, et ascendit super omnes coelos Filius Dei, ut non tantùm leges prophetasque compleret, sed et alias quasdam occultas dispensationes, quod solus ille novit cum Patre. Neque enim scire possumus, quo modo et angelis, et his qui in inferno erant, sanguis CHRISTI profuerit: et tamen quin profuerit nescire non possumus." [The Son of GOD therefore descended into the lower parts of the earth, and ascended above all heavens, that he might fulfil not only the law and the prophets, but also certain other hidden dispensations, which he only knows with the Father. For we can neither know *how* the blood of CHRIST advantaged both the angels, and those who were in hell; nor yet can we be ignorant that it *did* advantage them.]

[m] Matt. xix. 12.

7. They abstain from the Eucharist and from prayer, because they confess not the Eucharist to be the flesh of our Saviour Jesus Christ, which suffered for our sins, and which the Father, of his goodness, raised up (again from the dead). They therefore who contradict the gift of God, die in their disputes. But better would it be for them to receive it,[a] that they might rise also from the dead. It will become you, therefore, to abstain from such persons, and not to speak with them either in private or in public: but to hearken to the prophets, and especially to the Gospel, in which Christ's passion is manifested unto us, and his resurrection perfectly declared. But flee all divisions, as the beginning of evils.

8. See that ye all follow your Bishop, as Jesus Christ the Father: and the Presbytery, as the Apostles: and reverence the Deacons as the command of God. Let no one do any thing which belongs to the Church, separately from the Bishop. Let that Eucharist be looked upon as well established, which is either offered by the Bishop, or by one to whom the Bishop hath given his consent. Wheresoever the Bishop shall appear, there let the people also be: as, where Jesus Christ is, there is the Catholic[b] Church. It is not

---

[a] ἀγαπᾶν. This is the sense which Abp. Wake gives to the word. It may perhaps mean, to acquiesce, and no longer contradict the gift of God. Bp. Pearson considers it to refer to the *Agapæ*, or common feasts of the rich and the poor, which were held at the time of the celebration of the Eucharist. See below, § 8. This feast, in the early ages of the Church, seems to have preceded the Communion, (1 Cor. xi. 20, 21.) but at a later period, it was deferred till after the administration of the Holy Sacrament. In the council of Carthage, A.D. 252, it was decreed that the Eucharist should be received fasting, except at Easter. See Bingham, *Ecclesiastical Antiquities*, Book xv. ch. vii. 7. Cave, *Primitive Christianity*, Part I. ch. 11. Suicer's *Thesaurus* on the word 'Ἀγάπη. Tertullian, *Apol*. c. 39.

[b] This is the earliest instance of the use of the word *Catholic*, which was so soon adopted to distinguish the faith of the Christian Church diffused throughout the whole world from that of other sects, which wished to shelter themselves under the name of Christians. Pacian in his *Epistle to Sempronian* the Novatian heretic, in the fourth century, well describes the reason of this appellation. "Christian is my name, and Catholic my sirname: the first is my denomination, the second my distinction." (Christianus mihi nomen est, Catholicus cognomen. Illud me nuncupat, istud ostendit.) The word *Catholic* occurs in the introduction to the *Account of the Martyrdom of Polycarp*. See Bingham, *Eccles. Ant.* Book I. ch. i. 7.

lawful, without the Bishop, either to baptize, or to celebrate the Holy Communion.[p] But whatsoever he shall approve of, that is also pleasing unto GOD, that so whatsoever is done may be surely and well done.

9. For what remains, it is reasonable that we should repent, and, while there is yet time, return unto GOD. It is good to have due regard both to GOD and to the Bishop. He that honors the Bishop, shall be honored of GOD. But he that doeth any thing without his knowledge, ministers unto the Devil. Let all things therefore abound to you in charity, seeing ye are worthy. Ye have refreshed me in all things; so shall JESUS CHRIST you. Ye have loved me absent and present. May GOD repay you, for whom whilst ye undergo all things ye shall attain unto him.

10. Ye have done well, in that ye have received Philo, and Rheus Agathopus,[q] who followed me for the word of GOD, as the Deacons of CHRIST our GOD: who also give thanks unto the LORD for you, forasmuch as ye have refreshed them in all things. Nothing (that ye have done) shall be lost to you. May my soul be for yours, and my bonds, which ye have not despised, nor been ashamed of. Neither shall JESUS CHRIST, (our) perfect faith, be ashamed of you.

11. Your prayer is come to the Church of Antioch which is in Syria. Whence being sent bound with chains, which are the fittest ornament[r] of a servant of GOD, I salute all (the Churches), not as though I were worthy to take my name from that Church, being the least of them.[s] Nevertheless by the will of GOD I have been thought worthy (of this honor); not that I am at all conscious of deserving it, but by the grace of GOD, which I wish may be given unto me in perfection, that by your prayers I may attain unto GOD. In order, therefore, that your work may be fully accomplished, both upon earth and in heaven, it is fitting, that, for the honor of GOD, your Church should appoint some worthy

---

[p] ἀγάπην ποιεῖν. See note (n) on Sect. 7.

[q] Compare *Epistle to the Philadelphians*, Sect. 11.

[r] Θεοπρεπεστάτοις δεσμοῖς. Compare *Epistle of* POLYCARP, Sect. 1. IGNATIUS, *Epistle to the Ephes.* Sect. 11.

[s] Compare IGNATIUS' *Epistles, to the Romans*, Sect. 9., *to the Trallians*, Sect. 13.

delegate, who being come as far as Syria may rejoice with them, in that they were at peace,' and that they are again restored to their former greatness, and have again received their proper body. It hath appeared therefore to me a proper measure, that ye send some one from you, with an epistle, to congratulate them upon the calm which hath been given them of GOD, and that through your prayers they have already attained to a harbor. Being perfect, mind also that which is perfect. For when ye are desirous to do well, GOD is ready to enable you thereunto.

12. The love of the brethren that are at Troas salutes you. Whence also I write to you by Burrhus whom ye sent with me, together with the Ephesians your brethren; and who hath in all things refreshed me. And would that all imitated him, as being a pattern of the ministry of GOD. May (his) grace fully reward him. I salute your very worthy Bishop, and your venerable Presbytery, and your Deacons, my fellow-servants; and all of you in general, and every one in particular, in the name of JESUS CHRIST, and in his flesh and blood; in his passion and resurrection both fleshly and spiritually, in the unity of GOD with you. Grace be with you, and mercy, and peace, and patience, for evermore.

13. I salute the families of my brethren with their wives, and children, and the virgins that are called Widows.ᵘ Be strong in the power of the Holy Ghost.

' See the *Epistle to the Philadelphians*, Sect. 10. *to Polycarp*, Sect. 7.

ᵘ These were the *Deaconnesses*, whose office was very ancient in the Christian Church. St. Paul speaks of Phœbe, "a servant (διάκονος) of the Church which is at Cenchrea." Rom. xvi. 1. And PLINY evidently alludes to them, in his celebrated Epistle: (Lib. x. Ep. 97.) "Quo magis necessarium credidi, ex duabus ancillis, quæ *ministræ* dicebantur, quid esset veri et per tormenta quærere." [For which reason I the rather deemed it necessary to ascertain the truth from two maidens, who were called *servants*, even by torture.] They are frequently styled *Widows*; (TERTULL. Lib. i. *ad Uxorem*. c. 7.) and usually were so. The qualifications generally required for a Deaconness were, that she should be a widow, who had borne children, had been the wife of but one husband, and of mature age, from forty to sixty years old. TERTULLIAN (*De Velandis Virgin*. c. 9.) inveighs in strong terms against the abuse of introducing a virgin, under the age of twenty years, into the order of the Deaconnesses. " Planè

Philo, who is present with me, salutes you. I salute the house of Tavia, and pray that she may be strengthened in faith and charity, both of flesh and spirit. I salute Alce, my well-beloved; and the incomparable Daphnus, and Eutechnus, and all (others) by name. Farewell in the grace of God.

---

scio alicubi virginem *in viduatu* ab annis nondum viginti collocatam. Cui si quid refrigerii debuerat Episcopus, aliter utique salvo respectu disciplinæ præstare potuisset, ne tale nunc miraculum, ne dixerim monstrum, in Ecclesiâ denotaretur." [Indeed I know that in a certain place a virgin not yet twenty years old was placed *in the widowhood*. To whom if the bishop was bound to render any assistance, he might surely have done it in some other way with due regard to discipline, and so have preserved the Church from the stigma of such a wonderful, not to say monstrous transaction.]

It appears, however, from this passage of IGNATIUS, and from other authorities, that virgins were admitted into this order. Thus EPIPHANIUS (*Exposit. Fid.* n. 21.) says the Deaconnesses must be either virgins, or widows who had been but once married: ἢ χηρεύσασαι ἀπὸ μονογαμίας, ἢ ἀεὶ πάρθενοι οὖσαι. The same rule is laid down in the *Apostolical Constitutions*, Lib. vi. c. 17; the *preference* being there given to a virgin. See BINGHAM, *Eccles. Ant.* B. II. c. xxii. 1, 2. where several instances of virgin Deaconnesses are mentioned: and VALESIUS, on EUSEBIUS *de Laudibus Constantini*, c. 17.

THE

EPISTLE OF IGNATIUS

TO

POLYCARP.

IGNATIUS, who is also called Theophorus, to Polycarp, Bishop of the Church which is at Smyrna; (their overseer), but rather himself overseen by GOD the Father, and our Lord JESUS CHRIST; all happiness.

1. Having known that thy mind toward GOD is fixed as it were upon an immoveable rock, I exceedingly give thanks, that I have been thought worthy to behold thy blessed face, in which may I always rejoice in GOD. I beseech thee, by the grace of GOD, with which thou art clothed, to press forward in thy course, and to exhort all (others) that they may be saved. Maintain thy station with all diligence both of flesh and spirit.[a] Be careful (to preserve) unity, than which nothing is better. Bear with all men; even as the LORD with thee. Support all in love, as also thou dost. Find time to pray without ceasing. Ask more understanding than that thou already hast. Be watchful, having thy spirit always awake. Speak to every one, according as GOD shall enable thee. Bear the infirmities of all,[b] as a perfect combatant; where there is the greater labor, there is the greater gain.

2. If thou shalt love the good disciples, what thank is it? But rather do thou subject to thyself in meekness those that are mischievous. Every wound is not healed with the same remedy. Mollify severe attacks with lenient fomentations. Be in all things wise as a serpent, and harmless as a dove.[c] For this cause

---

[a] 1 Cor. vii. 34.   [b] Comp. Isa. liii. 4. Matt. viii. 17.
[c] Matt. x. 16.

thou art composed of flesh and spirit, that thou mayest treat mildly those things which appear before thy face. And, as for those that are not seen, pray to God that he would reveal them unto thee, that so thou mayest be wanting in nothing, but abound in every gift. The times demand thee, as (pilots) require the winds, and as he that is tossed in a tempest (desires) the haven; that thou mayest attain unto God. Be sober, as the combatant of God. The crown (proposed to thee) is immortality, and eternal life, concerning which thou art also fully persuaded. In all things I, and my bonds which thou hast loved, will be thy surety.

3. Let not those which appear worthy of credit, but teach other doctrines, disturb thee. Stand firm and immoveable as an anvil when it is beaten upon. It is the part of a brave combatant, to be wounded, and yet to overcome. But especially we ought to endure all things for God's sake, that he may bear with us. Become daily more diligent even than thou art. Consider the times, and expect Him, who is above all time, eternal, invisible, though for our sakes made visible: who cannot be perceived by our touch, neither is liable to suffering, although for our sakes he submitted to suffer, and endured evils of every kind for us.

4. Let not the widows be neglected. Be thou, after God, their guardian. Let nothing be done without thy knowledge and consent; neither do thou any thing but according to the will of God; as also thou dost in all constancy. Let your assemblies be more full :[d] inquire into all by name. Overlook not the men servants and maid-servants. Neither let them be puffed up, but rather let them be the more subject, to the glory of God, that they may obtain from him a better liberty. Let them not desire to be set free at the public cost, that they may not be slaves to their own lusts.

5. Flee evil arts: or rather, make not any mention of them.[e] Say to my sisters, that they love the Lord, and be satisfied with their husbands both in the flesh

---

[d] Compare Ignatius' *Epistle to the Ephesians*, Sect. 13.

[e] The Greek text, $μᾶλλον\ δὲ\ περὶ\ τούτων\ ὁμιλίαν\ ποιοῦ$. "Rather make frequent discourses respecting them." The old Latin version has the same sense. It seems probable, however, that the reading, $μὴ\ ποιοῦ$, which is preserved in the Interpolated Epistle, is correct.

and spirit. In like manner exhort my brethren, in the name of JESUS CHRIST, to love their wives, even as the LORD the Church.[f] If any one is able to remain in chastity, to the honor of Him, who is the LORD of (all) flesh,[g] let him remain so without boasting. If he boast, he is undone. And if he desire to be more esteemed than the Bishop, he is corrupted. It becomes also those who marry and are given in marriage to be united with the consent of the Bishop, that so the marriage may be according to godliness, and not in lust. Let all things be done to the honor of GOD.

6. Hearken ye (all)[h] unto the Bishop, that GOD also may hearken to you. My soul be security for those who submit to their Bishop, Presbyters, and Deacons. And may my portion be together with theirs in GOD. Labor ye one with another: strive together; run together; suffer together: together take rest, and together rise, as the stewards, and assessors, and ministers of GOD. Please him, under whom ye war, and from whom also ye receive your wages. Let none of you be found a deserter. Let your baptism remain, as arms, faith as a helmet, charity as a spear; patience as your whole armor. Let your works be that which is committed to your charge,[i] that so ye may receive a suitable reward. Be long-suffering, therefore, toward each other in meekness, as GOD is toward you. Let me have joy of you in all things.

7. Now, forasmuch as the Church of Antioch in Syria, is, as I have learned, at peace through your prayers,[k] I also have been the more comforted and without care in GOD, if so be that by suffering I shall attain unto GOD, that through your prayers I may be found a disciple (of CHRIST). It will be fit, most worthy Polycarp, to call a council of the most godly

---

[f] Eph. v. 25.   [g] Comp. Jer. xxxii. 27.

[h] Although this Epistle was written to Polycarp, Bishop of Smyrna, precepts are included in it addressed to the whole Church; as St. Paul, in his first Epistle to Timothy, introduces many instructions to Christians in general.

[i] τὰ δεπόσιτα ὑμῶν, τὰ ἔργα ὑμῶν. See that ye employ all the talents, committed to you as a sacred deposit, for which ye will be called upon to give an account.

[k] Trajan having put a stop to the persecution at Antioch. Compare the *Epistle to the Philadelphians*, Sect. 10.

men, and choose some one whom ye particularly love, and who is patient of labor, that he may be the messenger of GOD, and to appoint him to go into Syria, and glorify your unwearied love, to the praise of CHRIST. A Christian is not in his own power, but must be always at leisure for (the service of) GOD. And this is the work both of GOD, and of you, when ye shall have perfected it. For I trust, through the grace (of GOD) that ye are ready to every good work, that is fitting for you in the LORD. Knowing therefore your earnest affection for the truth, I have exhorted you by these short letters.[1]

8. But forasmuch as I have not been able to write to all the Churches, because I must suddenly sail from Troas to Neapolis, for so is the will of those to whom I am subject, write to the Churches which are near thee, inasmuch as thou art instructed in the will of GOD, that they also may do in like manner. Let those who are able send messengers; and the rest send (their) letters by those who shall be sent by you: that thou mayest be glorified to all eternity, even as thou art worthy.

I salute all by name: and (particularly) the wife of Epitropus, with all her house and children. I salute Attalus my well-beloved. I salute him who shall be thought worthy to be sent by you into Syria. Grace be ever with him, and with Polycarp who sends him. I wish you all happiness in our God JESUS CHRIST, in whom continue in the unity and protection of GOD. I salute Alce my well-beloved. Farewell in the LORD.

---

[1] The Epistle to the Smyrneans and this to himself.

THE MARTYRDOM

OF

IGNATIUS.

A RELATION OF THE MARTYRDOM OF IGNATIUS.

Soon after Trajan had succeeded to the Roman empire, Ignatius, the disciple of the apostle John, a man in all things like unto the Apostles, governed the Church of Antioch with all care. He had with difficulty escaped the former storms of the numerous persecutions, which happened under Domitian, like a skilful pilot, by the helm of prayer and fasting, by the constancy of his doctrine and spiritual labor, withstanding the raging floods, fearing lest he should lose any of those who wanted courage, or were not well-grounded in the faith. Wherefore, when the persecution was for the present somewhat abated, he rejoiced greatly at the tranquillity of the Church. Howbeit for himself he was troubled, that he had not yet attained to the true love of CHRIST, nor to the perfect rank of a disciple. For he thought that the confession, which is made by martyrdom, would bring him to a yet more close and intimate union with the LORD. Wherefore, having continued a few years longer with the Church, illuminating, like a divine lamp, the heart of every man by the exposition of the holy Scriptures, he attained the object of his wishes.

2. For, after this, in the ninth* year of his empire, Trajan elated with his victory over the Scythians and

---

* The Greek has ἐννάτῳ ἔτει, [in the *ninth* year;] the old Latin version, "post quartum annum," [after the *fourth* year.] Bp. PEARSON, in his dissertation on the year in which Ignatius was condemned at Antioch by Trajan, shows that there is some error in this date. He places the event as late as the *eighteenth* year of Trajan, A.D. 116.

Dacians, and many other nations, conceived that the religious company of Christians was yet wanting to complete his universal dominion. He therefore threatened them with persecution, unless they chose to submit to the worship of devils, with all other nations; so that terror compelled all men of godly lives either to sacrifice or to die. Then, therefore, this noble soldier of CHRIST, apprehensive for the Church of Antioch, was voluntarily brought before Trajan, who was at that time passing through the city, as he was hastening against Armenia, and the Parthians. As soon then as he stood in the presence of the Emperor Trajan, the Emperor said, "Who art thou, unhappy and deluded man,[b] who art so active in transgressing our commands, and beside persuadest others to their own destruction?" Ignatius replied, "No one ought to call (one who is properly styled) Theophorus,[c] unhappy and deluded; for the evil spirits (which delude men) are departed far from the servants of GOD. But if you so call me, because I am a trouble to those evil spirits, and an enemy to their delusions, I confess the justice of the appellation. For having (within me) CHRIST the heavenly King, I loosen all their snares." Trajan replied, "And who is Theophorus?" Ignatius answered, "He that hath CHRIST in his heart." Then said Trajan, "Thinkest thou, therefore, that we have not the gods within us, who also assist us in our battles against our enemies?" "Thou dost err," Ignatius replied, "in calling the evil spirits of the heathen, gods. For there is but one GOD, who made the heaven and the earth, the sea and all that are in them: and one CHRIST JESUS the only-begotten Son of GOD, whose kingdom may I enjoy." Trajan said, "Speakest thou of him who was crucified under Pontius Pilate?" Ignatius answered, "(I speak of) him who hath crucified my sin, with the inventor of it; and hath put all the deceit and malice of the devil under the feet of those who carry him in their

---

[b] τίς εἶ, κακόδαιμον. The word κακοδαίμων signifies both a person who is *unhappy*, or *ill-fated*, and one who is under the influence of evil spirits. Trajan uses the word in the first sense. Ignatius replies by a reference to the second. See PEARSON, *Vindiciæ Ignatianæ*, Part II. c. 12.

[c] See note on the introduction to IGNATIUS' *Epistle to the Ephesians*.

hearts." Then asked Trajan, "Carriest thou, then, within thee him who was crucified?" "Yea," replied Ignatius, "for it is written, I will dwell in them, and walk in them."[d] Then Trajan pronounced this sentence: "We decree that Ignatius, who hath confessed that he carries about within himself him that was crucified, shall be carried in bonds by soldiers to the great Rome, there to be thrown to the beasts for the gratification of the people." When the holy martyr heard this sentence, he cried out with joy, "I thank thee, O Lord, that thou hast vouchsafed thus to punish me, out of thy perfect love toward me, and hast made me to be put in iron bonds, with thine apostle Paul." Having thus spoken, he joyfully suffered his bonds to be put about him; and having first prayed for the Church, and commended it with tears unto the Lord, like a choice ram, the leader of a goodly flock, he was hurried away by the brutal and cruel soldiers, to be carried to Rome, and there to be devoured by blood-thirsty wild beasts.

3. Wherefore with much readiness and joy, out of his desire to suffer, he left Antioch, and came to Seleucia, whence he set sail. After (a voyage of) much labor he reached the city of Smyrna, and with great gladness left the ship, and hastened to see the holy Polycarp, Bishop of Smyrna, who had been his fellow disciple; for both of them had been instructed by St. John the apostle. Being hospitably received by him, and communicating to him spiritual gifts,[e] and glorying in his bonds, he entreated first of all the whole Church, (for the cities and Churches of Asia attended this holy man by their Bishops, and Priests, and Dea-

---

[d] 2 Cor. vi. 16.

[e] It is highly probable that, at this time, certain preternatural powers subsisted in the Church, especially in those who had been ordained to any holy office by the imposition of the hands of the Apostles themselves. Although IGNATIUS expresses in his Epistles the greatest humility, and the fullest sense of his inferiority to the Apostles, (*Ephesians*, Sect. 3. *Magnesians*, Sect. 11. *Romans*, Sect. 4,) he yet plainly implies that some revelations were made to him, (*Ephesians*, Sect. 20.) and that he possessed some knowledge of spiritual things which he was not then at liberty to communicate to those who were less advanced in Christian knowledge. (*Trallians*, Sect. 4, 5.) The writer of this account probably refers to some communications of this nature. See 1 Pet. iv. 10, 11.

cons, all hastening to him, if by any means they might receive some part of his spiritual gift) but more particularly Polycarp, to contend (with GOD) in his behalf: that being suddenly taken by the beasts from the world, he might appear before the face of CHRIST.

4. Thus, then, he spake, and thus he testified; extending so much his love for CHRIST, as one who was about to receive heaven, through his own good confession, and the earnest contention of those who prayed together with him: and to return a recompense to the Churches, who came to meet him by their governors, he sent letters of thanks to them which distilled spiritual grace, with prayer and exhortation. Seeing therefore all men so kindly affected toward him, and fearing lest the love of the brotherhood should prevent his hastening to the LORD, now that a fair door of martyrdom was opened to him, he wrote to the Church of the Romans the Epistle following.[f]

5. Having then by this Epistle prepared, according to his wishes, such of the brethren at Rome as were against his martyrdom, he set sail from Smyrna and came to Troas. For this faithful follower of CHRIST was pressed by the soldiers to arrive at the great city of Rome before the public spectacle, that he might be delivered to the wild beasts in sight of the Roman people, and so receive the crown for which he strove. From Troas, then, he proceeded and landed at Neapolis, and went (on foot) by Philippi through Macedonia, and that part of Epirus which is next to Epidamnus; and having found a ship in one of the sea-ports, he sailed over the Adriatic sea, and passing out of that into the Tyrrhene sea, and sailing by many islands and cities, at length he came in sight of Puteoli. As soon as this holy man saw the place, he was very anxious to disembark, wishing to tread in the footsteps of the apostle Paul. But a violent wind arising and driving back the ship, suffered him not to do so. Wherefore, commending the love of the brethren in that place, he sailed forward. For one whole day and night, then, we[g] were hurried on by a favorable wind. To us, this

---

[f] Here was inserted the Epistle of Ignatius to the Romans.
[g] This abrupt and inartificial change from the third to the first person is a strong internal mark of genuineness. It is exactly similar

was a subject of sorrow, inasmuch as we were grieved at our approaching separation from that holy man; but to him it was the accomplishment of his prayers, that he might the sooner depart out of this world, and attain unto the LORD whom he loved. Wherefore sailing into the Roman port, as that impure festival was approaching to an end, the soldiers began to be offended at our slowness, but the Bishop, with great joy, complied with their haste.

6. Being therefore hurried from the place which is called the Port, we forthwith met the brethren; for the report respecting the holy martyr was already spread abroad, who were full of fear and joy. For they rejoiced in that GOD had vouchsafed them the company of Theophorus, but were afraid when they considered that such a one was brought thither to die. Some of these who were the most zealous (for his safety), and promised to calm the people, that they should not desire the destruction of the just, he commanded to hold their peace: for he presently knew this by the Spirit, and saluted them all, entreating them to show true love toward him; expressing himself in discourse more fully even than he had in his epistle, and persuading them not to hinder him who was hastening to the LORD. And so, all the brethren kneeling down, he prayed to the Son of GOD for the Church, that he would cause the persecution to cease, and (continue) the love of the brethren toward each other. (This being done) he was hurried away with all haste into the amphitheatre, and was immediately thrown in, according to the previous command of Cæsar, the end of the spectacles being at hand. For it was then a very solemn day, called in the Roman tongue the thirteenth (of the Calends of January), upon which the people were more than ordinarily wont to be gathered together. Thus was he delivered to the wild beasts, near the temple, that so the desire of the holy martyr Ignatius might be accomplished, as it is written, the desire of the righteous is acceptable:[h] namely, that he might be

---

to that in Acts xvi. 8, 10. "And *they* passing by Mysia, came down to Troas. And after he had seen the vision, *we* immediately endeavored to go into Macedonia" — the first incidental intimation that St. Luke there became the companion of St. Paul.

[h] Prov. x. 24.

burdensome to none of the brethren, by the gathering of his remains, according as in his epistle he had before wished that so his end might be.[1] For only the more solid parts of his holy remains were left, which were carried to Antioch, and wrapped in linen, as an inestimable treasure left to the holy Church, by the grace which was in the martyr.

7. Now these things were done the day before the thirteenth of the Calends of January, that is on the twentieth day of December, Sura and Senecius being the second time consuls of the Romans.[k] We ourselves were eye-witnesses of these events, with many tears; and as we watched all night in the house, and prayed GOD in many words, with bended knees and supplication, that he would give us weak men some assurance of what was before done, it happened that, having fallen into a slumber for a little while, some of us on a sudden saw the blessed Ignatius standing by us and embracing us: and others beheld him praying for us; others saw him as it were dropping with sweat, as if he came out of great labor, and standing by the LORD. Having seen these things then with great joy, and comparing the visions of our dreams, we sang praises to GOD the giver of all good things, and pronounced the saint blessed; and have now made known unto you both the day and the time: that, being assembled together at the season of his martyrdom, we may communicate with the combatant and noble martyr of CHRIST, who trod under foot the devil, and perfected the course which he had piously desired, in JESUS CHRIST our Lord, by whom and with whom, all glory and power be to the FATHER with the HOLY SPIRIT for ever. Amen.

---

[1] See IGNATIUS' *Epist. to Romans*, Sect. 4.
[k] This corresponds to A.D. 107.

THE CIRCULAR EPISTLE OF THE CHURCH OF SMYRNA CONCERNING THE MARTYRDOM OF ST. POLYCARP.[a]

The Church of God which is at Smyrna to the Church of God which is at Philadelphia, and to all the other assemblies of the holy and Catholic Church, in every place; mercy, peace, and love from God the Father and our Lord Jesus Christ be multiplied.

1. We have written unto you, brethren, respecting the other martyrs, and (especially) the blessed Polycarp, who by his martyrdom has set, as it were, his seal, and put an end to the persecution. For almost all things that went before were done, that the Lord might show us from above a martyrdom truly such as became the Gospel. For he expected to be delivered up, even as the Lord also was, that we also should imitate his example; considering not only our own interest but that of our neighbor. For true and perfect charity desires not only that a man's self should be saved, but also all his brethren.

2. The sufferings, then, of all the other martyrs which they underwent according to the will of God, were blessed and generous. For so it becomes us, who who are more religious (than others) to ascribe the supreme power over all things unto Him. And who

---

[a] Eusebius, *Eccles. Hist.* iv. 15. has preserved the substance of this Epistle, from another copy, sent to the Church of Philomelium in Phrygia. He has transcribed the Epistle from Sect. 8. to the middle of Sect. 19. with some variations from the present Greek copy.

indeed would not admire the greatness of their mind, their patience and love of their LORD; who when they were so torn with scourges, that the very structure of their bodies to the inward veins and arteries was seen, did yet endure it; so that all who stood round pitied and lamented them? Others again attained to such a degree of fortitude, that no one uttered a cry or a groan, plainly showing to all of us, that those martyrs of CHRIST, in the same hour in which they were tormented, were absent from the body: or rather that the LORD stood by, and conversed with them. Wherefore being supported by the grace of GOD, they despised all the torments of the world, and by the sufferings of one hour redeemed themselves from everlasting punishment. Whence even the fire of their cruel murderers seemed cold to them: for they had before their eyes the prospect of escaping that which is eternal and unquenchable: and beheld with the eyes of their heart those good things which are reserved for them that endure, which neither ear hath heard, nor eye seen, nor have they entered into the heart of man.[b] But to them they were now revealed by the LORD, as being no longer men, but already become angels. In like manner they who were condemned to the wild beasts, (and kept) a long while (in prison,) underwent many grievous torments: being compelled to lie upon sharp spikes,[c] and tormented with divers other punishments, that, if it were possible, the tyrant might force them, by the length of their sufferings, to deny CHRIST.

3. The devil did indeed invent many things against them: but, thanks be to GOD; for he prevailed not over all. For the brave Germanicus[d] strengthened those

---

[b] 1 Cor. ii. 9.

[c] κήρυκας—These spikes might be natural or artificial. EUSEBIUS, (*Hist. Eccles.* iv. 15.) who has given only a brief abstract of the early part of this Epistle, paraphrases the expression thus:—"being sometimes laid upon whelk-shells from the sea, and upon sharp spikes." (τοτὲ δὲ τοὺς ἀπὸ θαλάττης κήρυκας, καὶ τινας ὀξεῖς ὀβελίσκους ὑποστρωννυμένους.) The shell of the κῆρυξ or *buccinum*, was armed with rough spikes: (Plin. Hist. Nat. ix. 36.) and an iron instrument, formed with sharp spikes projecting in every direction, used by the Romans as a defence against the enemy's horse, was called *Murex*, from its resemblance to the shell of the fish of that name.

[d] The Latin Church celebrate the memory of Germanicus on the 19th of January.

that feared, by his patience, and fought gloriously with wild beasts. For when the proconsul would have persuaded him, telling him, that he should consider his age, and spare himself, he forcibly drew the wild beast toward him,* being desirous the more quickly to be delivered from a wicked and unjust world. Upon this, the whole multitude, wondering at the courage of the holy and pious race of Christians, cried out, 'Away with the wicked wretches :† let Polycarp be sought out.'

4. Then one named Quintus, a Phrygian, having lately come from his own country, when he saw the wild beasts, was afraid. Now this was the same man who forced himself and some others, to present themselves of their own accord (to the trial). Him therefore the Proconsul induced, after much persuasion, to swear (by the Emperor) and to sacrifice. For which cause, brethren, we do not commend those who offer themselves (to persecution); since the Gospel teaches no such thing.

5. Now the most admirable Polycarp, when he first heard (that he was called for), was not disturbed in mind, but determined to remain in the city. But the greater part (of his friends) persuaded him to retire. Accordingly he went into a little village, not far distant from the city, and there remained, with a few others, doing nothing else, either by day or by night, but praying for all men, and for all the Churches throughout the world, according to his usual custom. And as he prayed, he saw a vision,‡ three days before

---

* Compare IGNATIUS' *Epistle to the Romans*, Sect. 5.

† ἀθέους—*Atheists.* This was a constant term of reproach against the early Christians, arising from their opposing the worship of the Heathen deities. Thus DIO, in his life of Domitian, speaks of the charge of Atheism being "very common against those who went over to the *Jewish* religion;" evidently alluding to Christianity; and of Acilius Glabrio being put to death on that account.

ATHENAGORAS says that the Gentiles brought three principal accusations against the Christians,—Atheism, banquetting on the bodies of children, and incest. (τρία ἐπιφημίζουσιν ἡμῖν ἐγκλήματα, ἀθεότητα, Θυέστεια δεῖπνα, Οἰδιποδείους μίξεις.) (ATHENAG. *Legatio pro Christianis*, p. 4. C. Colon. 1686.) JUSTIN MARTYR, *Apol.* c. 5. and elsewhere refers to the same charge. From Sect. 9. of this Epistle it is plain that the phrase, "away with the Atheists," was considered equivalent to "away with the Christians."

‡ EUSEBIUS describes this as a dream. For he says, "When he

he was taken; and, behold, the pillow under his head appeared to be on fire. Whereupon, turning to those who were with him, he said prophetically, "I must be burnt alive."

6. And when those who sought for him drew near, he departed into another village; and immediately his pursuers came thither. And when they found him not, they seized upon two young men, one of whom being tormented, confessed. For it was impossible he should be concealed, forasmuch as they who betrayed him were his own domestics. So the keeper of the peace, who was also magistrate elect, Herod by name,[b] hastened to bring him into the lists: that so Polycarp might receive his proper portion, being made partaker of CHRIST: and they that betrayed him might undergo the punishment of Judas.

7. The officers, therefore, and horsemen, taking the young lad along with them, departed about supper time, it being Friday, with their usual arms, as if they were in pursuit of a robber. And being come to the place where he was, about the close of the day they found him in a small house, lying in an upper chamber, whence he could easily have escaped into another place; but he would not, saying, "The will of the LORD be done." Wherefore, when he heard that they were come to the house, he went down and spake to them. And as they that were present wondered at his age and constancy, some of them began to say, "Was there need of all this care to take such an old man as this?" Immediately then he commanded to be set before them, the same hour, to eat and to drink, as much as they would: desiring them to give him one hour's

---

awoke from sleep, he immediately related what he had seen to those who stood by." Ἔξυπνον δὲ ἐπὶ τούτῳ γενόμενον, εὐθὺς ὑφερμηνεῦσαι τοῖς παροῦσι τὸ φανέν.

[b] καὶ ὁ εἰρήναρχος, ὁ καὶ κληρονόμος, τὸ αὐτῷ ὄνομα Ἡρώδης, ἐπιλεγόμενος. This is the manner, in which SMITH proposes to read and point the passage. The Proconsul was at that period the chief magistrate of the Province of Asia. But every year the names of ten principal men were sent to him out of each city, one of whom was appointed by the Proconsul to be keeper of the peace for the following year. See VALESIUS on EUSEB. *Hist. Eccles.* iv. 15. ARISTIDES *Orat.* iv. Herod appears to have been elected also to some other permanent office, implied by the title κληρονόμος.

liberty, that he might pray without disturbance. And when they had permitted him, he stood praying, being full of the grace of God, so that he ceased not for two whole hours, to the admiration of all that heard him; insomuch that many (of the soldiers) began to repent, that they were come out against so godly an old man.

8. As soon as he had finished his prayer, in which he made mention of all men who had ever been acquainted with him, whether small or great, honorable or obscure, and of the whole Catholic [i] Church, throughout the world; the time being come when he was to depart, they set him upon an ass, and led him into the city, it being the day of the great Sabbath.[k] And Herod, the keeper of the peace, with his father Nicetes, met him in a chariot. And having taken him up to them, and set him in the chariot, they began to persuade him, saying, 'What harm is there in saying, Lord Cæsar, and in offering sacrifice, and so being safe?' with other words which are usual on such occasions. But Polycarp at first answered them not: whereupon as they continued to urge him, he said, 'I shall not do as you advise.' They, therefore, failed to persuade him, spake bitter words against him, and then thrust him violently off the chariot, so that he hurt his thigh in the fall. But he, without turning back, went on with all diligence, as if he had received no harm at all: and so was brought to the lists, where there was so great a tumult, that no one could be heard.

9. Now as he going into the lists, there was a voice from heaven, 'Be strong, Polycarp, and quit thyself like a man.' No one saw who it was that spake to him: but those of our brethren who were present heard the voice. And as he was brought in, there was a great disturbance, when they heard that Polycarp was taken. And when he came near, the Proconsul [l] asked him,

[i] See note (o.) on the *Epistle* of IGNATIUS *to the Smyrneans*, Sect. 8. p. 92.

[k] The week in which the passion of our Saviour was celebrated was called *the Great Week:* and the Saturday of that week *the Great Sabbath.* This was the only Saturday which was observed as a fast, in the Eastern Church. BINGHAM, *Eccles. Ant.* xx. c. 3. 1. Other opinions on this point are stated by VALESIUS, in his notes on EUSEBIUS, *Eccles. Hist.* iv. 15.

[l] Statius Quadratus, who was consul, A. D. 142.

whether he were Polycarp. And, when he acknowledged (that he was), he persuaded him to deny (the faith), saying, 'Reverence thy old age;' with many other exhortations of a like nature, as their custom is, saying, 'Swear by the fortune of Cæsar; Repent, and say, Away with the wicked.'ᵐ Then Polycarp, looking with a severe countenance upon the whole company of ungodly Gentiles who were in the lists, stretched forth his hand to them, and said, groaning and looking up to heaven, 'Away with the wicked.' But the Proconsul urging him, and saying, 'Swear, and I will release thee: reproach CHRIST,' Polycarp answered, 'Fourscore and six years have I continued serving him, and he hath never wronged me at all; how then can I blaspheme my King and my Saviour?'

10. And when the Proconsul nevertheless still insisted, and said, 'Swear by the genius of Cæsar,' he answered, 'If thou art so vainly confident as to expect that I should swear by what thou callest the genius of Cæsar, pretending to be ignorant of what I am, hear

---

ᵐ Atheists. See note on Sect. 5.

It appears from the celebrated letter of PLINY to Trajan, that one of the customary trials, to which those accused of Christianity were exposed, was to urge them to sacrifice to the gods, or to the statue of the Emperor, to swear by the genius or fortune of Cæsar, and to reproach CHRIST. "Propositus est libellus, sine auctore, multorum nomina continens, qui negarent se esse Christianos, aut fuisse, quum, præeunte me, deos appellarent, et imagini tuæ, quam propter hoc jusseram cum simulachris numinum afferri, thure ac vino supplicarent, præterea maledicerent CHRISTO: quorum nihil cogi posse dicuntur, qui sunt revera Christiani." PLIN. *Ep.* x. 97.

TERTULLIAN's *Apology*, c. 32. shows that the Christians in his time were exposed to the same trial, and gives the reasons why they would swear neither by the fortune nor by the genius of Cæsar.

CHRYSOSTOM founds one of his eloquent appeals to the consciences of his hearers upon this well known fact. "Wherefore let us bear witness to CHRIST: for we, as well as the martyrs of old, are called upon to bear testimony to him. They obtained that appellation, because, when they were called upon to abjure, they endured every torment, sooner than deny the truth. Let us then be unsubdued, when various passions invite us to abjure our faith. Gold commands you, 'Say that CHRIST is not CHRIST.' Hear it not then, as if it were the voice of GOD, but set at nought its counsel. Evil lusts pronounce the same command. But be not thou persuaded by them, but stand firmly, that it be not said of us, 'They profess that they know GOD, but in works they deny him.' (Tit. i. 16.) For this becomes not martyrs, but the reverse." CHRYSOST. *Hom.* 47. *on the Acts of the Apostles*, (Opp. Tom. IV. p. 872. Savil.)

me freely professing unto thee, I am a Christian. And if thou further desirest to know what Christianity really is, appoint a day, and thou shalt hear it.' The Proconsul replied, 'Persuade the people.' Then said Polycarp, 'To thee have I freely offered to give even a reason of my faith; for we are taught to pay to the powers and authorities, which are ordained of God, the honor which is due, provided it be not injurious to ourselves. But for the people, I esteem them not worthy that I should give any account of my faith to them.'

11. The Proconsul said unto him, 'I have wild beasts ready; to those I will cast thee, unless thou repent.' He answered, 'Call for them, then: for we Christians are fixed in our minds, not to change from good to evil. But it will be good for me to be changed from my grievous (sufferings) to their just reward.' The Proconsul added, 'Seeing thou despisest the wild beasts, I will cause thee to be devoured with fire, unless thou shalt repent.'[a] Polycarp answered, 'Thou threatenest me with fire, which burns for an hour, and in a little while is extinguished: for thou knowest not the fire of the future judgment, and of that eternal punishment, which is reserved for the ungodly. But why tarriest thou? Bring forth what thou wilt.'

12. Having said this, and many other things, (of the like nature,) he was filled with confidence and joy, insomuch that his very countenance was full of grace, so that not only he was serene and undisturbed at what was spoken to him, but, on the contrary, the Proconsul was astonished, and sent his own herald to proclaim thrice, in the midst of the lists, "Polycarp hath confessed himself to be a Christian." When this was proclaimed by the herald, the whole multitude both of the Gentiles and of the Jews which dwelt at Smyrna, being full of fury, cried out with a loud voice, 'This is the teacher of Asia,[b] the father of the Christians, who

---

[a] It will be observed that the punishment of being burnt alive is here considered more severe than that of being exposed to wild beasts.

[b] The original words are, ὁ τῆς ἀσεβείας διδάσκαλος. But Eusebius, *Hist. Eccles.* iv. 15. Rufinus; and the old Latin version agree in putting 'Ἀσίας for ἀσεβείας. Jerome, in his *Catalogue of Ecclesias-*

hath overthrown our gods, and teaches so many not to sacrifice, nor to pay any worship to the gods.' And so saying, they cried out and desired Philip the president of the spectacles,[p] that he would let loose a lion against Polycarp. But Philip replied, that it was not lawful for him to do so, since that kind of spectacle was already over. Then it pleased them to cry out with one consent, that Polycarp should be burnt alive. For so it was necessary that the vision should be fulfilled which was made manifest to him by his pillow, when he saw it on fire, as he prayed, and said prophetically to the faithful that were with him, I must be burnt alive.

13. This then was done with greater speed than it was spoken; the whole multitude instantly gathering together wood and faggots, out of the work-shops and baths: the Jews especially, according to their custom, with all readiness assisting them in doing it. When the pile was ready, Polycarp laying aside all his upper garments, and loosing his girdle, endeavored also to loosen his sandals, which aforetime he was not wont to do; forasmuch as always every one of the faithful, that was about him, contended who should soonest

---

tical Writers, calls Polycarp, "Totius Asiæ princeps," [Chief (or primate) of all Asia.]

[p] 'Ασιάρχης. The *Asiarch* was chief priest of the whole province of Asia. He is called ἀρχιερεὺς in Sect. 21. Every year, about the period of the Autumnal equinox, an assembly was held in the several cities, in which one person of that city was nominated to the office. The common council of all Asia afterward elected about ten, out of those nominated by the several cities. It is doubtful whether all the ten filled the office during the year, or whether the Proconsul appointed one of the ten, as in the case of the Irenarch, or keeper of the peace. See note (h), Sect. 6.

VALESIUS (on EUSEB. *Hist. Eccles.* iv. 15.) is of opinion, from the conclusion of this Epistle, in which the martyrdom of Polycarp is said to have taken place "when Philip was chief priest," that one only was appointed. In Acts xix. 31. mention is made of "certain of the chiefs of Asia," ('Ασιαρχῶν) whence Abp. USHER concludes these were more than one. But those who had once discharged the office might still be called by the name, as was sometimes the case with the Jewish High Priests.

The office was accompanied with great expense. For which reason STRABO says that the Asiarch was often chosen, as in this instance, (Sect. 21.) from the opulent citizens of Tralles. καὶ δεῖ τινας ἢ αὐτῶν (Τραλλιανῶν) εἶσιν οἱ προτεύοντες κατὰ τὴν ἐπαρχίαν οὓς Ἀσιάρχας καλοῦσι. STRABO, Lib. xiv.

touch his flesh. For he was adorned by his good conversation with all kinds of piety, even before his martyrdom.ᵃ Immediately then they put upon him the instrumentsᵇ which were prepared for the pile. But when they would also have nailed him to the stake, he said, 'Leave me thus; for he who hath given me strength to endure the fire, will also enable me, without your securing me by nails, to remain without moving in the pile.'

14. Wherefore they did not nail him, but bound him (to the stake). But he, having put his hands behind him, and being bound as a ram, (chosen) out of a great flock for an offering, and prepared to be a burnt sacrifice, acceptable unto GOD, looked up to heaven, and said, 'O LORD GOD ALMIGHTY, the Father of thy well-beloved and blessed Son JESUS CHRIST, by whom we have received the knowledge of thee; the GOD of angels and powers and of every creature, and (especially) of the whole race of just men, who live in thy presence; I give thee hearty thanks that thou hast vouchsafed to bring me to this day and to this hour; that I should have a part in the number of thy martyrs, in the cup of thy CHRIST, unto the resurrection of eternal life, both of soul and body, in the incorruption of the HOLY SPIRIT: among which may I be accepted this day before thee, as a fat and acceptable sacrifice, as thou hast before ordained, and declared, and fulfilled, even thou the true GOD with whom is no falsehood at all. For this and for all things else, I praise thee, I bless thee, with the eternal and heavenly JESUS CHRIST, thy beloved Son, with whom to thee and the HOLY GHOST be glory, both now and to all succeeding ages. Amen.'ᶜ

ᵃ EUSEBIUS has, "For, even before he was grey-headed, (πρὸ τῆς πολιᾶς) he was adorned in all things by his good conversation."

ᵇ ὄργανα—the pitched shirt, in which the victim was wrapped, the stake, to which he was bound, the nails, and other implements, by which he was secured.

ᶜ The conclusion of this prayer is differently expressed in EUSEBIUS: "For this, and for all things else, I praise thee, I bless thee, I glorify thee, through the eternal High Priest, JESUS CHRIST thy beloved Son, through whom, to Thee with Him, in the HOLY GHOST, be glory both now and to all succeeding ages. Amen."
δι' οὗ σοὶ σὺν αὐτῷ ἐν πνεύματι ἁγίῳ δόξα, κ. τ. λ.
The old Latin version agrees nearly with EUSEBIUS. "Ob hanc

15. As soon as he had uttered 'Amen,' and finished his prayer, the men appointed for the purpose lighted the fire. And when the flame began to blaze to a very great height, a wonderful sight appeared to us, who were permitted to witness it, and were also spared, to relate to others what had happened. For the flame, making a kind of arch, like the sail of a ship filled with wind, encompassed the body of the martyr, which was in the midst, not as flesh which was burned, but as bread which is baked, or as gold or silver glowing in the furnace. Moreover we perceived as fragrant an odor, as if it came from frankincense, or some other precious spices.

16. At length, when these wicked men saw that his body could not be consumed by the fire, they commanded the executioner[a] to go near, and pierce him with his sword. Which being accordingly done, there came forth[b] so great a quantity of blood, as extinguished the fire, and raised an admiration among the people to consider what a difference there is between the infidels and the elect, one of which this admirable martyr Polycarp was, being in our times a truly apostolical and prophetical teacher, and the Bishop of the Catholic Church which is at Smyrna. For every word that proceeded out of his mouth either is (already) fulfilled, or will (in due time) be accomplished.

---

rem te benedico in omnibus, et glorior, per æternum, Pontificem omnipotentem JESUM CHRISTUM, per quem tibi, et cum ipso, et cum SPIRITU SANCTO, gloria nunc, et in futurum, et in sæcula sæculorum. Amen."

[a] Both the Greek text and EUSEBIUS, have here the Latin word κομφίκτορα. The *confectores* were persons appointed to kill the wild beasts, at the public games; if there was any apprehension of their injuring the people. They differed from the *bestiarii*, who fought with the beasts, in somewhat the same manner as the *matador* does from the combatant in the Spanish bull-fights.

[b] The original words are ἐξῆλθε περιστέρα καὶ πλῆθος αἵματος. 'There came forth *a dove*, and a quantity of blood.' EUSEBIUS, and his translator RUFINUS, make no mention of this prodigy; and no tradition of the kind is contained in any ancient Christian writer. It has been conjectured, with some probability, that the word περιστέρα is an error for ἐπ' ἀριστερᾷ, 'on the left side:' so that the sentence would be to this effect, "When the executioner wounded him with the sword, there came forth from the wound, which was inflicted in his left side, such a quantity of blood, as extinguished the fire."

§ 17, 18.] OF POLYCARP. 117

17. But when the emulous and envious and wicked adversary of the race of the just saw the greatness of his martyrdom, and considered how blameless his conversation had been from the beginning, and that he was now crowned with the crown of immortality, having without all controversy received his reward, he took all care that not the least relic of his body should be taken away by us, although many desired to do it, and to have a share in his holy flesh. And to that end he suggested to Nicetus, the father of Herod, and brother of Alce, to go to the governor, and hinder him from giving his body to be buried: lest, said he, forsaking him that was crucified, they should begin to worship this Polycarp. And this he said at the suggestion and instance of the Jews, who also watched us that we should not take him out of the fire: not considering that it is impossible for us, either ever to forsake CHRIST, who suffered for the salvation of all such as shall be saved throughout the whole world, (the righteous for the ungodly),* or to worship any other. For him indeed, as being the Son of GOD, we adore. But for the martyrs, we worthily love them,ˣ as the disciples and imitators of our LORD, on account of their exceeding great love toward their Master and King; of whom may we also be made companions and fellow-disciples.

18. The centurion, therefore, seeing the contention of the Jews, put his body into the midst of the fire, and burned it. After which, we, taking up his bones more precious than the richest jewels and tried above gold, deposited them where it was fitting. Where being

---

* 1 Pet. iii. 18. These words appear to be an interpolation. They are not found in EUSEBIUS nor in the old Latin version.

ˣ This valuable testimony of the Church of Smyrna, against the adoration of Saints, agrees with the sentiments of AUGUSTIN: "Non sit nobis religio cultus hominum mortuorum; quia, si piè vixerunt, non sic habentur ut tales quærant honores: sed Illum à nobis coli volunt, quo illuminante, lætantur meriti sui nos esse consortes. Honorandi ergo sunt propter imitationem, non adorandi propter religionem." [Let us not count the adoration of dead men a religious act; because, if they lived piously, they are not so thought of as if they desired such honors: but they wish us to adore Him, by whose illumination they rejoice that we are made partakers of His merits. They are therefore to be honored for their example's sake, not worshipped as a matter of religion.] AUGUSTIN, De Verâ Religione, c. 55.

gathered together as we have opportunity, with joy and gladness, the LORD will grant unto us to celebrate the anniversary [y] of his martyrdom, both in memory of

---

[y] τὴν τοῦ μαρτυρίου αὐτοῦ ἡμέραν γενέθλιον, 'the birth-day of his martyrdom.'—The celebration of the anniversary of the day on which a martyr suffered began thus to be observed, early in the second century. At the end of the fourth, and in the beginning of the fifth century, we find from CHRYSOSTOM and THEODORET (*Serm.* viii. *de Martyribus*) that these days were greatly increased in number. There are extant sixteen homilies of CHRYSOSTOM, preached on different days set apart for such commemorations. BINGHAM, *Eccles. Ant.* xiii. 9. 5. quotes CHRYSOSTOM, (*Hom.* xl. *in Jubentinum*,) to prove that the festival of Babylas and Jubentinus then occurred on two successive days. The passage, however, merely implies that the festival of Babylas occurred soon before that of Jubentinus: the one, indeed, on the 4th of September, the other on the 25th of January.

'Ο μακάριος Βαβύλας πρώην ἡμᾶς ἐνταῦθα μετὰ παίδων τριῶν συνήγαγε· σήμερον στρατιωτῶν ξυνωρὶς ἁγίων, τὸ τοῦ Χριστοῦ στρατόπεδον ἐπὶ τῆς παρατάξεως ἕστηκε., CHRYSOS. *Hom. in Juventin.* Tom. V. p. 533. Savil.

CHRYSOSTOM makes the same kind of allusion to the previous festival of Pelagia, on the 8th of October, in his *Homily upon the Martyrdom of Ignatius*, on the 20th of December.

Πρώην γοῦν ἡμᾶς κόρη κομιδῇ νέα καὶ ἀπειρόγαμος ἡ μακαρία μάρτυς Πελαγία μετὰ πολλῆς τῆς εὐφροσύνης εἱστίασε· σήμερον πάλιν τῆς ἐκείνης ἑορτῆς ὁ μακάριος οὗτος καὶ γενναῖος μάρτυς Ἰγνάτιος διεδέξατο. CHRYS. *Hom. in Ignat.* Tom. V. p. 498. Savil.

The only two festivals which appear to have occurred on consecutive days in the Eastern Church, in the time of CHRYSOSTOM, were those of Romanus and Barlaam on the 18th and 19th of November.

These anniversaries of the days on which the martyrs suffered were called their *birth-days*, as being the days on which they were freed from the trials of mortality, and born, as it were, into the joys and happiness of heaven. Thus TERTULLIAN (*de Coron. Militis*, c. 3.) says, "Oblationes pro defunctis pro natalitiis annua die facimus." [We make anniversary oblations for the dead on their *birth-days*.] CYPRIAN, Bishop of Carthage, writing to his Presbyters and Deacons respecting their treatment of the Confessors, then in prison, thus advises them; "Denique et dies eorum quibus excedunt annotate, ut commemorationes eorum inter memorias martyrum celebrare possimus." [Lastly, note the days of their departure, that we may be able to celebrate their commemorations among the memorials of the martyrs.] CYPRIAN, *Ep.* xii. p. 27. (Fell.) And, in another Epistle to the same persons, he says, with reference to Laurentius and Ignatius; "Sacrificia pro eis semper, ut meministis, offerimus, quoties martyrum passiones et dies anniversariâ commemoratione celebramus." [We always offer sacrifices for them, as ye remember, as often as we celebrate the passions and days of the martyrs in our anniversary commemoration.] Epist. xxxix. p. 77. Fell.

After Cyprian himself had suffered for the faith, we find PETER CHRYSOLOGUS, in his *Sermon on the Martyrdom of Cyprian*, using the like expressions: "Natalem sanctorum cùm audistis, fratres,

those who have suffered, and for the exercise and preparation of those that may hereafter (suffer).

19. Such were the sufferings of the blessed Polycarp; who, though he was the twelfth of those who, together with them of Philadelphia, suffered martyrdom, in Smyrna, is yet alone chiefly had in memory of all men; insomuch that he is spoken of by the very Gentiles themselves in every place, as having been not only an eminent teacher, but also a glorious martyr. Whose death all desire to imitate, as having been in all things conformable to the Gospel of CHRIST. For having by patience overcome the unjust governor, and so received the crown of immortality, he now, together with the apostles and all other righteous men, with great triumph glorifies GOD even the Father, and blesses our LORD the Governor of our (souls and) bodies,* and the

---

nolite putare illum dici, quo pascuntur in terram de carne; sed de terrâ in cœlum, de labore ad requiem, de tentationibus ad quietem, de cruciatibus ad delicias, non fluxas sed fortes et stabiles et æternas, de mundanis risibus ad coronam et gloriam. Tales *natales dies* martyrum celebrantur." [When ye hear of a *birth-day* of saints, brethren, do not think that that is spoken of, in which they are born on earth, of the flesh; but (that in which they are born) from earth into heaven, from labor to rest, from temptations to repose, from torments to delights, not fluctuating, but strong and stable and eternal, from the derision of the world to a crown and glory. Such are the *birth-days* of the martyrs that we celebrate.]

In the time of Constantine, the observation of the festivals of the martyrs was enforced by a decree of the Emperor. EUSEB. *de Vit. Constant.* iv. 23.

The manner of celebrating the memories of the Martyrs and Confessors, in the primitive Church, was this.

On the anniversary day, the people assembled, sometimes at the tombs where the martyrs had been buried. They then publicly praised GOD for those who had glorified him by their sufferings and death; recited the history of their martyrdom, and heard a sermon preached in commemoration of their patience and Christian virtues. They offered up fervent prayers to GOD, and celebrated the Eucharist, in commemoration of CHRIST's passion, and gave alms to the poor.

They kept also a public festival, provided by general contribution, to which the poorer brethren were freely admitted. In the early ages these feasts were frugal and temperate; but afterward degenerated into excess.

* The Greek has κυβερνήτην τῶν σωμάτων ἡμῶν. The old Latin version has, 'salvatorem animæ nostræ, gubernatorem corporum:' [Saviour of our soul, governor of (our) bodies:] and adds, at the conclusion of the sentence, 'et SPIRITUM SANCTUM, per quem cuncta cognoscimus.' [And the HOLY SPIRIT, by whom we know all things.]

Shepherd of the Catholic Church throughout the world.

20. Whereas, therefore, ye desired that we would at large declare to you what was done, we have for the present briefly signified it to you by our brother Marcus. When, therefore, ye have read this Epistle, send it also to the brethren that are more remote, that they also may glorify God, who makes such choice of his own servants, and is able to bring us all by his grace and help to his eternal kingdom, through his only begotten Son Jesus Christ; to whom be glory, honor, might, and majesty, for ever and ever; Amen. Salute all the saints. They that are with us salute you: and Evarestus, who wrote this Epistle, with his whole house.

21. Now the martyrdom of the blessed Polycarp was on the second day of the month Xanthicus, that is the seventh of the Calends of May,[a] on the great Sabbath, about the eighth hour. He was taken by Herod, Philip the Trallian being the chief priest,[b] Statius Quadratus proconsul; but our Saviour Christ reigning for evermore. To Him be honor, glory, majesty, and an eternal throne, from generation to generation; Amen.

22. We wish you, brethren, all happiness, by living according to the rule of the Gospel of Jesus Christ; with whom, glory be to God the Father, and the Holy Spirit, for the salvation of his chosen saints: after whose example the blessed Polycarp suffered; at whose feet may we be found in the kingdom of Jesus Christ.

This Epistle was transcribed by Caius out of the copy of Irenæus the disciple of Polycarp, who also lived and conversed with Irenæus. And I Socrates transcribed it at Corinth, out of the copy of the said Caius. Grace be with all.

After this, I Pionius again wrote it from the copy before mentioned, Polycarp having pointed it out to me

[a] The 26th of April. [b] Or *Asiarch*. See note on Sect. 12.

by a revelation, as I shall declare in what follows; having gathered these things together, already almost corrupted by length of time: that JESUS CHRIST our LORD may also gather me together with his elect. To whom with the FATHER and the HOLY GHOST, be glory for ever and ever. Amen.

THE FIRST APOLOGY

OF

JUSTIN MARTYR.

THE APOLOGY OF JUSTIN MARTYR

FOR THE

CHRISTIANS

TO ANTONINUS PIUS.

---

1. To the Emperor Titus Ælius Adrianus Antoninus Pius Augustus Cæsar, and to his son Verissimus the Philosopher, and to Lucius the Philosopher, the son[b] of (Ælius Verus) Cæsar by birth, and of

---

[a] The figures in the margin refer to the pages in the Paris Edition.
[b] The Emperor Adrian adopted Lucius Ælius Verus, and gave him the title of Cæsar. This Lucius died; leaving only one son Lucius Verus.

Adrian then adopted Titus Antoninus Pius, as his successor, upon condition that he should adopt both Marcus Aurelius Antoninus, who is here called Verissimus, his wife's brother's son, and Lucius Verus, the son of Ælius Verus.

The following scheme will show the relation in which Lucius Verus stood toward Antoninus Pius and Lucius Ælius Verus.

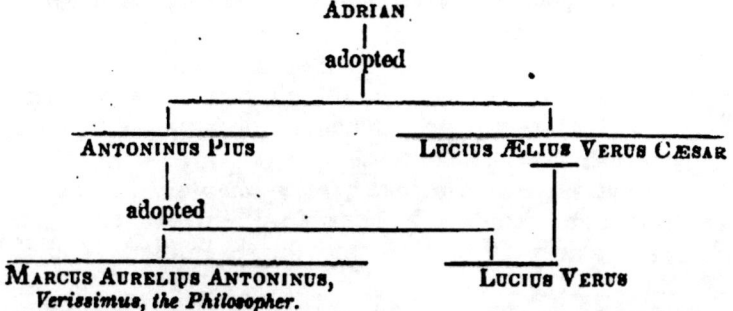

```
                    ADRIAN
                      |
                   adopted
         _____|_____
        |                         |
  ANTONINUS PIUS         LUCIUS ÆLIUS VERUS CÆSAR
        |                         |
     adopted                      |
        |_____|
        |                         |
MARCUS AURELIUS ANTONINUS,    LUCIUS VERUS
Verissimus, the Philosopher.
```

Thus Lucius Verus was by birth son of L. Ælius Verus Cæsar, and the *adopted* son of Antoninus Pius. The apology of Athenagoras is in like manner inscribed to Marcus Aurelius and Lucius Ælius, or Aurelius Verus, the philosophers.

Of Lucius Verus the following character is given by GIBBON, (*History of the Decline and Fall of the Roman Empire*, Book I. ch. 3.) "He was adopted by Pius; and on the accession of Marcus

Pius by adoption, the lover of learning; and to the sacred Senate, and to all the Roman people, in behalf of those of all nations who are unjustly hated and persecuted, I Justin, the son of Priscus, and grandson of Bacchius, natives of Flavia Neapolis[c] of Syria Palestine, being myself one of those (who are so unjustly used) offer this address and supplication.

2. Reason herself dictates that those, who can with propriety be denominated 'Pious' and 'Philosophers,' should love and honor truth alone, and refuse to follow the opinions of the ancients, if plainly erroneous. For right reason not only forbids us to assent to those who are unjust, either in practice or in principle, but commands the lover of truth, by all means, to choose that which is just in word and deed, even in preference to his own life, and under the threatened danger of immediate death. Now ye hear continually ascribed to yourselves the appellations, 'Pious,' 'Philosophers,' 'Guardians of Justice,' and 'Lovers of Learning:' but whether ye also really are such, the event will show. For we have come before you, not to flatter you in this address, nor to obtain favor by words of adulation, but to demand that judgment may be passed according to strict and well-weighed reason; that ye be not influenced by prejudice or the desire of pleasing superstitious men, nor, through inconsiderate passion, and the long prevalence of an evil report, pass a sentence, which would turn against yourselves. For we are fully persuaded that we can suffer no injury from any one, unless we are found guilty of some wickedness, or proved to be bad men: and kill us, ye may; but hurt us ye cannot.

3. That no one, however, may imagine this to be an unfounded and rash boast, we entreat that the charges against Christians may be examined; and if

---

was invested with an equal share of sovereign power. Among the many vices of this younger Verus, he possessed one virtue: a dutiful reverence for his wiser colleague, to whom he willingly abandoned the ruder cares of empire. The philosophic emperor dissembled his follies, lamented his early death, and cast a decent veil over his memory."

[c] Flavia Neapolis was, as its name implies, a new town, built near the ruins of Sychem, in Samaria. It derived its name Flavia from Flavius Vespasian, who sent a colony thither.

they be proved to be well founded, we are willing that they should be punished as they deserve, or even to punish them ourselves.[d] But if no one has any proof to bring against them, right reason requires that you should not, in consequence of an evil report, injure innocent men, or rather yourselves, since your decisions would be influenced not by judgment but by passion.

Every wise man will agree, that an appeal of this nature can then only be conducted equitably and well, when subjects have the privilege of giving, without interruption, a full account of their lives and opinions; and princes, on the other hand, pass sentence in all godliness and true philosophy, and not according to the dictates of violence and arbitrary power: since by so doing, both princes and subjects would secure their own interest. For even one of the ancients hath somewhere said, "Unless both princes and subjects be influenced by true philosophy, the state can never prosper."[e] It will be our care, therefore, to give all men the power of examining our lives and doctrines, that we may not suffer for the errors blindly committed by such as determine to be ignorant of our opinions: and it will be your duty, as right reason requires, when ye have heard the cause, to be just judges. For if, when ye shall have been so informed, ye do not what is just, ye will be inexcusable before GOD. A name in itself ought not to be judged favorably or unfavorably, without the actions which that name implies. Although, as to our name, which is made a subject of accusation against us, we are the best of men.[f] But as we should

---

[d] ἀξιοῦμεν——κολάζεσθαι ὡς πρέπον ἐστὶ, μᾶλλον δὲ κολάζειν.
The translation expresses the sense which FABRICIUS gives to this difficult passage. A similar sentiment is found at the end of Sect. 22. "We even entreat that those who live not agreeably to their doctrines, but are merely called Christians, may be punished by you."
Other explanations of the words are given by THIRLBY.

[e] PLATO *de Republicâ.* v. Tom. II. p. 473, D. This was a favorite maxim of Antoninus the philosopher, and was, therefore, judiciously introduced by Justin Martyr.

[f] Χρηστότατοι. The names CHRISTUS and Χρηστὸς were frequently confounded; sometimes fancifully enough. Thus THEOPHILUS *ad Autolycum,* p. 69, B. ἐγὼ μὲν οὖν ὁμολογῶ εἶναι Χριστιανός, καὶ φορῶ τὸ θεοφιλὲς ὄνομα τοῦτο, ἐλπίζων εὔχρηστος εἶναι τῷ Θεῷ. And again, p. 77, B. See TERTULLIAN, *Apol.* Sect. 3.

think it unjust that, if we are proved to be guilty, we should demand to be acquitted in consequence of possessing a good name, so on the other hand, if we are proved to be innocent of all offence both in the name which we bear, and in the lives which we lead, it will be for you to beware, lest, if you unjustly punish the guiltless, ye yourselves should be exposed to the vengeance of justice. From a mere name neither praise nor blame can justly arise, unless something either good or bad can be proved by actions. For you pass not sentence upon any that are accused among yourselves, until they are condemned; but against us you receive the very name as an accusation; whereas from our name you ought rather to punish our accusers. For we are accused of being Christians: but to hate that which is good, (which *Chrestus* implies,) is manifestly unjust. And again, if any one of those also who are so accused, denies it, asserting that he is not, ye dismiss him; ye release him as if ye had nothing whereof to accuse him. But if any one confesses that he is a Christian, ye punish him for his confession: whereas ye ought to inquire into the life both of him who confessed and of him who denied, that by their deeds it might be made manifest what kind of man each of them was.

4. For as some, who have been taught by our master CHRIST not to deny him, even when tortured, exhort (others to embrace the faith); so it may happen that men of evil lives may afford a pretence to others, who are anxious to accuse all Christians of impiety and injustice. But this too is unjustly done. For many assume the name and garb of Philosophy, who act not at all in conformity with their character. And ye well know that men holding opposite opinions and doctrines among the ancients, are styled by the common name of philosophers. Now some of these taught atheism; and some who were poets attributed even to Jupiter the grossest indulgences, with his own children. Yet those who give publicity to such opinions receive no prohibition from you. Nay, ye even propose prizes and honors to such as shall eloquently express these disgraceful histories of your gods.

5. Why then should we be thus treated, who openly

avow our determination not to injure any one, nor to hold these impious opinions? Ye judge not righteous judgment, but under the excitement of unreasonable passion, and lashed on by the scourges of evil demons, ye punish without judgment and without thought. For the truth must be spoken. Evil demons,[g] in times of old, assuming various forms, went in unto the daughters of men, and committed other abominations; and so astonished the minds of men with the wonders which they displayed, that they formed not a rational judgment of what was done, but were hurried away by their fears; so that, not knowing them to be evil demons, they styled them gods, and addressed them by the name which each demon imposed upon himself. And when Socrates, in a spirit of true wisdom and research, endeavored to bring all this to light, and to lead men away from the worship of demons, the demons themselves so wrought by the hands of men who delighted in wickedness, as to put him to death, as an atheist or impious, under the pretence that he was introducing new deities. And so in like manner do they act toward us. For not only was this declared to the Greeks by Socrates, at the suggestion of right reason, but also in other lands, by Reason, even the Word itself, which appeared in a bodily form, and was made man, and was called JESUS CHRIST. We, then, believing in him, declare that the demons, who did such things, not only are no gods,[h] but are evil and unholy spirits, whose actions are not even equal to those of virtuous men. Hence it is that we are styled Atheists.[i]

6. We confess, indeed, that we are unbelievers of such pretended gods, but not of the most true GOD, the Father of righteousness and temperance, and of all other virtues, in whom is no mixture of evil. But we worship and adore Him, and his Son, who came out from Him, and hath taught us respecting these things,[k]

---

[g] Ἐπεὶ τὸ παλαιὸν δαίμονες φαῦλοι ἐπιφανείας ποιησάμενοι, καὶ γυναῖκας ἐμοίχευσαν καὶ παῖδας διέφθειραν, καὶ φόβητρα ἀνθρώποις ἔδειξαν.

[h] οὐ μόνον μὴ θεοὺς εἶναι φαμὲν, ἀλλὰ κακοὺς καὶ ἀνοσίους δαίμονας. The common reading is μὴ ὀρθοὺς, which is plainly erroneous.

[i] See the note on the *Martyrdom of Ignatius*, c. 3.

[k] Ἀλλ' ἐκεῖνόν τε, καὶ τὸν παρ' αὐτοῦ υἱὸν ἐλθόντα καὶ διδάξαντα ἡμᾶς ταῦτα καὶ τὸν τῶν ἄλλων ἑπομένων καὶ ἐξομοιουμένων ἀγαθῶν ἀγγέλων στρατὸν,

and respecting the host of the other good angels, who follow Him and are made like unto Him; and the

---

πνεῦμά τε τὸ προφητικὸν σεβόμεθα, καὶ προσκυνοῦμεν, λόγῳ καὶ ἀληθείᾳ τιμῶντες.

The sense given in the translation is that usually affixed to these words, and supported by Bp. BULL, *Defensio Fid. Nicenæ*, Sect. ii. c. iv. 8. Justin had observed, in § 5. that Socrates fell a victim to the cruelty of his countrymen instigated by evil demons; and that the same spirits caused the Gentiles to accuse the Christians of atheism. He shows, therefore, that the religion of CHRIST taught them that those spirits were no gods. "The object of our worship," he says, "is GOD the Father of righteousness and temperance, the author of every good thing. We adore Him, and his Son, who came out from Him. He it was who taught us fully what hath before been observed respecting evil angels, and their delusions, and hath also taught us that there is an innumerable host of good angels, who follow him and are made like unto Him. We worship also the Prophetic Spirit."

The parenthetic mention of evil and good angels is certainly harsh; but may perhaps be justified when the words are considered in connexion with the context.

The statement respecting the three persons of the blessed Trinity, as the only objects of worship, is repeated in Sect. 16.

"We worship the Creator of the universe.—Again we have learned, that he, who taught us these things and for this end was born, even JESUS CHRIST—was the Son of Him who is truly GOD; and we esteem him in the second place. And that we with reason honor the Prophetic Spirit, in the third place, we shall hereafter show."

Τὸν δημιουργὸν τοῦδε τοῦ παντὸς σεβόμενοι—τὸν διδάσκαλόν τε τούτων γενόμενον ἡμῖν, καὶ εἰς τοῦτο γεννηθέντα Ἰησοῦν Χριστὸν—υἱὸν αὐτοῦ τοῦ ὄντως Θεοῦ μαθόντες, καὶ ἐν δευτέρᾳ χώρᾳ ἔχοντες, πνεῦμά τε προφητικὸν ἐν τρίτῃ τάξει, ὅτι μετὰ λόγου τιμῶμεν, ἀποδείξομεν. *Apol.* p. 60, D.

GRABE follows CAVE (*Primitive Christianity*, Part I. ch. i. p. 9,) by connecting τὸν ἀγγέλων στρατὸν with ἡμᾶς. "Who instructed us, and the whole society of angels, in these divine mysteries." GRABE supports this version by a reference to Eph. iii. 10. Ἵνα γνωρισθῇ νῦν ταῖς ἀρχαῖς καὶ ταῖς ἐξουσίαις ἐν τοῖς ἐπουρανίοις, διὰ τῆς ἐκκλησίας, ἡ πολυποίκιλος σοφία τοῦ Θεοῦ· and quotes IRENÆUS ii. 55. "Semper autem coexistens Filius Patri, olim et ab initio semper revelat Patrem, et angelis et archangelis et potestatibus et virtutibus, et omnibus quibus vult revelare Deus."

ASHTON, in a note subjoined to his edition of this apology, supposes that there is a dislocation in the words of the text, the clause—καὶ τὸν τῶν ἄλλων—ἀγγέλων στρατὸν—having been removed from the end of the sentence into the middle. The passage, with this alteration, will stand thus. Ἀλλ' ἐκεῖνόν τε, καὶ τὸν παρ' αὐτοῦ υἱὸν ἐλθόντα καὶ διδάξαντα ἡμᾶς ταῦτα, πνεῦμά τε τὸ προφητικὸν σεβόμεθα καὶ προσκυνοῦμεν, λόγῳ καὶ ἀληθείᾳ, τιμῶντες καὶ τὸν τῶν ἄλλων ἑπομένων καὶ ἐξομοιουμένων ἀγαθῶν ἀγγέλων στρατόν.

"But we worship and adore, in reason and truth, Him, and his Son who came out from Him, and taught us these things, and the HOLY SPIRIT; honoring also the host of the other good angels who follow him and are made like unto him."

Roman Catholic writers adduce this passage, as favoring the worship

Prophetic Spirit; honoring them in reason and in truth. And to every one who wishes to learn, we freely deliver our opinions, even as we have been taught.

7. But, some one will say, already some of those who have been taken have been proved guilty of crimes. And, in fact, ye do frequently condemn many, after having made diligent inquiry into the life of each one that is accused, and not in consequence of such charges as have been mentioned.[1] Moreover, this we readily confess, that in the same manner as among the Greeks, those who hold any peculiar system of opinions, are all called by the name of philosophers, although their tenets be opposed to each other, so, in other countries, the name assumed by all those, who either have or profess true wisdom, is the same; for all are called Christians. Wherefore we require that the actions of all those who are accused before you may be examined; that he who is convicted may be punished as an evil doer, but not as a Christian.[m] And if any one appears to be innocent, that he may be dismissed, as a Christian who hath done no evil. For we require you not to

---

of angels. They place a comma after ταῦτα, and render the words to this effect: "We worship in reason and in truth, with all honor, Him, and his Son who came out from Him, and taught us these things, and the host of good angels which follow him and are made like unto Him, and the Prophetic Spirit."

In the passage, however, above quoted, and in many others, Justin plainly points out three persons only, the Creator, the Son, and the Prophetic Spirit, as the objects of Christian worship. Compare *Apol.* Sect. 77, 79, 85, 87.

See Bp. KAYE's *Account of the Writings and Opinions of Justin Martyr*, Ch. II. p. 53.

[1] καὶ γὰρ πολλοὺς πολλάκις, ὅταν ἑκάστοτε τῶν κατηγορημένων τὸν βίον ἐξετάζητε, ἀλλ' οὐ διὰ τοὺς προλεχθέντας, καταδικάζετε. If this passage is correct, its sense seems to be this:

"In the course of your various and discursive inquiries into the lives of so many as are brought before you under the general accusation of being Christians, there are doubtless many who are guilty of some crime, for which they may justly suffer punishment, although they would deserve no blame for the charge first alleged against them." The last clause, ἀλλ' οὐ διὰ τοὺς προλεχθέντας, is, however, so harsh, that we might almost suspect that Justin wrote, ἀλλ' οὐδ' αὐτοὺς οὐκ ἐλεγχθέντας, or, if the word might be allowed, οὐ προελεγχθέντας. "Ye frequently condemn many, after ye have made inquiry into the life of each, but not even those, unless they have been first convicted of some crime."

[m] 1 Pet. iv. 15.

57 punish our accusers:ⁿ they are sufficiently recompensed by their own malice, and their ignorance of what is good.

8. Moreover, bear in mind that it is for your sakes that we thus speak; since it is in our power to deny, when we are questioned. But we choose not to live by falsehood. For out of our great love of an eternal and pure life, we desire to converse with GOD, the Father, and Creator of all things; and hasten to confess, inasmuch as we believe and are sure, that such as show by their works that they follow GOD, and earnestly long to converse with him, in the place where no evil assaults them, shall be able to attain to those blessings. Such, then, to speak briefly, are our expectations: such are the doctrines, which through CHRIST we have learned, and teach. Now Plato° in like manner declared that Rhadamanthus and Minos will punish the wicked who shall come to them. The event, of which we speak, is the same; but we say that it will be accomplished by CHRIST: and that both souls and bodies will be united, and punished with eternal torments, and not, as he declares, for a thousand years only.ᵖ If, notwithstanding, any one should say that all this is incredible or impossible, this error regards ourselves only, and no one else,ᵠ as long as we are not proved guilty of any evil action.

ⁿ This is probably an allusion to the rescript of the Emperor Adrian, subjoined to this Apology, in which punishment is threatened against any who should calumniate the Christians.
° PLATO, *Gorgias*, p. 524.
ᵖ PLATO, *de Republ.* Lib. x. p. 615.
Justin here plainly maintains the eternity of future punishments. When Justin M. speaks in his own person, he always describes the punishment of the wicked as eternal. See c. 12, 24, 29 at the end, 60 at the end. See also Apol. 2, p. 41, C. E. 45, E. 46, D. 47, D. There is a passage in his Dialogue with Trypho, however, in which his instructer describes the happiness of the righteous and the punishment of the wicked as enduring as long as GOD shall will:
οὕτως αἱ μὲν (ψυχαὶ) ἄξιαι τοῦ Θεοῦ φανεῖσθαι οὐκ ἀποθνήσκουσι ἔτι, αἱ δὲ κολάζονται ἕς τ' ἂν αὐτὰς καὶ εἶναι καὶ κολάζεσθαι ὁ Θεὸς θέλῃ. p. 223, C.
If Justin is here to be considered as expressing his own sentiments, the apparent contradiction will be reconciled by supposing his opinion to be, that the eternity of the soul of man is not inherent, but that GOD wills the punishment of the wicked to be eternal. See Bp. KAYE's *Account of Justin Martyr*, Ch. v. p. 102.
ᵠ Compare Job xix. 4.

9. Neither again do we honor with numerous sacrifices and garlands of flowers, those, whom men have invested with a bodily shape, and placed in temples, and then denominated gods. We well know that these are senseless and dead, possessing not the form of God. We imagine not that God hath such a bodily shape as some pretend to imitate, to his honor; and are persuaded that these images have not the form of God, but the names and figures of those evil demons which have appeared. For why should I repeat to you, who know so well, in what manner the workmen treat their materials, polishing, cutting, melting, and hammering, and frequently out of the meanest vessels, by merely changing their form, and fashioning them anew, giving them the name of gods?[r] In our opinion this is not only unreasonable, but offers great dishonor to God, who, although he possesses a glory and form which are inexpressible, is thus named after corruptible things and such as require care to preserve them. Ye well know, also, that those who are occupied in these works lead most impure lives, and, not to dwell upon particulars, practise all kinds of wickedness, so that they even corrupt the women who assist them in their works. O astonishing blindness! that men thus impure should be said[s] to form and change the fashion of gods, for the purpose of worship; and that such men should be placed as guards of the temples where they are set up, not considering that it is impious either to imagine or to say, that men are the keepers of gods.

10. But we are firmly persuaded that God requires not from men material offerings, seeing that he hath given us all things. And we have been taught, and believe, and are sure, that they only are accepted of him, who imitate the perfections of his holy nature, chastity, justice, humanity, and whatever other virtues belong to God, to whom no name can be ascribed.[t] We have

---

[r] Compare Isa. xliv. 12–19. It might be conceived that Justin Martyr had in view the history told of Amasis, in HERODOTUS, Lib. ii. 172.

[s] λέγεσθαι is the reading of H. Stephanus, instead of λέγεσθε.

[t] Justin expresses the same thought in c. 80, and in his *Second Apology*, p. 44. ὄνομα δὲ τῷ πάντων πατρὶ θετὸν, ἀγεννήτῳ ὄντι, οὐκ ἔστιν. In the persecution, which took place after the death of Antoninus Pius, Attalus, in the midst of his torments, while being roasted in an iron chair by a slow fire, was asked, what was the name of God? his reply

been taught also, that he, of his goodness, did in the beginning make all things of unformed matter, for the sake of men; who shall, we know, be admitted to his presence, there to reign with him, in immortality and freedom from all suffering, if they show themselves worthy, by their actions, in obedience to his will. For in the same manner as he created us from nothing, so we believe that they who choose such things as are well-pleasing in his sight, shall, in consequence of that choice, be deemed worthy of immortality and communion with him. For to exist, at the beginning, was not in our own power. But to obey what is conformable to his will, making our choice by means of the rational faculties with which he hath endowed us, persuades us and leads us to faith." And we consider it to be of the utmost importance to every man, that he be not forbidden to learn these things, but be exhorted and persuaded to embrace them. For that which human laws never could have effected, the Word, which is divine, would have (already) performed, had not the evil demons disseminated many false and impious accusations, of which we are entirely guiltless, availing themselves of the assistance of that proneness to all evil, which, although various in its kind, exists in every man.

11. Now ye, when ye hear that we look for a kingdom, assume, without inquiry, that we speak of a human kingdom; whereas we speak of that which is with GOD: as plainly appears from this, that when we are questioned by you, we confess that we are Christians; when we know that the punishment of death will be inflicted upon all who confess. For if we expected a human kingdom, we should deny, that we might escape death; and should seek to remain concealed, that we might obtain what we expect. But since our hopes are not fixed upon this present world, we care not for our murderers, knowing that at all events we must die.

12. Moreover, we aid and assist you to preserve peace, more than all other men: for we are firmly

---

was, "GOD is not like men, he hath no name." Ὁ Θεὸς ὄνομα οὐκ ἔχει ὡς ἄνθρωπος. EUSEB. *Hist. Eccles.* v. 1. The same sentiment is found in the *Cohortatio ad Græcos*, ascribed to JUSTIN, p. 19, B.

ᵘ Compare John vii. 17.

persuaded, that it is impossible that any man should escape the notice of GOD, whether he be an evil doer, or covetous, or a traitor, or a virtuous man: and that every one shall go into eternal punishment or happiness, according to that which his deeds deserve. For if all men knew this, no one would choose evil for a little time, knowing that he must go into everlasting punishment by fire; but each would restrain himself, and adorn himself with all virtue, that so he might attain unto the good things which are of GOD, and be free from those torments. They, who offend against the laws and are exposed to the punishments which you impose, may endeavor to escape detection, knowing well that it is possible to elude the notice of human beings like yourselves. But if they had learned and were well assured, that it is impossible for GOD not to know every thing which is done, nay even every thing which is thought, they would by all means live circumspectly, if it were but to avoid the punishment hanging over their heads, as even ye yourselves will confess.

13. But, it would seem, ye fear lest all should be just and holy in their lives, and ye should have none to punish. This would be an apprehension worthy of an executioner, but not of good princes. And we are persuaded that such suggestions arise, as we have before said, from those evil demons, who demand even offerings and worship from those who live a life contrary to reason. Neither do we suspect that ye, who follow after piety and philosophy,[x] would do any thing against reason. But if ye also, in like manner with those inconsiderate men, honor established practices more than truth, then do what ye can: and the utmost that even princes can do, who honor the opinions (of men) more than the truth, is but as much as robbers in the desert could.[y] And that your labor will be in vain the Word himself declares, than whom, with GOD his Father, we know no prince more royal and more just. For as all avoid the inheritance of the poverty, or

---

[x] Justin alludes to the appellations of the two Antonines, 'Pius' and 'Philosopher.' See Sect. 2.
[y] That is, 'put us to death.' Compare Sections 2 and 60.

60 disease, or disgrace of their parents, so will every one who is wise reject that which right reason commands him to refuse.*

14. Our teacher the Son and Apostle* of GOD the Father and LORD of all things, even JESUS CHRIST, from whom also we have obtained the name of Christians, hath foretold to us that all these things would come to pass. Wherefore we cleave steadfastly to all things which were taught of him, since whatsoever he before declared should happen, hath indeed been fulfilled. For this is the work of GOD (only); to declare events before they happen; and manifestly to bring them to pass, even as they were predicted.

15. We might now rest satisfied with what hath been said, and add nothing more, in the full assurance that our demands are perfectly consistent with justice and truth. But being well aware that the mind, once held captive by ignorance, doth not without great difficulty change, in an instant, its whole train of thought, we have determined to add a few words, to persuade those who are really lovers of truth; for, although difficult, we are persuaded that it is not impossible, that a plain representation of the truth should be sufficient to dissipate error.

16. With respect to the charge of impiety: what man of consideration will not confess that this accusation is falsely alleged against us? since we worship the Creator of this Universe, declaring, as we have been taught, that he requires not sacrifices of blood, and libations, and incense; and praise him to the utmost of our power, with words of prayer and thanksgiving, for all things which we enjoy. For we have learned, that the only honor which is worthy of him is, not to consume with fire what he hath given to us for our nourishment, but to distribute them to ourselves and to those

---

* Children inherit the property of their parents, and they justly claim it as their right. But no one requires to succeed to the poverty, or disease, or disgrace of his parent. In like manner, although established prejudices may have descended to us, we shall exercise our own judgment upon them: we shall consider whether right reason declares them to be part of the wealth, or of the weakness of antiquity: and accordingly accept or reject them.

* Heb. iii. 1.

who have need: and that our thankfulness to him is best expressed, by the solemn offering of prayers and hymns. Moreover we pour forth our praises[b] for our creation, and every provision for our well-being; for the various qualities of all creatures, and the changes of seasons; and (for the hope) of rising again in corruption, through faith which is in him. Again we have learned, that he who taught us these things, and for this end was born, even JESUS CHRIST, who was crucified under Pontius Pilate, the procurator of Judea, in the time of Tiberius Cæsar, was the Son of Him who is truly GOD, and we esteem him in the second place. And that we with reason honor the prophetic Spirit, in the third place, we shall hereafter show.[c] For upon this point they accuse us of madness, saying that we give the second place after the unchangeable and eternal GOD, the Creator of all things, to a man who was crucified; (and this they do) being ignorant of the mystery which is in this matter; to which we exhort you to take heed while we explain it.[d]

17. For we have forewarned you to beware, lest those demons, whom we have before accused, should deceive you, and prevent you from reading and understanding what we say. For they strive to retain you as their slaves and servants, and sometimes by revelations in dreams, and at other times again by magical tricks, enslave those who strive not at all for their own salvation. In like manner as we also, since we have been obedient to the Word, abstain from such things, and, through the Son, follow the only unbegotten GOD. We, who once delighted in fornication, now embrace chastity only: we, who once used magical arts, have consecrated ourselves to the good and unbegotten GOD: we, who loved above all things the gain of money and possessions, now bring all that we have into one common stock, and give a part to every one that needs: we, who hated and killed one another, and permitted not those of another nation, on account of their different

---

[b] The true reading is probably αἰνέσεις, not αἰτήσεις.
[c] Compare Sect. 6.
[d] Justin here digresses after his usual manner, and does not resume his argument till Sect. 31.

customs, to live with us under the same roof, now, since the appearing of CHRIST, live at the same table, and pray for our enemies, and endeavor to persuade those who unjustly hate us; that they also, living after the excellent institutions of CHRIST, may have good hope with us to obtain the same blessings, with GOD the LORD of all.

18. And, that we may not seem to deceive you, we think it right to remind you of some few of the doctrines which we have received from CHRIST himself, before we proceed to the proof (which we have promised): and be it your care, as powerful princes,* to inquire whether in truth we have thus been taught and teach. His words were short and concise; for he was no sophist, but his word was the power of GOD.f With respect, then, to chastity, he spake thus: "Whosoever shall look on a woman to lust after her, hath already committed adultery in his heart before GOD."g And "If thy right eye offend thee, cut it out;h for it is profitable for thee to enter into the kingdom of heaven with one eye, rather than with the two, to be sent into everlasting fire."i And, "Whosoever marrieth a wife that is put away from another man, committeth adultery:"k and, "There are some, which were made eunuchs of men: and there are some which were born eunuchs; and there are some which have made themselves eunuchs, for the kingdom of heaven's sake: but all receive not this."l Hence they who, under the sanction of human laws, marry again, and they who look on a woman to lust after her, are sinners in the sight of our master. For not only he, who is an adulterer in fact, is cast out by him, but he who wishes to commit adultery: since not only the deeds but the very desires are manifest to GOD. Nay many, both men and women, of the age of sixty and seventy years, who have been disciples of CHRIST from their youth,

---

* ὡς δυνατῶν βασιλέων. H. STEPHANUS proposes to read ὡς δὴ συνετῶν βασιλέων, "as wise princes."
f 1 Cor. i. 24.   g Matt. v. 28.
h Justin has Ἔκκοψον αὐτόν — the word ἔκκοψον being taken from the following verse, for ἔξελε.
i Matt. v. 29. Mark ix. 47.
k Matt. v. 32. Luke xvi. 18.   l Matt. xix. 11, 12.

continue in immaculate virginity; and it is my boast to be able to display such before the whole human race. For why should we mention also the innumerable multitude of those, who have been converted from a life of incontinence, and learned these precepts? For CHRIST called not the righteous nor the chaste to repentance, but the ungodly, and the incontinent, and the unjust. For thus he said; "I came not to call the righteous, but sinners to repentance."[m] For our heavenly Father prefers the repentance of a sinner to his punishment.

19. Again, concerning the love of all men he thus taught: "If ye love those who love you, what new thing do ye? for even the fornicators also do the same. But I say unto you, Pray for your enemies, and love those that hate you, and bless those that curse you; and pray for those that despitefully use you."[n] And that we should give to them that are in need, and do nothing for the sake of vain-glory, he thus said; "Give to every one that asketh of you, and from him that would borrow of you turn not ye away:"[o] "For if ye lend to them from whom ye hope to receive, what new thing do ye? for even the publicans do the same."[p] "But lay not ye up for yourselves treasures upon earth, where moth and rust doth corrupt, and thieves break through: but lay up for yourselves treasures in the heavens, where neither moth nor rust doth corrupt."[q] "For what is a man profited, if he shall gain the whole world, and lose his own soul? Or what shall he give in exchange for it?"[r] "Lay up therefore treasure in the heavens, where neither moth nor rust doth corrupt." And, "Be ye good and merciful, as your Father also is good and merciful; and maketh his sun to rise upon the sinners, and the righteous, and the wicked."[s] "Take no thought what ye shall eat, or what ye shall put on: are ye not better than the fowls and the beasts? Yet GOD feedeth them. Therefore take no thought, what ye shall eat, or what ye shall put on;

---
[m] Matt. ix. 13. Luke v. 32.
[n] Matt. v. 44, 46. Luke vi. 27, 28, 32.
[o] Matt. v. 42. Luke vi. 30.   [p] Luke vi. 34.
[q] Matt. vi. 19, 20.   [r] Matt. xvi. 26. Luke ix. 25.
[s] Luke vi. 35, 36. Matt. v. 45,

for your heavenly Father knoweth that ye have need of these things. But seek ye the kingdom of heaven, and all these things shall be added unto you.' For where the treasure is, there also is the mind of man."ᵃ And, "Do not these things to be seen of men: otherwise ye have no reward with your Father which is in heaven."ˣ

20. That we should also patiently endure evil, and be kind to all, and not give way to wrath, he taught us in these words: "Unto him that smiteth thee upon the cheek, turn also the other: and him that taketh away thy coat or thy cloak hinder not."ʸ "And whosoever is angry is in danger of the fire."ᶻ "And whosoever shall compel thee to go a mile, follow him twain."ᵃ "Let your good works shine before men, that they may see them, and glorify your Father which is in heaven."ᵇ For we must not oppose: neither would he that we should imitate bad men, but hath commanded us by patience and meekness to withdraw all men from shameful and evil lusts. Which also we can show to have actually taken place among us, in many, who have been subdued and changed from violent and tyrannical men, either by imitating the constancy of their neighbors' lives, or by observing the unusual patience of those with whom they travelled, when they were defrauded on the way, or by experiencing the faithfulness of those with whom they had any dealings.

21. That we should not swear at all, but speak the truth always, he thus commanded us: "Swear not at all: but let your yea be yea, and your nay, nay: for whatsoever is more than these cometh of evil."ᶜ And that we should worship GOD only, he thus taught us, saying, "The greatest commandment is, Thou shalt worship the LORD thy GOD, and him only shalt thou serve, with all thy heart, and with all thy strength, even the LORD who created thee."ᵈ And when a certain man came to him, and said, "Good master;" he an-

---

' Matt. vi. 25, &c. Luke xii. 22, 24, &c.
ᵃ Matt. vi. 21. Luke xii. 34.   ˣ Matt. vi. 1, 9.
ʸ Matt. v. 39. Luke vi. 29.   ᶻ Matt. v. 22.
ᵃ Matt. v. 41.   ᵇ Matt. v. 16.
ᶜ Matt. v. 34, 37.   ᵈ Matt. iv. 10. Mark xii. 30.

swered and said, "There is none good save one, that is GOD, who created all things."ᵉ

22. Now whosoever are found not to live as CHRIST taught them, let it be publicly known that they are not Christians, although they should profess with their tongue the doctrines of CHRIST. For he declared, that not they who only profess, but they who do his works shall be saved. For thus he said: "Not every one that saith unto me, LORD, LORD, shall enter into the kingdom of heaven, but he that doeth the will of my Father which is in heaven,"ᶠ "For he that heareth me, and doeth what I say, heareth him that sent me."ᵍ "And many shall say unto me, LORD, LORD, have we not eaten, and drunk,ʰ and done mighty works, in thy name? and then will I say unto them, Depart from me, ye workers of iniquity."ⁱ "Then shall be weeping and gnashing of teeth; when the righteous shall shine as the sun: but the unrighteous shall be sent into eternal fire."ᵏ "For many shall come in my name, covered outwardly with sheep's clothing, but inwardly being ravening wolves: by their works ye shall know them. But every tree, which bringeth not forth good fruit, is hewn down, and cast into the fire."ˡ And we even entreat, that those who live not agreeably to their doctrines, but are merely called Christians, may be punished by you.

23. We make it also our principal endeavor in every place to pay tribute and custom to such officers as are appointed by you, even as we have been taught by him. For "at that time certain came unto him, and asked him, whether it were lawful to pay tribute unto Cæsar. And he answered, Tell me, whose image doth the tribute money bear? They said unto him Cæsar's. Then again answered he them, Render therefore unto Cæsar the things which are Cæsar's, and unto GOD the things which are GOD's."ᵐ Wherefore we worship

---

ᵉ Matt. xix. 16, 17. ᶠ Matt. vii. 21.
ᵍ Matt. vii. 24; x. 40.
ʰ The Greek has οὐ τῷ σῷ ὀνόματι ἐφάγομεν καὶ ἐπίομεν, καὶ δυνάμεις ἐποιήσαμεν; Ashton proposes to read οὐκ ἐνώπιον σοῦ ἐφάγομεν καὶ ἐπίομεν, καὶ τῷ σῷ ὀνόματι δυνάμεις ἐποιήσαμεν. Compare Luke xiii. 26.
ⁱ Matt. vii. 22. Luke xiii. 26. ᵏ Matt. xiii. 42, &c.
ˡ Matt. vii. 15, 16, 19. ᵐ Matt. xxii. 17, &c.

GOD only: but in all other matters we joyfully serve you, confessing that ye are kings and rulers; and praying that ye may be found to possess, together with your royal power, a sound and discerning mind. If, however, notwithstanding we thus pray, and openly lay every thing before you, ye yet treat us with contempt, we shall receive no injury, believing, yea rather being firmly persuaded, that every one, if his deeds shall so deserve, shall receive the punishment of eternal fire; and that an account will be required of him, in proportion to the powers which he hath received from GOD; as CHRIST hath declared, saying, "To whomsoever GOD hath given much, of him shall be much required."[a]

24. For look to the end of each of the Emperors who have already reigned, that they died the common death of all men: and well would it be for the wicked,[o] if this were merely a passage into a state of insensibility. But since both sense remains in all who have ever lived, and eternal punishment is reserved (for the wicked), take heed that ye be persuaded and believe that these things are true. For the very acts of necromancy,[p] the inspection of the bodies of pure children,[q] (for the purpose of divination,) the calling

---

[a] Luke xii. 48.

[o] ἕρμαιον ἂν ἦν τοῖς ἀδίκοις πᾶσιν. Justin seems to allude to a similar phrase in his master PLATO: εἰ μὲν ἦν ὁ θάνατος τοῦ παντὸς ἀπαλλαγή, ἕρμαιον ἂν ἦν τοῖς κακοῖς ἀποθανοῦσι. *Phædo.* p. 107.

[p] See TERTULLIAN's *Apology*, Sect. 23.

[q] Justin here refers to a barbarous practice frequently alluded to by writers both of ecclesiastical and profane history. Immaculate children of both sexes were slain, and their entrails inspected for the purpose of divination, under the persuasion that the souls of the victims were then present, and revealed the knowledge of futurity to those who consulted them.

Thus Dionysius, Bishop of Alexandria, as preserved by EUSEBIUS, *Hist. Eccles.* Lib. vii. c. 10, relates that, in the ninth persecution under Valerian, the emperor was instructed by the chief of the Magi of Egypt, in many abominable rites, and taught "to murder wretched infants, and sacrifice the children of miserable parents; and to examine their tender entrails." Τελετὰς δὲ ἀνάγνους καὶ μαγγανείας ἐξαγίστους καὶ ἱερουργίας ἀκαλλιερήτους ἐπιτελεῖν ὑποτιθέμενος, παῖδας ἀθλίους ἀποσφάττειν, καὶ τέκνα δυστήνων πατέρων καταθύειν, καὶ σπλάγχνα νεογενῆ διαιρεῖν. EUSEBIUS also, in two places, mentions among the enormities perpetrated by the tyrant Maxentius, that he filled up the measure of his guilt by having recourse to magical arts, among which was the inspection of the entrails of new-born children. Ἡ δὲ τῶν κακῶν τῷ τυράννῳ κορωνὶς ἐπὶ γοητείαν ἤλαυνε· μαγικαῖς ἐπινοίαις τοτὲ μὲν γυναῖκας

forth of human souls, and those whom your magicians call senders of dreams, and familiar spirits,[r] and the practices of those who are skilled in such matters, may induce you to believe that souls after death are still in a state of sensibility. To these may be added the men who are seized and thrown down by the souls of the departed,[s] who are commonly called demoniac and mad; and what are styled oracles among you, such of those of Amphilochus, and Dodone, the Pythian, and the like: the opinions also of writers, such as Empedocles, Pythagoras, Plato, and Socrates: the trench mentioned by Homer,[t] and the descent of Ulysses to see

---

ἐγκύμονας ἀνασχίζοντας, ποτὲ δὲ νεογνῶν σπλάγχνα βρεφῶν διερευνωμένον. EUSEBIUS, *Hist. Eccles.* Lib. viii. c. 14. *Vit. Const.* Lib. i. c. 36.

SOCRATES states the same brutal treatment to have been used by the Pagans toward the Christians, in the time of Julian, in various cities, and particularly at Athens and Alexandria. "At that time, the Gentiles made a furious attack upon the Christians: and those who called themselves philosophers were gathered together. They established also certain horrid rites, so that they even slew many young children, both male and female, for the purpose of inspecting their entrails, and also tasted their flesh." Τηνικαῦτα καὶ οἱ Ἕλληνες τῶν χριστιανιζόντων κατέτρεχον. σύρροιά τε τῶν φιλοσοφεῖν λεγόντων ἐγίνετο. Καὶ τελετάς τινας συνίστασαν, ὡς καὶ σπλαγχνοσκοπούμενοι παῖδας καταθύειν ἀφθόρους, ἄρρενας καὶ θηλείας, καὶ τῶν σαρκῶν ἀπογεύεσθαι. SOCRAT. *Hist. Eccles.* Lib. iii. c. 13.

In the work called the *Recognitions of Clement*, which is at least as old as the time of ORIGEN, by whom it is cited, (*Philocal.* c. 23,) Simon Magus is made to say; "By means of ineffable adjurations I called up the soul of an immaculate boy, who had been put to a violent death, and caused it to stand by me: and by its means whatever I command is effected." And again, ("The soul freed from the body) possesses the faculty of foreknowledge: whence it is called forth for necromancy." "Pueri incorrupti et violenter necati animam adjuramentis ineffabilibus evocatam adsistere mihi feci; et per ipsam fit omne quod jubeo." "Statim et præscientiam habet (anima), propter quod evocatur ad necromantiam." *Recognit. Clementis*, Lib. ii. c. 13.

[r] πάρεδροι. VALESIUS in his notes on EUSEBIUS, *Hist. Eccles.* Lib. iv. c. 17, shows that by this word were meant spirits, who assisted the Magicians and performed their orders. IRENÆUS, *Adv. Hær.* Lib. i. c. 20, says that the followers of Simon Magus had both the kinds of spirits here mentioned. "Qui dicuntur *paredri* et oniropompi et quæcunque sunt alia perierga apud eos studiosè exercentur."

[s] Such as the demoniacs, described in Matt. viii. 28. Mark v. 3. Luke vii. 25. JOSEPHUS, (*Bell. Jud.* VII. vi. 3,) in like manner describes demons as the spirits of wicked men. Τὰ γὰρ καλούμενα δαιμόνια, ταῦτα δὲ πονηρῶν ἐστιν ἀνθρώπων πνεύματα, τοῖς ζῶσιν εἰσδυόμενα καὶ κτείνοντα τοὺς βοηθείας μὴ τυγχάνοντας, αὕτη (ἡ ῥίζα Βαάρας) ταχέως ἐξελαύνει.

[t] *Odyss.* λ. 25, 37, &c.

these things; together with the tenets of those who have spoken to the same effect. Give us, now, but the same degree of credit which you give to them; inasmuch as our confidence in (the power of) GOD is not less, but greater, than theirs: for we expect that we shall each again take upon us our bodies which are dead and cast into the earth, holding that nothing is impossible to GOD.

25. And if any one considered the matter well, would this appear more incredible than it would, if we were not in the body, and any one should assert that it was possible for bones, and tendons, and flesh to be formed, as we see in the human body, out of a minute drop of seminal matter? For let us suppose an imaginary case. If ye were not such as ye are, nor of such an origin, and any one should show you the generating substance, and a painted representation (of the human form), and should persist in affirming that the one could be produced from the other, would ye believe him before ye saw the effect produced? No one would be bold enough to assert, that ye would. In the same manner, ye now disbelieve, because ye never saw a dead man raised to life. But even, as ye would not at first have believed, that from a little drop of seminal matter such bodies could be formed, which yet, ye see, are formed; so consider that it is not impossible for human bodies, decomposed, and, like seed, resolved into earth, to arise, in due season, at the command of GOD, and to put on incorruption."[u] We pretend not to say, how

---

[u] The argument here used by Justin, is frequently employed by the early Christian writers. TERTULLIAN *de Resurrect. Carnis*, c. 11, says, "Idoneus est reficere (carnem), qui fecit: quantò plus est fecisse, quàm refecisse: initium dedisse, quàm reddidisse. Ita restitutionem carnis faciliorem credas institutione." See also TERTULLIAN, *Apol.* c. 48. IRENÆUS argues, with a plain reference to this passage of Justin, how much more difficult it is that bones, and tendons, and veins, and the rest of the body made after the fashion of a man, should be caused to exist, and to become a pious and rational being, when as yet it existed not, than that, having once been made and resolved into earth, it should be restored to a form which it once possessed, even if it should have been reduced to the same state in which it was, before it was first made man. — Καίπερ πολλῷ δυσκολώτερον καὶ ἀπιστότερον ἦν, ἐκ μὴ ὄντων ὀστέων τε καὶ νεύρων — καὶ τῆς λοιπῆς τῆς κατὰ τὸν ἄνθρωπον οἰκονομίας, ποιῆσαι εἰς τὸ εἶναι, καὶ ἔμψυχον, καὶ λογικὸν ἀπεργάσασθαι ζῷον, ἢ τὸ γεγονὸς, ἔπειτα ἀναλυθὲν εἰς τὴν γῆν — αὖθις ἀποκαταστῆσαι, εἰς ἐκεῖνα

worthy an estimate of divine power they form, who maintain that every thing returns to its original whence it proceeded, and that beyond this even GOD can do nothing: but we plainly see this, that they would not have believed it possible, for beings like themselves, and for the whole world, to have existed, and to have had their origin, in the manner which their own observation now discovers. 66

26. We have already assumed that it is better to believe things, which in their own nature and by the power of men are impossible, than to disbelieve as others do. Since we know how our master JESUS CHRIST said, "The things which are impossible with men, are possible with GOD."[x] He said also, "Fear ye not them that kill you, and after that are able to do nothing: but fear him, who after death, is able to cast both soul and body into hell."[y]

27. Now hell is the place, where those shall be punished who have lived unrighteously, and have not believed that the things shall come to pass, which GOD hath taught through CHRIST. And even the Sibyl[z] and Hystaspes declared that there should be a destruction of corruptible things by fire. And those who are styled Stoic philosophers[a] teach, that GOD himself will

---

χωρῆσαν ὅθεν τὴν ἀρχὴν μηδέπω γεγονὼς ἐγεγόνει ὁ ἄνθρωπος. IRENÆUS, *Adv. Hær.* Lib. v. c. 3. p. 401, 32.

ATHENAGORAS, in his argumentative treatise on the Resurrection of the body, lays great stress upon the same reasoning. ATHENAG. *de Resurrectione Carnis*, p. 43, A. 59, A. See also the *Apostolical Constitutions*, Lib. v. Sect. 43. 7. p. 308.

[x] Luke xviii. 27.   [y] Matt. x. 28. Luke xii. 45.

[z] ——— ῥεύσει δὲ πυρὸς μαλεροῦ καταρράκτης
'Ακάματος· φλέξει δὲ γαῖαν, φλέξει δὲ θάλασσαν,
Καὶ πόλον οὐράνιον, καὶ ἤματα, καὶ κτίσιν αὐτὴν
Εἰς ἓν χωνεύσει, καὶ εἰς καθαρὸν διαλέξει.
                                    CARM. SIB. Lib. iii.

THEOPHILUS (*ad Autolycum*, Lib. ii. p. 114, D. 116, A.) appeals in like manner to the Sibyl. The author of the *Quæstiones et Responsiones ad Orthodoxos*, a work falsely ascribed to Justin, says that CLEMENT of Rome, in his Epistle to the Corinthians, appeals to the writings of the Sibyl, as testifying that the world should be destroyed by fire. In the present Epistle of Clement there is no such allusion. GROTIUS (*de Veritate Rel. Christ.* I. 22,) has accumulated several instances of the same tradition.

[a] See Justin Martyr's *Second Apology*, p. 45.—CICERO *De Natura Deorum*, ii. 46.

be resolved into fire; and affirm that the world shall be renewed by a change. But we entertain far higher notions respecting GOD, the Creator of all things, than that he should be subject to any change.

28. If then in some things we hold the same opinions with the poets and philosophers, whom ye honor, and in others entertain views more sublime and more worthy of the divine nature, and if we alone are able to prove what we say, why are we unjustly hated above all men? For when we affirm that all things were ordered and made by GOD, we hold apparently the same doctrine as Plato: when we speak of a destruction by fire, we agree with the Stoics: in maintaining that the souls of the unjust are punished, retaining their consciousness even after death, and the souls of good men live happily, free from pain, we assent to what your poets and philosophers declare:[b] when we say that we ought not to worship the works of men's hands, we agree with Menander the comic poet, and others who hold the same opinions; for they have shown that the Creator is greater than the creature. And when we affirm that the Word, which is the first-begotten of GOD, was born without carnal knowledge, even JESUS CHRIST our Master, and that he was crucified, and died, and rose again and ascended into heaven, we advance no new thing different from what is maintained respecting those, whom ye call the sons of Jupiter.[c]

29. For ye well know how many sons your approved writers attribute to Jupiter: Mercury, the word of interpretation and the teacher of all men; Esculapius, who was a physician, and yet struck with lightning and taken up into heaven; Bacchus, who was torn in

---

[b] THEOPHILUS of Antioch, (*ad Autolycum*, Lib. ii. p. 115,) and CLEMENS Alexandrinus, (Stromata, Lib. iv. p. 541,) have collected many passages of Heathen poets and philosophers, agreeing with different tenets of the Christian religion.

[c] The object which Justin has in view, in the ensuing part of his Apology, although now void of interest, was important at the time in which it was written, when the Heathen world was given up to idolatry. He endeavors to show that the Gentiles could not consistently make it a matter of accusation against the Christians, that they believed in the incarnation of JESUS CHRIST the Son of GOD, when they themselves held opinions, which were fully as incredible, respecting their false gods.

pieces; Hercules, who burned himself upon the pile to escape his torments; Castor and Pollux, the sons of Leda; Perseus the son of Danäe; and Bellerophon, born of human race, and carried away upon the horse Pegasus.[d] For why should I speak of Ariadne, and others also, like her, who were said to be raised among the stars of heaven? Nay, ye determine that the very Emperors, who die among you, shall always become immortal; and bring forward some one to swear that he saw Cæsar, who was burnt, going up to heaven out of the funeral pile. Neither is it necessary that I should relate to you, who already know well, of what kind were the actions of each of those who were called the sons of Jupiter; I need only say, that the writings, in which they are recorded, tend only to corrupt and pervert[e] the minds of those who learn them: for all take a pride in being imitators of the gods. Now far be from every sound mind such conceptions concerning the gods, that even the very leader and father of them all, as they account Jupiter, should be a parricide, as his father also was;[f] should be a slave of the worst and basest passions, as in the instance of Ganymede and his adulteries with many women, and receive with approbation his sons who acted in like manner. But, as we have before said, the evil spirits did these things. And we have been taught that they only are immortalized, who live holily and virtuously before God: believing also that they who live an unjust life, and repent not, shall be punished in eternal fire.

30. But Jesus, who is called the Son of God, even if he had been but a man, in the ordinary sense, would yet by his wisdom have deserved to be called the Son of God; for all writers call Him God, who is the Father of gods and men: but if we say that he was begotten of God, in a manner far different from ordi-

---

[d] Justin alludes to the same story respecting Bellerophon in Sect. 71. The mythological history was not, however, that Bellerophon was carried to heaven on Pegasus, but that he made the attempt and failed.

[e] εἰς διαφθορὰν καὶ παράτροπήν.

[f] The word "parricide" does not always strictly mean the murderer of a parent. Jupiter was said to have dethroned, and, by some, to have imprisoned Saturn; and Saturn was accused of using still greater violence to his own father, Cœlus or Uranus.

nary generation, being the Word of God, as we have before said, let this be considered a correspondence with your own tenets, when ye call Mercury the word who bears messages from God. And if any one objects to us, that he was crucified; this too is a point of correspondence with those whom ye call the sons of Jupiter, and yet allow to have suffered, as we before stated. For the sufferings of their deaths are related to have been not similar to his, but different;[g] so that he seems not to have been inferior to them even in the peculiar manner of his death: nay, in the progress of our address we shall show, as we promised, that he is even superior: or rather this is already shown; for he that is superior appears to be so from his deeds. Again, if we affirm that he was born of a virgin; let this be considered a point in which he agrees with what you (fabulously) ascribe to Perseus. And whereas we say that he made those whole, who were lame, palsied, and blind[h] from their birth, and raised the dead; in this too we ascribe to him actions similar to those which are said to have been performed by Esculapius.

31. We desire also to make it fully apparent to you, that those things only which we affirm, and have learned from Christ and the prophets who went before him, are the truth, and more ancient than (what is recorded by) all other writers; and we do not require to be believed, because in some particulars we agree with them, but because we say the truth; and Jesus Christ, who alone was properly born the Son of God, being his Word, and First-begotten and Power, and by his counsel made man, hath taught us these things, for the reformation and improvement of the human race. Before he was made man and dwelt among men, some,[i]

---

[g] In Sect. 72, Justin argues that the mystery of the cross was never imitated by any of the false gods.

[h] πηροὺς. This seems a better reading than πονηροὺς. Thirlby shows that the word is used by Justin to signify "the blind" as in *Trypho*, p. 295.

[i] φθάσαντές τινες διὰ τοὺς προειρημένους κάκους δαίμονας, διὰ τῶν ποιητῶν ὡς γενόμενα εἶπον, ἃ μυθοποιήσαντες ἔφησαν· ὃν τρόπον καὶ τὰ καθ' ἡμῶν λεγόμενα δύσφημα καὶ ἀσεβῆ ἔργα ἐνήργησαν.—There is probably some omission or error in the Greek text. The assertion of Justin seems to be, that the demons, whom he supposes to have inspired the Heathen

at the instigation of those evil spirits of which we have spoken, declared through the fictions which the poets uttered, that these events had already happened; as also they have fabricated those infamous and impious actions which are reported of us, without witness or proof. Of this our refutation follows.

32. In the first place, we alone, although we express nothing but what is similar to the professions of the Greeks, are hated on account of the name of CHRIST, and, although innocent, are put to death as transgressors: whereas other persons, in different places, worship trees and rivers, and mice, and cats, and crocodiles, and (many) other brute beasts. Yet the same animals are not held sacred by all, but some in one place and some in another; so that all are accounted impious one to the other, for not worshipping the same objects.—And this is the only thing of which ye can accuse us, that we worship not the same gods which ye worship, and offer not libations, and the perfume of the fat of beasts, to the dead, nor crowns and sacrifices to images.[k]—or ye well know that the same things are regarded by some as gods, by others as beasts, and by others again as victims.

33. In the second place, we out of every nation, who formerly worshipped Bacchus the son of Semele, and Apollo the son of Latona, whose infamous abominations it is a shame even to mention, together with Proserpine and Venus, who were inflamed with passion for Adonis, and whose mysteries ye celebrate, or any others of those who are called gods, do now for the sake of JESUS CHRIST despise all these, even under the threat of death: and dedicate ourselves to GOD who is unbegotten[1] and without passions; of whom we believe not (as ye believe of Jupiter) that under the influence of base passion he followed Antiope, or others in like manner, or Ganymede, nor that he was loosed from

---

poets and mythologists, had obtained some imperfect knowledge of the actions which CHRIST should perform, and purposely framed the stories of the false gods so as to anticipate them.

[k] *ἐν γραφαῖς στεφάνους.* SALMASIUS reads *ἐν ῥαφαῖς στεφάνους,* crowns sewed together.

[1] *ἀγεννήτω.* See note (q) on IGNATIUS' *Epistle to the Ephesians,* Sect. 7, p. 58.

bonds by (Briareus) with a hundred hands at the solicitation of Thetis; nor on that account was anxious that Achilles, the son of Thetis, should slay many of the Greeks,[m] for his concubine Briseis. Nay we pity those who believe such fables, and are persuaded that evil spirits are the authors of them.

34. In the third place, even after the ascension of CHRIST into heaven, the evil spirits have put forward certain men, who said that they were gods: and these men were so far from being persecuted by you, that they were thought worthy even of honors. For instance, there was one Simon, a Samaritan, from a village named Gitton, who under Claudius Cæsar performed magical wonders in your imperial city Rome, through the art and agency of evil spirits; and was regarded as a god, and had a statue erected to him among you. This statue stood by the river Tiber, between the two bridges, having upon it this Latin inscription,

SIMONI DEO SANCTO.[n]

And almost all the Samaritans, and some also in other nations, confess him to be the first of the gods, and

---

[m] *Iliad*, B. 4.
[n] The account which Justin here gives of the statue erected to Simon Magus, is followed by TERTULLIAN, (*Apol.* Sect. 13;) IRENÆUS, (*Adv. Hæres.* Lib. i. c. 20;) EUSEBIUS, (*Hist. Eccles.* Lib. ii. c. 13,) and many others of the Fathers; and was not doubted till the year 1574, when a stone was dug up in the island of the Tiber, with the inscription, SEMONI SANCO (or SANGO) DEO FIDIO SACRUM SEX. POMPEIUS S. P. F. COL. MUSSIANUS QUINQUENNALIS DECUR BIDENTALIS DONUM DEDIT.

Since that time, many have supposed that the similarity of names led Justin into an error; and that he attributed to Simon Magus an honor which was really paid to Semo Sancus, a god of the Sabines.

It is certainly possible enough that Justin should have been mistaken. But it must be observed that the inscriptions, although similar, are not the same, the order of the words being different: that the statue to Simon Magus is said (JUSTIN, *Apol.* Sect. 73,) to have been dedicated by the Roman people, whereas that to Semo Sancus is a private offering of Sextus Pompeius. The statue of Simon Magus was in the form of Jupiter: (IREN. *Adv. Hæres.* Lib. i. c. 20. p. 95, 25. "Imaginem quoque Simonis, habent *factam ad figuram Jovis.*"— CYRIL. *Cateches.* vi. p. 87. Oxon. ἐν εἴδει Διὸς EPIPHAN. *Hær.* xxi. c. 3;) that of Semo represented Hercules.

The objections of VALESIUS (in EUSEB. *Hist. Eccles.* Lib. ii. c. 13,) and of Basnage, (*Exercit. Hist.* p. 573,) founded on the assertion that

§ 35.] *JUSTIN MARTYR.* 151

even worship him; and say that a certain Helena, who travelled with him at that time, and formerly had been a prostitute, was the first Intelligence ° which proceeded from him. We know also that one Menander,ᵖ a Samaritan also, from the village of Capparetæa, a disciple of Simon, received power from the evil spirits, and being in Antioch deceived many by magical art. He persuaded also his followers that he should never die; and still there are some of his sect who profess to believe this.

70

35. There is also Marcion of Pontus,ᵠ who is even

---

the Romans never attached the epithet *sanctus* to their gods, nor employed the words *Deo Sancto* in an inscription, are proved to be incorrect. There are numerous passages of the poets, and of Cicero, (*) in which *sanctus* is so used: and inscriptions are extant with the words, *Apollini Sancto, Æsculapio Sancto,* and the like; and with the very words in dispute, *Deo Sancto Apollini Pacifero.* GRUTER, *Inscript.* xxxviii. 7.

It is also said, but I know not on what authority, that the statue attributed to Simon Magus was of *brass*, whereas that discovered was of *stone*.

The accuracy of Justin is questioned by BASNAGE, *Exercit. Histor.* p. 570; by ANTONIUS VAN DALE, in his *Dissertatiuncula de statuâ Simoni Mago erectâ;* by VALESIUS, GRABE, and many others. The defenders of Justin's correctness on this point are BARONIUS, *Eccles. Hist.* Ann. xliv. 55; HALLOIX, in his life of Justin; TILLEMONT, Tom. II. Part I. p. 341, and p. 176, and JENKIN, in his *Defensio S. Augustini adversus Joan. Phereponi Animadversiones,* p. 176. THIRLBY, in his notes on the passage, pretends to defend the accuracy of Justin; and, in his usual way between jest and earnest, brings much information to bear upon the point.

° IRENÆUS *Adv. Hæres.* Lib. i. c. 20, and after him, TERTULLIAN *de Animâ,* c. 34, and THEODORET *de Fabulis Hæreticorum,* Lib. i. ii. give an account of the strange doctrines maintained by Simon Magus.   *   *   *   *   *   *   *

ᵖ Menander was the disciple of Simon Magus, and the master of Saturninus. For an account of his doctrines, see IRENÆUS *Adv. Hæres.* Lib. i. c. 21. TERTULLIAN *de Animâ,* c. 23, 50. *De Resurrect. Carnis,* c. 5. EUSEBIUS *Hist. Eccles.* iii. 26.

ᵠ Marcion lived in the reign of Antoninus: (TERTULLIAN *de Præscript.* c. 30,) and that this was Antoninus *Pius,* appears from IRENÆUS *Adv. Hæres.* Lib. iii. c. 4, who states that he flourished in the time of Anicetus, the tenth Bishop of Rome, who lived in the reign of Antoninus Pius. EUSEB. *Hist. Eccles.* Lib. iv. c. 10, 11, and *Chronicon.*—IRENÆUS gives an account of his tenets. *Adv. Hæres.* Lib. i. c. 29. TERTLLUIAN wrote five books against Marcion: and the best account of the opinions of that heretic is given by the Bp. of Lincoln,

(a) CATULLUS lxiv. 269, lxviii. 5.—TIBULLUS i. 3, 52.—OVID, *Met.* i. 372.— CICERO *pro P. Sestio,* 68.—*Pro Milone* 31.—*In Verrem,* i. 19, v. 72.

now teaching his followers to profess, that there is some other God, greater than he who created the world. This man, through the assistance of evil spirits, hath caused many in every nation to speak blasphemies, and to deny that the Creator of the universe was God; maintaining that some one else, of superior power, hath exceeded that Creator by executing greater works. And yet all, who have sprung from these sects, as we have stated, are called Christians. In the same manner as those, who do not hold the same opinions as the philosophers, are still included under the common appellation of philosophy. Now whether they are guilty of any of those infamous acts which are reported,[r] such as the putting out of the lights, and promiscuous intercourse, and feeding on human flesh, we know not; but we know that they are not persecuted nor put to death by you, even on account of their peculiar doctrines. We have also a treatise composed against all the heresies which have arisen, which, if you wish to peruse it, we will produce.

36. But we are so far from committing any (such) injustice or impiety (as is implied in the charge of devouring children), that we have learned that none but wicked men expose infants when they are born. First, because we see, that almost all such are brought up in the vilest manner, and for the basest purposes, whether they be male or female: and are every where publicly exposed, even as men of old reared

---

in his luminous epitome of those books. Bp. KAYE's *Account of Tertullian*, c. vii. pp. 474–505. EUSEBIUS, (*Hist. Eccles.* Lib. iv. c. 11,) in quoting this passage, expresses himself as if it occurred in a book of Justin written against Marcion.

[r] These calumnies were constantly brought against the Christians; and are refuted in all their apologies. Compare JUSTIN, *Second Apology*, p. 50. *Dial. cum Tryph.* p. 227. TERTULLIAN, *Apol.* Sect. 2, 7, 8. *Ad Nationes* i. c. 2. MINUCIUS FELIX, *Octavius*, Sect. 9, 30. They are mentioned also by the martyrs, who suffered in the persecution after the death of Antoninus Pius, (EUSEB. *Hist. Eccles.* Lib. v. c. i. p. 133, A,) by ATHENAGORAS (*Legat.* p. 4,) and by ORIGEN (*Contra Celsum*, Lib. vi. p. 293, 4,) as having been advanced at the beginning of Christianity. He attributes the origin of the accusation to the Jews. Καὶ δοκεῖ μοι παραπλήσιον Ἰουδαίοις πεποιηκέναι (Κέλσος) τοῖς κατὰ τὴν ἀρχὴν τοῦ Χριστιανισμοῦ διδασκαλίας κατασκεδάσασι δυσφημίαν τοῦ λόγου· ὡς ἄρα καταθύσαντες παιδίον μεταλαμβάνουσιν αὐτοῦ τῶν σαρκῶν. κ. τ. λ.

for sale herds of oxen, or goats, or sheep, or horses. And ye receive the hire* and tribute and custom of these persons, when ye ought to cut them off from the face of your empire. I abstain from mentioning the horrible, and even incestuous, offences which hence frequently occur; the manner in which men sometimes prostitute their children and their wives: or the shocking offerings which are made to her, whom ye call the mother of the gods. And, indeed, in the worship of all those who are accounted gods among you, a serpent is represented as a great symbol and mystery. (Ye accuse us also of extinguishing the lights, that we may give way to gross indulgences:) thus what ye openly practise and hold in honor, as if the divine light (of reason and natural sense of right and wrong) were overthrown and extinguished in you, ye falsely attribute to us: but this brings no blame upon us, who are free from all such abominations, but rather upon those who do them, and bear false witness. For, as ye may learn, by inquiry, from our Scriptures, the leader of the evil demons is by us called the Serpent, and Satan, and the Devil,[t] who, as Christ hath foretold, shall be sent into fire with all his host, and such men as follow him, to be punished for endless ages. For the cause why God hath hitherto delayed the execution of this is the human race. For he foreknows that some shall be saved by repentance, and some perhaps who are not yet born: and at the first he formed the human race intelligent, and able to choose the truth and to be happy,[u] so that all men should be without excuse before God; for they are made capable of reason and foresight. But if any one believes not that God cares for such things, such a man must either profess that God exists not at all,[x] or affirm that, if He exists, he delights in evil; or else that he remains as insensible as a stone: and that

71

---

* Compare Suetonius, *Caligula:* c. 40. This disgraceful tribute was finally removed by a law contained in the code of Justinian, tit. xl. Lib. xi.

[t] Rev. xx. 2. See Justin's *Dial. with Trypho*, p. 331.

[u] εὖ πράττειν.

[x] ἢ μὴ εἶναι αὐτὸν διὰ τέχνης ὁμολογήσει. For διὰ τέχνης should probably be read either ἀτέχνως or δι' ἀνάγκης.

virtue and vice are nothing; but that men judge actions to be good or bad merely by their own opinion; which is the greatest impiety and injustice.

A second reason[7] for our not exposing infants is, lest any one so exposed should not be taken up, but perish; and thus we should be murderers.

37. Moreover, we either marry at first, for no other object than to rear children, or else abstaining from marriage, continue to live in a state of continence. And already one of our religion, in order to persuade you that promiscuous concubinage is not a religious mystery with us, (as ye falsely allege,) presented a written petition to Felix the governor, at Alexandria, praying that he would permit a physician to mutilate his person; an operation which the physicians there said they were not at liberty to perform, without the governor's leave. And when Felix altogether refused to grant his permission, the young man still persisted in his resolution of continence, satisfied with his own conscience, and that of his Christian brethren. Here also we may mention Antinous, who lately died, and whom all, through fear (of offending the Emperor Adrian) were eager to worship as a god, knowing well what kind of character he bore, and whence he was.

And that no one may advance this objection against us, "What should hinder us from believing, that he who by us is called CHRIST, was a man of merely human origin, who performed the wonders, which we speak of, by magical art,[a] and on that account was

---

[7] Justin here takes up again the subject of exposing children, from which, in his usual discursive manner, he had deviated, at the beginning of this Section.

[a] Absurd as this objection may appear, it was one which the early Christian Apologists thought it necessary to anticipate, and on that account sometimes laid greater stress on prophecy than on the miracles of CHRIST. Compare IRENÆUS *Adv. Hæres.* Lib. ii. c. 57, LACTANTIUS v. 3. "Disce igitur, si quid tibi cordis (cordi) est, non idcirco à nobis Deum creditum Christum, quia mirabilia fecit, sed quia vidimus in eo facta esse omnia quæ nobis annunciata sunt vaticinio prophetarum. Fecit mirabilia: magum putassemus, ut et vos nuncupatis, (nunc putatis) et Judæi tunc putaverunt, si non illa ipsa facturum Christum prophetæ uno spiritu prædixissent."—In another place (iv. c. 13,) LACTANTIUS replies to the objection, said to have been made by the oracle of Apollo, and assented to by some of the

considered to be the Son of God?" we will proceed now to bring forward a proof. We will not rely upon testimony, but shall necessarily be persuaded by prophecies delivered before the events; since we see with our own eyes that events have taken place, and are now taking place, according to the predictions. And this proof will, we imagine, appear to you also the most perfect and most true.

38. There were, then, among the Jews certain men, who were Prophets of God, by whom the prophetic Spirit proclaimed future events before they came to pass. And the kings, who were over the Jews in those days, possessed and preserved with great care the prophecies of these men, as they were first delivered, in books composed by the prophets themselves, in their own Hebrew language. Now when Ptolemy, king of Egypt, was forming his library, and endeavoring to collect the writings of all men, he heard of these prophecies, and sent to Herod[b] who then ruled over the Jews, desiring that the books of the prophecies might be sent to him. And Herod the king sent them written in their aforesaid Hebrew language. But since what was thus written in them could not be understood by the Egyptians, he again sent, and desired him to send men to translate them into the Greek language. This being done, the books have remained with the Egyptians even to this day: and they are also with all the Jews in every place. Yet the Jews who read, under-

---

Jews, that the miracles of Jesus were performed by magic, by an appeal to the fulfilment of prophecy, as a continual miracle going on before their eyes.—Origen meets the same objection, with different reasons. *Contra Cels.* Lib. ii. p. 88, seq.

[b] This is a mistake either of Justin, or of some of his transcribers. The person to whom Ptolemy sent was Eleazar, who, according to Philo Judæus (*Lib.* 2, *de Vitâ Mosis*) was high-priest and king of Judea. Josephus (*Ant.* XI. iv. 8,) says that the high-priests had the supreme power, till the posterity of the Asamoneans established a monarchical authority.

Grabe supposes we should here read ἱερεῖ for Ἡρώδῃ.

The account of the Septuagint version of the Old Testament given in the *Cohortatio ad Græcos*, p. 13, 14, which is ascribed to Justin, is somewhat different from this. It follows Philo, (*De Vit. Mosis*, Lib. ii.) in asserting that the seventy interpreters were each shut up in a different cell, and composed so many distinct versions, which all literally agreed.

stand not what is written; but regard us with hatred and enmity, slaying and punishing us, even as ye do, whenever they are able; as ye may easily learn. For in the late Jewish war,[c] Barchochebas, the leader of the Jewish insurrection, commanded the Christians only to be led away to severe tortures, unless they denied JESUS CHRIST and blasphemed.

39. Now in the books of the prophets we find it predicted, that JESUS, our CHRIST, should come, should be born of a virgin, and be made man; that he should heal every disease, and all manner of sickness, and raise the dead: that he should be enviously treated, and not be known; that he should be crucified, and die, and rise again, and ascend into heaven; that he should be the Son of GOD; and so be called: that some should be sent by him to preach these things to every nation of mankind, and that men of the Gentiles should more especially believe on him. Some of these prophecies also respecting him were delivered five thousand years before his appearing,[d] some three thousand, some two thousand; and some again one thousand, and others eight hundred years. For in the course of successive generations, different prophets succeeded one another.

40. Moses then, who was the first of the prophets,[e] wrote in these very words: "A prince shall not fail from Judah, nor a ruler from between his feet,[f] until He shall come, for whom it is reserved;[g] and He shall be the expectation of the Gentiles, binding his colt to a vine, washing his garment in the blood of the grape."[h]

---

[c] In the 17th year of Adrian: EUSEBIUS, *Hist. Eccles.* Lib. iv. c. 6, and *Chronicon.* EUSEBIUS says the cause of his enmity to the Christians was their refusal to unite with him against the Romans.

[d] According to the chronology of Justin Martyr, somewhat more than 5000 years elapsed between the Creation and the birth of CHRIST. THEOPHILUS (ad *Autolycum*, Lib. iii. p. 138,) makes it 5515 years. Justin here, therefore, considers Adam as one of the prophets; agreeing with THEOPHILUS, (Lib. ii. p. 104.) CLEMENS Alexandrinus, (*Strom.* i. p. 335,) in like manner regards the names which Adam bestowed upon Eve, and upon all animals, as prophetic.

[e] The first, whose writings are preserved. Here, and in Sect. 71, the prophecy of Jacob is apparently ascribed to Moses who records it.

[f] ἐκ τῶν μηρῶν αὐτοῦ.

[g] ᾧ ἀπόκειται—that this, and not ὃ ἀπόκειται, is the true reading, is plain from JUSTIN's *Dial. with Trypho*, pp. 348, 349.

[h] Gen. xlix. 10.

Now it is for you to inquire diligently, and to learn how long the Jews continued to have a ruler and a king of their own. It was until the appearing of JESUS CHRIST, our Master, and the interpreter of the prophecies which were not understood: as it was declared by the divine holy spirit of prophecy, in the writings of Moses, that a prince should not fail from the Jews, until he should come, for whom the kingdom was reserved. For Judah was the ancestor of the Jews, from whom also they have received their name. And ye, since CHRIST hath appeared, have both reigned over the Jews, and possessed all their country. Moreover, the expression, "He shall be the expectation of the Gentiles," implied, that men of all nations should expect him to come again; and this ye may see with your own eyes, and be persuaded of by the fact itself. For out of all nations of men, they look for Him who was crucified in Judea; after whom the land of the Jews was immediately subjugated and given up to you.

41. The words,[1] "Binding his colt to a vine, and washing his garment in the blood of the grape," were a sign representing what should be done to CHRIST, and what he should himself perform. For an ass's colt was standing in a certain village bound to a vine, which he then commanded his disciples to lead to him; and when it was brought, he sat thereon, and entered into Jerusalem, where was that most magnificent temple of the Jews, which was afterward thrown down by you. And after these things, he was crucified; that the rest of the prophecy might be fulfilled. For the words, "Washing his garment in the blood of the grape," predicted his passion which he was to undergo, cleansing by his blood those who believe in him. For that which is called by the prophet in the holy spirit, his garment, are the men which believe in him, in whom dwells the seed which is from GOD, even the word. And that, which is called "the blood of the grape," indicates that he who was to appear should have indeed blood, but that he should have it by divine power, and not of human seed. And the principal power, after

---

[1] This passage is explained in a similar manner, in the *Dialogue with Trypho*, pp. 272, 348.

God the Father and the Lord of all things, is the Son, the Word; the manner of whose incarnation, and how he was made man, we shall hereafter show. For as not man, but God, hath made the blood of the vine, so this intimated that the blood should not be of human seed, but of the power of God, as we before said.

42. Isaiah also, another prophet, predicting the same things in different words, thus spake:[k] "There shall come a star out of Jacob, and a flower shall spring from the branch of Jesse:" "and upon his arm shall the Gentiles hope."[l] Now a shining star did rise, and a flower did spring from the root of Jesse, even this Christ. For through the power of God, he was born of a virgin, of the seed of Jacob, the father of Judah, who hath been shown to be the father of the Jews. Moreover Jesse was his progenitor, according to the prophecy; and he was the son of Jacob and Judah, by natural descent.

43. And again, hear how expressly it was predicted by Isaiah, that he should be born of a virgin. For thus it was spoken: "Behold a virgin shall conceive and bear a son: and they shall say of his name, God with us."[m] For the things which appeared to be incredible and impossible with men, those did God predict by the prophetic Spirit; that when they came to pass, they should not be disbelieved, but believed, inasmuch as they were before declared. But lest some,[n] not understanding the prophecy which hath been advanced, should bring the same charge against us, which we make against your poets, who say that Jupiter came down to women, under the influence of impure passions, we will endeavor to explain these words. Now, when it is said, "Behold a virgin shall conceive," it is implied that the virgin conceived without carnal intercourse with any one; or otherwise she would no longer have been a virgin. But the power of God coming upon the virgin overshadowed her, and caused her to conceive, although still a virgin. Moreover the angel of God, who was sent to the virgin at that very

---

[k] Justin here unites the prophecy of Balaam, Numb. xxiv. 17, with that of Isaiah xi. 1.
[l] Isa. xi. 1, 10. — [m] Isa. vii. 14. Matt. i. 23.
[n] ὅπως δὲ μή τινες μὴ νοήσαντες, κ. τ. λ.

time, saluted her saying, " Behold, thou shalt conceive in thy womb, by the HOLY GHOST, and shalt bear a son, and he shall be called the Son of the Highest; and thou shalt call his name JESUS: for he shall save his people from their sins."° Thus they, who have recorded ᵖ all things concerning our Saviour JESUS CHRIST, have taught: whom we believe; since the prophetic Spirit also declared, as we have shown, by the above-mentioned Isaiah, that he should be so born. Moses, therefore, the prophet already quoted, declares,ᵈ that we are not permitted to consider the Spirit, and the Power which is from GOD, to be any other than the Word,ʳ which is also the first-begotten of GOD. And this, coming upon the virgin and overshadowing her, not by carnal knowledge, but by (divine) power, caused her to conceive. The name also of JESUS, in the Hebrew tongue, hath the same meaning as Soter (Saviour), in the Greek language.ˢ Wherefore also the angel said to the virgin, "And thou shalt call his name JESUS; for he shall save his people from their sins."ᵗ

° Luke i. 31, 33. Matt. i. 21.

ᵖ ἀπομνημονεύσαντες.—In Sect. 86, the Gospels are styled ἀπομνημονεύματα, memoirs.

ᵈ Moses nowhere makes such an assertion; unless we suppose Justin to have alluded to some mystical interpretation of such a passage as Exod. iv. 22: "Israel is my son, my first-born." GRABE supposes that Justin may have written 'Ησαίας instead of Μωσῆς.

ʳ The SPIRIT and the WORD (Λόγος) seem here to be confounded. Compare Sect. 61, 85. Bp. KAYE observes, with reference to the passages of the early Fathers, in which πνεῦμα is used to signify the Divine Nature of CHRIST, " Perhaps the idea present to their minds was, that as, in the mystery of the Incarnation, the HOLY GHOST came upon the Virgin, and the Power of the Highest overshadowed her, and the Λόγος thereby became flesh, the HOLY SPIRIT, the 'power of the Highest,' and the Λόγος were the same. But Justin attributes the inspiration of the ancient Prophets sometimes to the Λόγος, sometimes to the HOLY SPIRIT. Here it is difficult to interpret the latter of the Divine nature in CHRIST; and yet the two appear to be identified. I know of no other mode of explaining this fact, than by supposing that, as the Λόγος was the conductor of the whole Gospel economy, Justin deemed it a matter of indifference, whether he said that the Prophets were inspired by the Λόγος, or by the HOLY SPIRIT who was the immediate agent. The Holy Spirit is called in Scripture the 'Spirit of CHRIST.' (Rom. viii. 9. Gal. iv. 6. Phil. i. 19. 1 Pet. i. 11. In the last passage the immediate reference is to the inspiration of the prophets.)" Bp. KAYE's Account of Justin Martyr, ch. II. p. 72.

ˢ Compare Dial. with Trypho, p. 44.   ᵗ Matt. i. 21.

44. Even ye yourselves, I imagine, will concede, that they who prophesy are inspired by nothing else but the divine word. Hear also how another prophet, Micah, predicted the very place where CHRIST should be born. For he spake thus: "And thou Bethlehem, in the land of Judah, art not the least among the princes of Judah: for out of thee shall come a governor, that shall rule my people Israel."[u] Now Bethlehem is a village in the country of the Jews, five and thirty furlongs distant from Jerusalem; as ye may also learn from the taxing, which took place under Cyrenius who was your first prefect[x] in Judea.

Hear, again, what was foretold, to show that JESUS, when he was born, should not be known by other men, until he came to man's estate, even as it came to pass. The prophecies are these.[y]

* * * * * *

45. "Unto us a child was born: unto us a young man was given: whose government is upon his shoulders."[z] This is a prophecy of the power of the cross, against which he placed his shoulders when he was crucified, as shall be more clearly shown as we proceed. And again the same prophet Isaiah, inspired by the Spirit of prophecy, declared, "I have stretched forth my hands unto a disobedient and gain-saying people, unto those who walked in a way that was not good."[a] "They ask of me now justice: and dare to draw nigh unto GOD."[b] And again in other words he saith by another prophet, "They pierced my feet and my hands, and cast lots for my vesture."[c] Now David, the king and prophet who said thus, suffered none of these things; but the hands of JESUS CHRIST were stretched out, when he was crucified by the Jews who spake against him, and said that he was not the CHRIST. For, as the prophet said, they in derision placed him upon a judgment seat, and said, "Judge over us."

---

[u] Micah v. 2, as quoted Matt. ii. 6.

[x] ἐπίτροπος—GROTIUS, on Luke ii. 2, shows that Cyrenius could not have been procurator. The word ἐπίτροπος is of general signification.

[y] There is here probably an omission of some passages from the prophets.

[z] Isa. ix. 6.   [a] Isa. lxv. 2. Rom. x. 21.
[b] Isa. lviii. 2.   [c] Ps. xxii. 16, 18.

The words also, "They pierced my hands and my feet," were a reference to the nails, which were fixed in his hands and feet upon the cross. And, after his crucifixion, they who crucified him cast lots for his vesture, and divided it among themselves. And that these things were done, ye may learn from the records of what took place under Pontius Pilate.[d] To show that it was expressly predicted, that he should sit upon the foal of an ass, and come into Jerusalem, we will mention the prophetic writings of another prophet, Zephaniah. The words are these: "Rejoice greatly, O daughter of Sion; shout, O daughter of Jerusalem: behold, thy king cometh unto thee, meek, and riding upon an ass, and upon a colt the foal of an ass."[e]

46. Now, when ye hear the sayings of the prophets, as if they were delivered by some one person, imagine not that they are said by the inspired writers themselves, but by the divine word which moved them. For sometimes it prophetically declares what shall come to pass hereafter; sometimes it speaks as in the person of GOD the Father, and Lord of all; sometimes as in the person of CHRIST; and sometimes as in the person of the people who answer to the LORD, or to his Father. In the same manner as ye may see also in your own writers, that one person writes the whole, but introduces different persons as holding discourse. The Jews who had the books of the prophets, not observing this, knew not CHRIST, when he came; and moreover hate us, who say that he is come, and prove that he was crucified by them, as it was predicted.

47. And that this also may be plain to you; these words were spoken, in the person of the Father, by Isaiah the prophet, whom we have before mentioned: "The ox knoweth his owner, and the ass his master's crib: but Israel doth not know me; and my people

---

[d] Compare Section 63. TERTULLIAN, *Apol.*, Sect. 5, 21, appeals to the information respecting JESUS CHRIST conveyed to the Emperor Tiberius by Pontius Pilate. These acts, or records, of Pilate were the memoranda of the daily transactions of his government.

[e] Zech. ix. 9. Matt. xxi. 5. Justin Martyr, in his *Dialogue with Trypho*, p. 273, quotes this prophecy correctly, from Zechariah, not from Zephaniah, as here.

doth not consider. Ah, sinful nation, a people full of iniquity, an evil seed, wicked children: ye have forsaken the LORD."ᶠ And again in another place, where the same prophet speaks in like manner in the person of the Father. "What house will ye build me, saith the LORD. Heaven is my throne, and earth my footstool."ᵍ And again in another place; "Your new moons and your sabbaths my soul hateth, and the great day of fasting and rest I endure not; even if ye come to present yourselves before me, I will not hear you. Your hands are full of blood: even if ye bring fine flour and incense, it is an abomination unto me. I desire not the fat of lambs and the blood of bulls. For who hath required this at your hands."ʰ "But loosen every band of wickedness, rend asunder the ties of violent contracts: cover the naked and him that hath no house: deal thy bread to the hungry."ⁱ Thus, then, may ye understand what kind of precepts are delivered from GOD by the prophets.

48. When, again, the prophetic spirit speaks in the person of CHRIST, it expresses itself thus: "I have stretched forth my hands unto a disobedient and gainsaying people, unto those who walked in a way that was not good."ᵏ And again, "I gave my back to stripes, and my cheeks to buffetings: I turned not away my face from the shame of spitting. And the LORD was my helper. Wherefore I turned not: but I set my face as a solid rock; and I knew that I should not be ashamed, for he is near that justifieth me."ˡ And again, when he saith, "They cast lots for my vesture; and pierced my feet and my hands."ᵐ "But I lay down and slept and rose up again: for the LORD sustained me."ⁿ And again, when he saith, "They spake with their lips, they shook the head, saying, let him save himself."ᵒ All which things, as ye may learn, were done to CHRIST by the Jews. For when he was crucified, they pouted their lips, and shook their heads, saying, Let him that raised the dead save himself.ᵖ

ᶠ Isa. i. 3, 4.
ʰ Isa. i. 11–14.
ᵏ Isa. lxv. 2. Rom. x. 21.
ᵐ Ps. xxii. 16–18.
ᵒ Ps. xxii. 7, 8

ᵍ Isa. lxvi. 1.
ⁱ Isa. lviii. 6, 7.
ˡ Isa. l. 6–8.
ⁿ Ps. iii. 5.
ᵖ Matt. xxvii. 39.

49. Moreover, when the prophetic spirit speaks to foretell things to come, it is in this manner. "For out of Sion shall go forth the law, and the word of the LORD from Jerusalem. And he shall judge among the nations, and shall rebuke many people. And they shall beat their swords into ploughshares, and their spears into pruning-hooks. And nation shall not lift up sword against nation, neither shall they learn war any more."ᵠ And that it did so come to pass, ye may readily learn. For from Jerusalem twelve men went forth into the world, and they unlearned,ʳ not knowing how to speak. But by the power of GOD they preached to every nation of men, that they were sent by CHRIST to teach all men the word of GOD. Wherefore we who formerly killed one another, now not only abstain from fighting against our enemies, but are ready to meet death with cheerfulness, confessing the faith of CHRIST, rather than lie, or deceive those who persecute us. For we might, on such an occasion, have acted according to that saying (of the poet),˙

"My tongue alone hath sworn, and not my mind."

However it would be absurd, while soldiers, once engaged and enrolled by you, adhere to the oath which they have made, in preference even to their own lives, their parents, their country, and all their families, when ye can offer them nothing immortal; that we, ardently desirous of immortality, should not endure every thing, in order to obtain the object of our wishes, from him who is able to fulfil them.

50. Hear also in what manner prophecy was made concerning those who preached his doctrine, and declared his appearing; the aforesaid prophet and king having thus spoken by the prophetic spirit: "Day unto day uttereth speech; and night unto night showeth knowledge. There is no speech nor language whose voices are not heard. Their sound is gone out through all the earth, and their words unto the ends of the world. In the sun he hath placed his tabernacle: and he (is)

ᵠ Isa. ii. 3, 4.
ʳ ιδιώται. Acts iv. 13. 1 Cor. ii. 1, 4, 6, 13; 2 Cor. xi. 6.
˙ EURIPIDES *Hippolytus*, 608.

as a bridegroom going out of his chamber: he will rejoice as a giant to run his course."[t]

51. In addition to these, we have thought it right and appropriate to mention some other prophecies, delivered by the same David; whence ye may learn in what manner the prophetic spirit exhorts men to live: and how it speaks of the conspiracy which was formed against CHRIST by Herod, king of the Jews, and the Jews themselves, and Pilate who was your procurator among them, with his soldiers: declaring that all nations of men should believe in Him; showing that GOD calls him his Son, and hath promised to put all his enemies under him: in what manner the devils endeavor, as far as is possible, to escape the power of GOD the Father and LORD of all things, and that of CHRIST himself: and how GOD calls all men to repentance, before the day of judgment shall come. The words are to this effect:[u] "Blessed is the man, who hath not walked in the counsel of the ungodly, and hath not stood in the way of sinners, and hath not sat upon the seat of the scornful.[x] But his will is in the law of the LORD, and in his law will he meditate day and night. And he shall be like a tree planted by the watercourses, which shall give its fruit in its season: and the leaf whereof shall not fall off, and all which it beareth[y] shall prosper. Not so the wicked, not so; but (they are) even as the chaff, which the wind scattereth from the face of the earth. Therefore the ungodly shall not stand in the judgment, nor sinners in the council of the righteous. For the LORD knoweth the way of the righteous, and the way of the ungodly shall perish."
"Why did the heathen rage, and the people imagine vain things? The kings of the earth stood up, and the rulers were gathered together against the LORD, and against his Anointed, saying, Let us break their bonds asunder, and cast away their yoke from us. He that dwelleth in the heavens shall laugh them to scorn; and the LORD shall have them in derision. Then shall he speak unto them in his wrath, and in his anger he shall trouble them. But I am set up by him as a king, upon

---

[t] Ps. xix. 2–5. Rom. x. 18.   [u] Ps. i. ii.
[x] λοιμῶν. Of pestilences.   [y] ὅσα ἂ ποιῇ.

Sion his holy mountain, declaring the command of the LORD. The LORD hath said unto me, Thou art my Son, to-day have I begotten thee. Ask of me, and I shall give thee the heathen for thine inheritance, and for thy possession the extremities of the earth. Thou shalt rule them with a rod of iron; as vessels of a potter shalt thou dash them in pieces. And now, ye kings, be wise; be instructed, all ye that judge the earth. Serve the LORD with fear, and rejoice in him with trembling. Receive instruction,[a] lest haply the LORD be angry, and so ye perish from the right way, when his wrath is quickly kindled. Blessed are all they that put their trust in him."

52. And again the prophetic spirit, declaring by the same David that CHRIST should reign after his crucifixion, spake thus: "Sing unto the LORD, all the earth, and show forth his salvation from day to day. For the LORD is great, and greatly to be praised; he is to be feared above all gods. For all the gods of the nations are idols of devils: but GOD made the heavens. Glory and praise are before his face; and strength and majesty[a] in the place of his holiness. Give glory unto the LORD, the Father of the worlds:[b] bring an offering,[c] and come in before his face, and worship in his holy courts. Let the whole earth fear before his face, and be established, and not be shaken. Let them rejoice among the nations. The LORD hath reigned from the wood."[d]

---

[a] Δράξασθε παιδείας. This is the version of the Septuagint. CAPPELLUS, (*Critica Sacra*, Lib. iv. Sect. 5, p. 243,) endeavors to show how the difference between the present Hebrew reading and the Greek may have arisen.

[a] Καύχημα.

[b] τῷ πατρὶ τῶν αἰώνων. The Sept. has αἱ πατριαὶ τῶν ἐθνῶν, "O ye kindreds of the people;" and Justin so quotes the passage in the *Dialogue with Trypho*, p. 299, A.

[c] λάβετε χάριν.

[d] Ps. xcvi. 1, 2, 4–10. Compare Col. ii. 14, 15.

The passage is thus quoted by many of the Fathers. TERTULLIAN *adv. Jud.* c. 11, says, "Age nunc, si legisti penes prophetam in psalmis, DEUS regnavit *à ligno*, expecto quid intelligas, ne forté lignarium aliquem regem significari putetis, et non Christum, qui exinde à passione CHRISTI (crucis) superatâ morte regnavit." And again, c. 13, "Unde et ipse David regnaturum *ex ligno* Dominum dicebat." See also TERTULLIAN *adv. Marcion.* iii. c. 19. BARNABAS,

53. But whereas the prophetic spirit speaks of future events, as if they were already past, as may have been observed in what hath been said, we will explain this also, that it may not perplex those who meet with it. (The spirit) speaks of things which it assuredly knows shall happen, as if they had already taken place. And that we must so receive these writings will be evident, if ye attend to the following considerations. David spake the words which have been recited, fifteen hundred years* before CHRIST was made man and crucified: and yet no one, of those who lived either before David or after him, gave occasion of rejoicing to the heathen by his sufferings upon the cross. But now, in our days,ᶠ JESUS CHRIST was crucified, and died, and rose again, and ascended into heaven, and reigned there; and, in consequence of what hath been preached in all nations, by the apostles sent from him, there is great joy to those who look for the immortality, which he hath promised.

54. And that no persons may imagine, from what we have now advanced, that we conceive events to happen by fatal necessity, because, as we have said, they are foreknown, we will explain this also. We have learned from the prophets, and declare it for a truth, that punishment and torments, as well as rewards, will be given to every one according to his works. For if this is not so, but every thing takes place by irresistible necessity, then there is nothing at all in our own power. For if it is fated that one man must be good, and another bad, neither is the one to be praised, nor the other to be blamed. And again, if the human race hath

---

(*Epist.* c. 8,) is supposed to recognise the words, when he says, ὅτι δὲ τὸ ἔριον ἐπὶ τὸ ξύλον; ὅτι ἡ βασιλεία τοῦ Ἰησοῦ ἐπὶ τῷ ξύλῳ. Justin Martyr, in his *Dialogue with Trypho*, p. 298, accuses the Jews of having erased the words ἀπὸ τοῦ ξύλου. There is no trace, however, of the words in any Hebrew or Greek MS. of the Old Testament, or in Origen or Jerome.

* In Sect. 39, Justin appears to allude to David, when he says, in round numbers, that some of the prophets lived one thousand years before CHRIST. THEOPHILUS, (ad *Autolycum*, p. 138,) places David eleven hundred years before CHRIST. The chronology of Justin seems to have been rather loose; but it is probable that the numbers here have been altered by an error of a transcriber.

ᶠ Ὁ καθ' ἡμᾶς Ἰησοῦς Χριστός.

no power, by its free-will, to avoid the evil and to choose the good, it is not responsible for any actions of any kind. But that men do stand and fall by free-will is thus shown. We see that the conduct of the same man is different at different times. But if it was fated, that he should be either bad or good, he could never act so differently, nor change so frequently. Neither indeed would some be good, and some bad: since in that case, we should represent fate as the cause of evil, and at variance with itself: or else we must profess that opinion to be true, which we have before mentioned,[f] that virtue and vice are nothing, but actions are reckoned to be good or bad by opinion only; which, as true reason plainly shows, is the greatest impiety and injustice.

55. But we say that this only is irreversibly determined, that they who choose what is good shall be proportionably rewarded, and in like manner, they who choose the reverse shall be punished as they deserve. For God did not make man like the other creatures, such as trees and four-footed beasts, incapable of doing any thing by free choice; since he would not be a fit object of reward or praise, if he did not himself choose the good, but were so made; nor, if he were bad, would he deserve punishment, if he were not such by his own act, but were unable to become in any respect different from what he was made.

56. Now the holy prophetic Spirit taught us this, saying by Moses, that God thus spake to the man who was first created: "Behold, before thy face is good and evil; choose the good."[h] Again it is thus spoken by another prophet, Isaiah, as in the name of God the Father and Lord of all things: "Wash you, make you clean, put away the evil from your souls; learn to do well: do justice to the fatherless, and avenge the widow; and come and let us reason together, saith the Lord. Even if your sins should be as scarlet, I will make them as white as wool: and if they should be as crimson, I will make them white as snow. And if ye

---

[f] Section 36.
[h] Deut. xxx. 15, 19. Justin Martyr erroneously attributes to Moses an application made in Ecclesiasticus xv. 14–17.

will, and will hearken unto me, ye shall eat the good of the land. But if ye will not hearken unto me, the sword shall devour you. For the mouth of the LORD hath spoken these things."[i] Now that which is said above, "The sword shall devour you," implies not, that they who are disobedient shall perish by the sword; but the sword of the LORD is the fire, by which those shall be consumed who choose to do evil. Wherefore he saith, "The sword shall devour you; for the mouth of the LORD hath spoken it." But if he had spoken of the sword which cuts, and immediately ceases, he would not have said, 'it shall devour.'[k]

57. Wherefore also when Plato said,[l] "The fault lies with him who chooses, but GOD is blameless;" he took it from the prophet Moses, who was more ancient than all the writers of the Greeks. And in all, which philosophers or poets have said concerning the immortality of the soul, or punishments after death, or the contemplation of heavenly things, or the like opinions, they could conceive and explain such notions only as they first derived from the prophets. Whence there appear to be the seeds of truth among them all: but they are proved not to have thoroughly understood them, since they so speak as to contradict themselves.

58. When therefore we say, that prophecies have been delivered respecting future events, we assert not that they were foreseen, because they happened by a fatal necessity; but that GOD, well knowing what the actions of all men would be, and having determined that he would reward every man according to his deeds, declared by his prophetic spirit, that his dealings with them would correspond with those actions, thus always leading the human race to reflection and repentance, and showing his care and providence for them.

59. But the evil spirits denounced death against those who read the books of Hystaspes, or the Sibyl, or the prophets, that they might deter them from improving

---

[i] Isa. i. 16–20.

[k] Justin's interpretations are sometimes fanciful enough. The mouth of the sword, פי־חרב is a common Hebrew expression. Jer. xxi. 7. Job i. 15, 17.

[l] *De Republ.* x. p. 617. H. Steph.

such an opportunity of learning what was for their real good, and retain them in slavery to themselves. But this purpose they could not entirely effect. For we not only fearlessly study these books, but as ye perceive, offer them for your consideration, being assured that they will be well-pleasing to all men. And even if we persuade but a few, our gain will be great: for as good husbandmen we shall receive the reward from our Master.

60. Hear also what was spoken by David the prophet, to show that GOD the Father of all things would receive CHRIST into heaven, after having raised him from the dead, and retain him there, until he should tread under foot his enemies the devils, and the number of those should be fulfilled, who, as He foreknew, would be good and virtuous; for whose sake also the final destruction[m] of all things by fire is yet delayed. The words are these: "The LORD said unto my LORD, Sit thou on my right hand, until I make thine enemies thy footstool. The LORD shall send the rod of thy strength out of Jerusalem: and rule thou in the midst of thine enemies. With thee shall be the rule in the day of thy power, in the splendors of thy saints. From the womb, before the day-star, have I begotten thee."[n] The words, "The LORD shall send the rod of thy strength out of Jerusalem," are a prophecy of that powerful word, which the apostles of CHRIST, who went out from Jerusalem, preached every where, although death was threatened against those who taught, or even confessed the name of CHRIST, and which we now every where embrace and teach. And if ye too receive what we now offer, in a hostile manner, ye can do no more, as we have already said,[o] than slay us: which brings, in fact, no evil upon us, but will procure everlasting punishment by fire upon yourselves, and all those who hate us without reason, and repent not.

---

[m] ἐκπύρωσιν for ἐπιπύρωσιν, as in Sect. 28, 74, 77, and *Second Apol.* p. 45, C.

[n] Ps. cx. 1–3. This is the reading of the Septuagint. See CAPPELLUS, *Critica Sacra*, Lib. iv. c. 2, 8, c. 11, 3.

[o] Sections 2, 13.

VOL. IV.—15

61. But, lest any one should unreasonably object to what is taught by us, saying that CHRIST was born but a hundred and fifty years since, in the time of Cyrenius, and taught what we ascribe to him still later, under Pontius Pilate, and should accuse us of maintaining that all men, who lived before that time, were not accountable for their actions, we will anticipate and solve the difficulty. We have learned, and have before explained, that CHRIST was the first-begotten of GOD, being the Word, or Reason, of which all men were partakers.[p] They then who lived agreeably to reason, were really Christians, even if they were considered Atheists, such as Socrates, Heraclitus, and the like among the Greeks; and among other nations Abraham, Ananias, Azarias, Misael, and Elias, and many others, the actions and even the names of whom we at present omit, knowing how tedious the enumeration would be. Those therefore who of old lived without right reason, the same were bad men,[q] and enemies to CHRIST, and the murderers of those who lived agreeably to reason. Whereas they who ever lived or now live, in a manner which reason would approve, are truly Christians, and free from fear or trouble. From what we have already so fully stated, any intelligent man may understand, for what cause He was made man, and born of a virgin, by the power of the Word[r] and the counsel of GOD the Father and LORD of all things, and was named JESUS, and died on the cross, and rose again, and went up again into heaven. But since any further disquisition for the explanation of this point is not now necessary, we will proceed to the proof of that which is more closely connected with our present purpose.

62. Hear, then, what was spoken by the prophetic

---

[p] Justin's notion was, that every degree of intelligence which men possessed, respecting the nature of the Deity, and their relation to him, was derived from a portion of the Divine reason, λόγος, communicated to them; but that the true believer in CHRIST only possesses this quality in perfection. He uses the word λόγος in different senses. Sometimes it denotes the Second person of the Trinity, the Word; sometimes reason or intelligence; and sometimes word or speech. This necessarily creates ambiguity in determining the sense of the term in any particular passage.

[q] ἄχρηστοι, καὶ ἐχθροὶ τῷ Χριστῷ ἦσαν.

[r] See note (r) on Sect. 43. Compare Phil. ii. 7.

spirit, declaring that the whole land of Judea should also be laid waste. The words, it will be observed, are spoken in the person of the people themselves wondering at what was done; and they are these. "Sion is become a wilderness; Jerusalem is become as a wilderness: the house, our holy place, is accursed; and the glory, which our fathers blessed, is burned with fire. And all its glories are fallen down. And in these things thou didst refrain thyself, and didst hold thy peace, and afflict us very sore."[s]

Now that Jerusalem is laid waste, as it was predicted it should be, ye have good proof. It was also thus spoken by Isaiah the prophet, concerning its desolation, and that no one should return thither to dwell: "Their land is desolate: their enemies devour it before their face:[t] and none of them shall dwell therein."[u] Ye well know also that ye have forbidden any man to dwell there: and that the punishment of death is denounced against any Jew who shall be found within the place.[x]

63. Hear also in what manner it was predicted that our CHRIST should heal all manner of diseases, and raise the dead. Thus it is said, "At his coming the lame man shall leap as a hart, and the tongue of the stammerer shall be eloquent, the blind shall receive their sight, and the lepers shall be cleansed, and the dead shall arise and walk."[y] And that CHRIST did these things ye may learn from the records of what was done under Pontius Pilate.[z] Hear again what was said by Isaiah, foretelling by the prophetic spirit that CHRIST should be slain, together with those men who hoped in him. The words are these. "Behold, how the just man perisheth, and no man layeth it to heart: and merciful men are taken away, and no one considereth.

---

[s] Isa. lxiv. 10–12.   [t] Isa. i. 7.
[u] Justin adds what is spoken, Jer. l. 3, respecting Babylon.
[x] TERTULLIAN (*Apol.* Sect. 21,) speaks of the Jews as banished from their country; and not even permitted as strangers to set foot upon their own land. He repeats the same assertion, *adv. Judæos*, c. 15. EUSEBIUS, (*Hist. Eccles.* Lib. iv. c. 6, and in his *Chronicon*,) states that an edict was made, in the eighteenth year of the Emperor Adrian, forbidding any Jew to approach within sight of Jerusalem. VALESIUS, in his notes on EUSEBIUS, *Hist. Eccles.* shows that there was one day in the year, on which the restriction was removed.
[y] Isa. xxxv. 5, 6.   [z] See Section 45.

The just man is taken away from before injustice: and his grave shall be in peace: he is taken away from the midst."ᵃ And again, how is it declared by the same Isaiah that the people of the Gentiles who expected him not, should worship him; but the Jews, who constantly expected him, should know him not when he came. The words were spoken as in the person of CHRIST; and are to this effect. "I was made known to them that looked not for me; I was found of them that sought me not: I said, Behold, here am I, to a people who called not upon my name. I stretched forth my hands to a disobedient and gain-saying people: to those that walked in a way which was not good, but after their own sins: a people that provoketh to anger before me."ᵇ For the Jews, who had the prophecies, and always expected the CHRIST to come, not only knew him not, but evil entreated him. But they of the Gentiles, who had never heard any thing of CHRIST, until the apostles who went forth from Jerusalem declared what he had done, and delivered the prophecies respecting him, were then filled with joy; and renounced their belief in idols; and dedicated themselves to the unbegotten GOD through CHRIST.ᶜ Hear also what was briefly spoken by Isaiah, to show that these harsh accusations should be brought against those who confessed CHRIST; and how wretched those should be who spoke ill of him, and maintained that the ancient customs ought to be preserved. His words are these: "Wo unto them that call sweet bitter, and bitter sweet."ᵈ

64. Hear also in what manner it was prophesied, that he should be made man for us; and submit to suffer, and be set at naught; and should come again with glory. The words are these. "Becauseᵉ he hath given up his soul unto death, and was numbered with

---

ᵃ Isa. lvii. 1, 2.   ᵇ Isa. lxv. 1–3.   Rom. x. 21.

ᶜ GRABE observes, that this is a formula in which Catechumens, who were subsequently to be baptized, were dismissed from the Church. Such a formula is given by the author of the *Apostolical Constitutions*, (Lib. viii. c. 6,) as part of the bidding prayer, [directions how to pray,] which the Deacon was to use for the Catechumens. Compare similar expressions in Sections 17, 33, 79.

ᵈ Isa. v. 20.   ᵉ Compare *Epistle of* CLEMENT, Sect. 16.

the transgressors; he hath borne the sins of many, and shall make intercession for the transgressors. For behold my Son shall understand, and shall be exalted, and shall be exceedingly glorified. As many shall be astonished at thee; so shall thy appearance be without honor, more than any men, and thy glory more than any men: so shall many nations wonder at thee; and kings shall shut their mouths at thee; for they to whom nothing had been told of thee, and who had not heard, shall understand. Lord, who hath believed our report, and to whom is the arm of the Lord revealed? We have declared before him, as (if he were) a child; as a root in a thirsty ground. There is no form in him, nor glory. Yea we saw him; and he had no form nor comeliness: but his form was without honor, and marred more than men. He was a man in stripes, and knowing how to bear infirmity. For his face was turned away, he was despised, and esteemed not. He beareth our sins and for us is he afflicted. And we considered him to be in trouble, in stripes, and in affliction. But he was wounded for our iniquities, and bruised for our sins. The chastisement of peace was upon him: by his stripes we were healed. All we like sheep have gone astray. Man hath erred from his way. And (the Lord) gave him for our sins: and he opened not his mouth through his suffering. He was led as a sheep to the slaughter, and as a lamb before her shearers is dumb, so he openeth not his mouth. In his affliction his judgment was taken away."[f] Wherefore after his crucifixion even all his disciples forsook him, and denied him. But afterward, when he arose from the dead, and appeared to them, and taught them that they should read the prophecies in which all these events were predicted, and when they had seen him going back into heaven, they believed, and received power which was thence sent down upon them from him, and went into all the world, and preached these things, and were themselves called apostles.

65. Again, these are the words of the prophetic spirit, declaring to us that he, who suffered thus, hath an origin which cannot be expressed, and rules over

---

[f] Isa. lii. liii. Septuagint.

his enemies: "Who shall declare his generation; for his life is taken from the earth. For their transgressions he comes to death. And I will give the wicked for his tomb, and the rich for his death. Because he did no iniquity, neither was guile found in his mouth: and the LORD will cleanse him from his stripes. If he shall be given an offering for sin, your soul shall see a long-lived seed. And the LORD is pleased to take his soul out of travail, to show him light, and to form him in understanding, to justify the just one who ministereth well to many. And he himself shall bear our sins. For this cause he shall inherit many; and shall divide the spoil of the strong. Because his soul was given up to death, and he was numbered with the transgressors; and he bare the sins of many, and he himself was given for their transgressions."[g] Hear also in what manner it was predicted that he should ascend up to heaven. For thus it was spoken: "Lift up the gates of heaven; be ye opened, that the King of glory may come in. Who is this King of glory? The LORD mighty, even the LORD powerful."[h] Hear also what was spoken by Jeremiah[i] the prophet, to show that he should also come again from heaven with glory. His words are these: "Behold how the Son of man cometh upon the clouds of heaven, and the angels with him."

66. Since, then, we have shown that all things which have already happened were foretold by the prophets, before they came to pass, we must necessarily believe with full faith, that those things, which are in like manner foretold, but are still to happen, will assuredly come to pass. For in the same manner as past events, which were predicted and not known, did come to pass, so events which are yet to happen, even if they be unknown and disbelieved, will come to pass. For the prophets foretold two comings of CHRIST; the first, which hath already taken place, as of a man without honor and exposed to suffering; and the second, when it is declared he will come with glory from heaven, with his angelic host; when also he shall raise again the bodies of all men who have ever lived, and shall

---

[g] Isa. liii. 8–12.   [h] Ps. xxiv. 7, 8.
[i] The passage alluded to is in Dan. vii. 13. See Matt. xxv. 31.

clothe with incorruption the bodies of those who so deserve, but shall send those of the wicked into everlasting fire, there to dwell in endless consciousness with the evil spirits.

67. Now that these things also are foretold, we will proceed to show. Thus, then, was it spoken by Ezekiel the prophet: "There shall be brought together joint to joint, and bone to bone: and flesh shall grow upon them."[k] And, "Every knee shall bow to the LORD, and every tongue shall confess to him."[l] Hear also what is in like manner foretold, to show in what degree of sensibility and punishment the wicked shall be. The words are these: "Their worm shall not cease, and their fire shall not be quenched."[m] And then shall they repent, when it will avail them nothing. Moreover what the people of the Jews shall say and do, when they see him coming in glory, is foretold in these words by the prophet Zechariah:[n] "I will command the four winds to bring together my children that are scattered: I will command the north to bring and the south to oppose not. And then in Jerusalem shall there be great wailing; not the wailing of the mouth or of the lips, but wailing of the heart. And they shall rend not their garments but their consciences. One tribe shall mourn to another: and then shall they look on him whom they pierced, and shall say, Wherefore, LORD, hast thou caused us to wander from thy way? The glory, which our fathers blessed, is turned to our reproach."

68. Although we might mention also many other prophecies, we here pause, persuaded that these are sufficient to convince such as have ears to hear, and hearts to understand; and nothing doubting that they will perceive, that we are not like those, who devise fables concerning the supposed sons of Jupiter, asserting what we are unable to prove. For how should we believe of a man who was crucified, that he was the first-born of the unbegotten GOD, and should himself be the judge of all the human race, unless we

---

[k] See Ezek. xxxvii. 6–8.   [l] Isa. xlv. 23. See Rom. xiv. 11.
[m] Isa. lxvi. 24. Mark ix. 44.
[n] See Zech. ii. 6; xii. 2, 10, 12. Isa. xi. 12; xliii. 5, 6; lxiii. 17; lxiv. 11. Joel ii. 13.

found testimonies of him foretold, before he came and was made man, and saw also that it so came to pass? For we have witnessed the desolation of the land of the Jews, and have seen such men, as we ourselves are, men out of every nation, persuaded by the teaching of his apostles, and renouncing their former manner of life, in which they had gone astray; and that Christians more numerous and more true have been made from the Gentiles, than from the Jews and Samaritans. For all other nations of mankind are called Gentiles, by the prophetic spirit; but the tribes of Judea and Samaria are denominated Israel and the house of Jacob.

69. And to show that it was foretold that there should be a greater number of believers from the Gentiles, than from the Jews and Samaritans, we will produce the prophecies, which are these. "Rejoice, thou barren that bearest not, break out and cry, thou that travailest not: for the children of the barren are more than those of her which hath a husband."[o] For all the nations were barren of the knowledge of the true GOD, worshipping the works of their own hands: but the Jews and Samaritans, who by the prophets had the word delivered to them from GOD, and continually looked for the CHRIST, knew him not when he came, except a certain few, who should be saved; even as the prophetic spirit foretold, by Isaiah. For he said, in their name, "Except the LORD had left us a seed, we should have been as Sodom and Gomorrha."[p] These are related by Moses to have been cities of wicked men, which GOD overthrew, and burned with fire and brimstone, so that no one who was in them was saved, except one man of another nation, a Chaldean by birth, named Lot, with whom his daughters also were saved. And any who wish, may now see the whole of that country desolate and burnt up, and still remaining unproductive. Moreover to show that it was foreseen that they of the Gentiles should be more true and more
89 faithful, we will state what was thus spoken by the prophet Isaiah:[q] "Israel is uncircumcised in heart, but the Gentiles (are uncircumcised) in the flesh."

---

[o] Isa. liv. i. Gal. iv. 27. [p] Isa. i. 9.
[q] This quotation is from Jer. ix. 26.

70. What, then, hath now been so fully seen may reasonably produce conviction and faith in those who embrace the truth, and are not vain-glorious, nor governed by their passions. Whereas they who teach the fables which have been invented by the poets, offer no proof to the young men who learn them: and we have shown that such tales are spoken, by the influence of evil demons, to deceive the human race, and lead them astray. For having heard that it was declared by the prophets that CHRIST should come, and that wicked men should be punished by fire, they put forward many, whom we have already mentioned,[r] to be called the sons of Jupiter; supposing that thus they might persuade men to consider what was related respecting CHRIST to be merely fabulous prodigies, of the same nature with those related by the poets. And these inventions were circulated both among the Greeks and all other nations, where they understood the prophets to declare that the belief in CHRIST should most prevail. We shall show, however, that when they thus heard what was spoken by the prophets, they did not perfectly understand it, but erroneously imitated what was really performed by CHRIST, in whom we believe.

71. Moses, then, the prophet, was, as we have before stated,[s] more ancient than all other writers; and he delivered this prophecy, which hath been already quoted:[t] "A prince shall not fail from Judah, nor a ruler from between his feet,[u] until He shall come for whom it is reserved: and He shall be the expectation of the Gentiles, binding his colt to a vine, washing his garment in the blood of the grape."[x] The demons then, hearing these prophetic words, asserted that Bacchus was born the son of Jupiter; they ascribed to him also the invention of the vine, and in the celebration of his mysteries led an ass[y] in procession, and taught that Bacchus was torn in pieces, and taken up

---

[r] Sect. 29.   [s] Sect. 57.   [t] Sect. 40.
[u] ἐκ τῶν μηρῶν. See also the note (g) on Sect. 40, p. 156.
[x] Gen. xlix. 10.
[y] οἶνον (ὄνον) ἐν ταῖς μυστηρίαις αὐτοῦ ἀναγράφουσι (ἀναφέρουσι.) Compare *Dial. with Trypho*, p. 295, where the same argument is used, and the same instances adduced. PLINY, *Hist. Nat.* xxiv. 1, says that the ass was sacred to Bacchus.

into heaven. And since, in the prophecy of Moses, it was not plainly expressed, whether he who should come was to be the Son of GOD, (or of man,) and whether, thus riding upon a colt, he should remain upon earth, or ascend into heaven; since also the word, colt, might imply the foal either of an ass or of a horse, and they doubted whether he who was predicted should lead an ass's colt, or that of a horse, as the sign of his coming, and whether he should be the Son of GOD or of man, they said that Bellerophon also, a man born of a human parent, went up to heaven[f] upon the horse Pegasus. When also they heard that it was said by another prophet, Isaiah, that CHRIST should be born of a virgin, and should ascend to heaven by himself, they devised the story of Perseus. Knowing, again, that it was said, as hath been already shown by reference to the prophets, "He shall be strong as a giant to run a race,"[a] they told of Hercules, who was strong, and wandered over the whole earth. And when again they learned that it was prophesied, that CHRIST should heal all manner of disease, and raise the dead, they introduced Esculapius.[b]

72. But in no instance, nor in the history of any of those who were called the sons of Jupiter, did they imitate his crucifixion: for since all that was spoken respecting this was figuratively expressed, as we have shown, it was unintelligible to them. Now the cross, as the prophet hath predicted, is the greatest sign of his might and dominion; as is plain from what falls under our own observation. For observe how impossible it is that any thing in the world should be regulated, or any mutual intercourse carried on, without employing this figure. The sea cannot be navigated, unless this symbol, as the mast and yard-arm of the sail, remains firm in the ship. Without an instrument in this form, the land cannot be ploughed: neither can they who dig exercise their labor, nor handicraft-men pursue their occupations, without implements which are fashioned in like manner. The human figure also differs from those of irrational animals in no respect but this, that it is erect, and hath the hands extended:

---
[f] Sect. 29.   [a] Ps. xix. 5.   [b] Compare Sect. 30.

and in the countenance also hath the nose reaching downward from the forehead, by which we are able to breathe. This again shows no figure but that of the cross. It is spoken also by the prophet, "The breath before our nostrils is CHRIST the LORD."[c] The signs also in use among yourselves show the force of the same figure,[d] [as in the instance of standards] and trophies, by which your progress is every where marked. In all these, ye show the true sign of authority and power, although ye do it ignorantly. Moreover by the use of the same figure, ye set up the figures of your deceased emperors, and denominate them gods, by the accompanying inscriptions. Having then thus exhorted you, to the utmost of our power, both by an appeal to your reason, and to these sensible signs, we know that we shall henceforth be blameless, even if ye believe not. For we have done our duty, and brought our work to an end.

73. It was not sufficient, however, for the evil demons to declare, before the coming of CHRIST, that those sons, who have been spoken of, were born to Jupiter: but afterward, when CHRIST had appeared and dwelt with men, and they learned in what manner he was predicted by the prophets, and knew that men of all nations believed on him and expected him [to come again to judgment], they again raised up others, as we

---

[c] Lament. iv. 20. πνεῦμα πρὸ προσώπου ἡμῶν Χριστὸς Κύριος. The Septuagint version now has πνεῦμα προσώπου, "the breath of our nostrils." And the words are so quoted by TERTULLIAN, *Adversus Marcion*: iii. 6, *Advers. Praxeam*. c. 14. IRENÆUS, *Adv. Hæres.* Lib. iii. c. 11, p. 315. In the *Apostolical Constitutions*, Lib. v. c. 20, the words are quoted in the same manner as by Justin. TERTULLIAN argues from this passage, that it was CHRIST, who spake by the prophets, and appeared at various times, before his coming in the flesh. The mystical senses, which Justin and others of the Fathers have applied to this passage, depend upon the Greek version, in which is found Χριστὸς Κύριος, and not Χριστὸς Κυρίου, "the Anointed of the LORD;" by which term probably Zedekiah was meant.

[d] Καὶ τὰ παρ' ὑμῖν δὲ σύμβολα τὴν τοῦ σχήματος τούτου δύναμιν δηλοῖ· . . . . λλωμεν καὶ τῶν τροπαίων.—Some words are here lost. Among the different conjectures, that of THIRLBY seems as probable as any:— δηλοῖ· λέγω δὲ τὰ τῶν καλουμένων παρ' ὑμῖν οὐιξίλλων· καὶ τῶν τροπαίων.

Notions of the same fanciful kind, respecting the universal use of the figure of the cross, are found in MINUCIUS FELIX, *Octavius*, c. 29, and in JUSTIN's *Dialogue with Trypho*, p. 317, 318, 332. He finds it exemplified, among other instances, in the horn of the unicorn!

have before shown, as Simon and Menander from Samaria:[*] who by the display of magical arts deceived, and continue to deceive, many. For Simon being with you, as we have already said, in the imperial city of Rome, under Claudius Cæsar, did so astonish the sacred senate and the people of Rome, that he was considered to be a god, and honored with a statue, even as the other gods who are worshipped among you. Wherefore we request that the sacred senate and your people would join with you in considering this our address; that if there be any one who hath been seduced by his doctrine, he may learn the truth, and be able to avoid error: and, if it please you, destroy the statue.

74. For the evil demons can never persuade men that the wicked shall not be punished in fire; even as they were unable to cause CHRIST to be unknown, when he did come; but this only: they can cause those men who oppose right reason by their lives, and have been brought up in depraved habits of sensuality, and are puffed up with vain-glory, to destroy and hate us. Yet we not only bear no malice against these men, but, as is hereby manifest, pity them and endeavor to persuade them to repentance. For we fear not death, since it is acknowledged that at all events we must die: and there is nothing new,[f] but a continual repetition of the same things in this life. And if they who partake of these delights are satiated with them in one year, they must surely hearken to our instruction, that they may live for ever, free from suffering and fear. But if they believe that there will be nothing after death, and are of opinion that they who die pass into a state of insensibility, then they act as our benefactors, in liberating us from sufferings and privations, while they yet show themselves to be influenced by hatred and enmity and vain-glory: for their object in thus removing us is not to relieve us from distress, but by our death to deprive us of life and all its pleasures.

75. The evil demons also, as we have already shown, raised up Marcion of Pontus, who even now continues to teach men to deny GOD the Creator of all things in heaven and earth, and CHRIST his Son, who was fore-

---

[*] See c. 34.   [f] Eccles. i. 9, 10.

told by the prophets: and asserts that there is some other God, beside the Maker of all things, and also another Son. And many, believing his pretensions to be the only one acquainted with the truth, deride us, although they can produce no proof of what they assert, but contrary to all reason are hurried away, as lambs are by wolves, and become a prey to wicked doctrines and to demons. For the demons, which we have spoken of, strive to do nothing else but to lead men away from God the Creator and Christ his first-begotten Son. Wherefore they have fixed and continue to fix down to earthly things and such as are made with hands, those men who cannot raise themselves from the earth: but as for those who turn to the contemplation of heavenly things, they mislead them, and cast them into ungodly living, unless they have a wise judgment, and lead a life of purity free from human passions.

76. Further, that you may be convinced that when Plato asserted, that God made the world by a change wrought in matter previously unformed, he was indebted to our teachers, that is to the word of God delivered by the prophets, hear the very words of Moses, whom we have before mentioned as the first prophet, and more ancient than any writers among the Greeks. The prophetic spirit, declaring by him in what manner, and from what materials, God in the beginning made the world, spake thus:[g] "In the beginning God created the heaven and the earth. And the earth was invisible and unformed; and darkness was upon the face of the deep: and the Spirit of God moved upon the face of the waters. And God said, Let there be light; and it was so."[h] Wherefore Plato and they who agree with him, as well as we ourselves, have all learned that the whole world was made by the word of God, from what was related and made known by Moses; as ye also may be convinced. Moreover we know that what is called Erebus by the poets, was before spoken of by Moses.[i]

77. Moreover, when Plato discussing the physical nature of the Son of God, saith in his Timæus,[k] "He

---

[g] Gen. i. 1–3.   [h] καὶ ἐγένετο οὕτως. (φῶς)   [i] ערב Gen. i. 5.
[k] The passage, to which Justin alludes, relates to the creation of the

impressed him upon the universe in the form of a cross," he here also borrowed his assertion from Moses. For in the writings of Moses it is recorded, that at the time when the Israelites came out of Egypt, and were in the desert, venomous creatures, vipers and asps, and all kinds of serpents, met them, and destroyed the people: and that Moses by the inspiration and power which were given him from GOD, took brass, and made it into the form of a cross, and placed this upon the holy Tabernacle, and said to the people, "If ye look upon this figure, and believe, ye shall be saved by it." He related also, that as soon as this was done, the serpents perished and the people escaped death. Plato reading this relation, and not fully comprehending it, nor aware that it was a type of the cross, but conceiving only a division in that form,[l] said that the virtue which was next to the supreme GOD was impressed upon the universe in the form of a cross. And he spoke also of that third quality, since, as we have already said,[m] he read what Moses related of the Spirit of GOD being carried over the waters. For he assigns the second place to the Word of GOD, whom he declares to have been impressed upon the universe in the form of a cross, and the third, to the Spirit, which is said to have been borne over the water, when he saith, "And what is in the third place about the third."[n] Hear also in what manner the prophetic spirit declared by Moses that there should be a destruction of all things by fire. For he spake thus; "There shall go down an ever-living fire, and shall consume even unto the abyss beneath."

78. It is not therefore that we hold the same opinions with others, but that all others speak in imitation of

---

soul of the universe. Ταύτην οὖν τὴν ξύστασιν πᾶσαν, διπλῆν κατὰ μῆκος σχίσας, μέσην πρὸς μέσην ἑκατέραν ἀλλήλαις, οἷον Χ προσβαλὼν, κατέκαμψεν εἰς κύκλον. *Timæus*, Tom. III. p. 36, b.

[l] χίασμα, the form of the Greek letter Chi,—X.   [m] Sect. 76.

[n] Ὧδε γάρ ἔχει· περὶ τὸν πάντων βασιλέα πάντ' ἐστί, καὶ ἐκείνου ἕνεκα πάντα· καὶ ἐκεῖνο αἴτιον ἁπάντων τῶν καλῶν· δεύτερον δὲ πέρι, τὰ δεύτερα, καὶ τρίτον πέρι, τὰ τρίτα. PLATO Epist. 2. Tom. III. p. 312, E. "For thus it is: around the King of the universe are all things, and all things for him; and he is the cause of every good thing: and about the second are those which are in the second place; and about the third those which are in the third place."

ours. For with us information may be obtained upon these points, from those who have not received even the rudiments of learning, who, although unlearned, and speaking a strange language,° had wisdom and faith in their hearts: though some of them were lame and blind, so as to make it evident that these things were not done by human wisdom, but spoken by the power of GOD.

79. We will state also in what manner we are created anew by CHRIST, and have dedicated ourselves to GOD: that we may not, by omitting this, appear to dissemble any thing in our explanation. As many as are persuaded and believe that the things which we teach and declare are true, and promise that they are determined to live accordingly, are taught to pray, and to beseech GOD with fasting, to grant them remission of their past sins, while we also pray and fast with them. We then lead them to a place where there is water, and there they are regenerated in the same manner as we also were: for they are then washed in that water in the name of GOD the Father and Lord of the universe, and of our Saviour JESUS CHRIST, and of the HOLY SPIRIT. For CHRIST said, "Except ye be born again, ye shall not enter into the kingdom of heaven:"[p] and that it is impossible, that those who are once born should again enter into their mothers' wombs is evident to all. Moreover it is declared by the prophet Isaiah, as we have before written, in what manner they who sinned and repent may escape (the punishment of) their sins. For thus it is said; "Wash you, make you clean, put away the evil from your souls; learn to do well; do justice to the fatherless, and avenge the widow: and come and let us reason together, saith the LORD. Even if your sins should be as scarlet I will make them as white as wool: and if they should be as crimson I will make them white as snow. But if ye will not hearken unto

---

° ἰδιωτῶν μὲν καὶ βαρβάρων τὸ φθέγμα. IRENÆUS, *Adv. Hæres.* Lib. iii. c. 4, expresses the same sentiments: "Hanc fidem qui sine literis crediderunt, quantùm ad sermonem nostrum, barbari sunt, quantùm autem ad sententiam et consuetudinem, et conversationem, propter fidem perquàm sapientissimi sunt, et placent DEO, conversantes in omni justitiâ et castitate et sapientiâ."

[p] John iii. 3, 5.

me the sword shall devour you: for the mouth of the Lord hath spoken these things."q

80. The apostles have also taught us for what reason this new birth is necessary. Since at our first birth, we were born without our knowledge or consent, by the ordinary natural means, and were brought up in bad habits and evil instructions,r in order that we may no longer remain the children of necessity or of ignorance, but may become the children of choice and judgment, and may obtain in the water remission of the sins which we have before committed, the name of God the Father and Lord of the universe is pronounced over him who is willing to be born again, and hath repented of his sins; he who leads him to be washed in the laver of baptism, saying this only over him:s for no one can give a name to the ineffable God; and if any man should dare to assert that there is such a name, he is afflicted with utter madness. And this washing is called illumination,t since the minds of those who are thus instructed are enlightened. And he who is so enlightened is baptized also in the name of Jesus Christ, who was crucified under Pontius Pilate, and in the name of the Holy Spirit, who by the prophets foretold all things concerning Jesus.u

81. The demons also, who heard that this washing of baptism was predicted by the prophet, caused that those who entered into their holy places, and were about to approach them, to offer libations and the fat of victims, should sprinkle themselves. Moreover, they cause them to wash themselves, as they depart (from the sacrifice), before they enter into the temples where

---

q Isa. i. 16–20.   r ἀνατροφαῖς.

s The translation follows the reading proposed by Thirlby, αὐτὸ τοῦτο μόνον ἐπιλέγοντος τοῦ τὸν λουσόμενον ἄγοντος ἐπὶ τὸ λουτρόν. They pronounced over the new convert the name of the Father, and of the Son, and of the Holy Spirit, according to the apostolical precept, Matt. xxviii. 19, but did not presume to give any other name to God, whose name is ineffable.
See note on Sect. 10.

t φωτισμός. Justin in *Dial. cum Tryph.* p. 258, A, uses the same anguage, φωτιζόμενοι διὰ τοῦ ὀνόματος τὸν Χριστοῦ τούτου. Terms of a like import were constantly applied to baptism. Instances are given by Suicer, (*Thesaurus*,) on the word φωτισμός: and Bingham, *Eccles. Ant.* XI. i. 4.

u Justin resumes this subject in Sect. 85.

their images are placed. Again, the demons having learned what happened to Moses, the prophet of whom we have spoken, and wishing to imitate him, introduced the practice, that those who enter into their temples, and worship the gods there, should be exhorted by the priests to loose their shoes from off their feet. For at the time when Moses was commanded to go down to Egypt, and lead out the people of the Israelites who were there, as he was feeding the flock of his mother's brother,[x] in the land of Arabia, CHRIST, whom we worship, spake with him in the appearance of fire out of a bush, and said, "Put off thy shoes, and come and hear."[y] And he put off his shoes, and went; and heard that he must go down to Egypt, and lead out the people of the Israelites who were there; and received great power from CHRIST who spake with him in the appearance of fire. So he went down, and led out the people, and performed great and wonderful miracles; which, if ye wish to hear them, ye may learn perfectly from his writings.

82. Now all the Jews to this day, teach that GOD, who cannot be named, spake to Moses.[z] Whence the prophetic spirit reproached them by Isaiah the aforementioned prophet, as we have already declared, thus saying, "The ox knoweth his owner, and the ass his master's crib: but Israel doth not know me; and the people doth not consider me." And in like manner JESUS CHRIST himself also said, upbraiding the Jews for that they knew not what the Father is, and what the Son is: "No one knoweth the Father, but the Son; neither knoweth any one the Son, but the Father, and they to whomsoever the Son shall reveal it."[a] And the Word of GOD is his Son, as we have before said. He is called also the Angel,[b] (who declares,) and the Apostle,[c] (who is sent;) since he declares whatever is

---

[x] Exod. iii. 1. Jethro was the father-in-law of Moses. Justin was perhaps led into the error by thinking of Jacob feeding the flock of Laban, his mother's brother. Gen. xxix. 10; xxx. 29.
[y] Exod. iii. 5.
[z] Justin treats on this subject, in his *Dialogue with Trypho*, p. 282.
[a] Matt. xi. 27. This passage is quoted in the same manner in the next Section,—§ 83.
[b] Exod. iii. 2.   [c] Heb. iii. 1, 2.

necessary to be known, and is sent to publish whatever is intrusted to him: as our LORD himself said, "He that heareth me, heareth him that sent me."[d] This also will plainly appear from the writings of Moses. For in them it is thus said: "And the Angel of the LORD spake unto Moses in a flame of fire out of the bush, and said, I am he who is; the GOD of Abraham, the GOD of Isaac, the GOD of Jacob, the GOD of thy fathers. Go down to Egypt, and lead out my people."[e] Ye may learn what follows from the writings themselves; since it is impossible to comprise every thing in the present address.

83. Now these words have been spoken, to show that the Son of GOD, and Apostle, is JESUS CHRIST, who before was the Word, and appeared sometimes in the form of fire, and sometimes in the image of incorporeal beings, but hath now by the will of GOD, and for the sake of mankind, been made man; and endured whatsoever the demons caused to be inflicted upon him by the senseless Jews: who, when they find it expressly declared in the writings of Moses, "And the Angel of GOD spake to Moses in a flame of fire in a bush, and said, I am he who is; the GOD of Abraham and the GOD of Isaac, and the GOD of Jacob,"[f] say that it was the Father and Creator of all things who so spake. Whence also the prophetic spirit reproached them, saying, "But Israel doth not know me, and the people doth not consider me."[g] And again JESUS, while he was with them, said, as we have already shown, "No one knoweth the Father but the Son: neither knoweth any one the Son, but the Father, and they to whomsoever the Son shall reveal it."[h] The Jews, therefore, who always thought that it was the Father of all things who spake to Moses, whereas he who spake to him was the Son of GOD, who is also called the Angel and the Apostle, are justly upbraided both by the prophetic spirit, and by CHRIST himself, as knowing neither the Father nor the Son. For they who say that the Son is the Father, are proved not to know the Father, nor that the Father of all things hath

---

[d] Matt. x. 40. [e] Exod. iii. 2, 14, 15. [f] Ibid.
[g] Isa. i. 3. [h] Matt. xi. 27.

a Son, who, being the first-begotten Word of God, is also God. He also formerly appeared to Moses and the prophets in the form of fire, and of an incorporeal image: but now in the time of your empire, as we have already said, was made man, and born of a virgin, according to the will of the Father, for the salvation of those who believe in him. He permitted himself also to be set at naught, and to suffer, that by dying and rising again he might conquer death. Moreover when he spake out of the bush to Moses, saying, "I am he who is; the God of Abraham, and the God of Isaac, and the God of Jacob, and the God of thy fathers," he intimated that they who were dead, did still exist and were men of Christ himself. For they were the first of all men who diligently sought after God, Abraham being the father of Isaac, and Isaac of Jacob, as Moses also hath recorded.

84. Ye may also, from what hath been already said, perceive, that it was in imitation of that which was written by Moses, that the demons caused to be placed by fountains of water, the statue of her who is called Proserpine, and said to be the daughter of Jupiter. For Moses said, in the words which have been already adduced,[i] "In the beginning God created the heaven and the earth: and the earth was invisible and unformed: and the Spirit of God moved upon the face of the waters." They therefore said, that Proserpine was the daughter of Jupiter, in imitation of the spirit of God, which was said to have moved over the water. By a similar perversion, they spake of Minerva as being the daughter of Jupiter, but not by natural generation. But having learned that God after deliberation made the world by the Word,[k] they spake of Minerva as the first Intelligence. Now this we consider most absurd, to carry about the image of Intelligence in a female form. In like manner, the actions of the others, who are called sons of Jupiter, prove what they really are.

85. We, then, after having so washed him who hath expressed his conviction and professes the faith, lead him to those who are called brethren, where they are gathered together, to make common prayers with great

---

[i] Sect. 76. Gen. i. 1, 2.   [k] See note on Sect. 34.

earnestness, both for themselves and for him who is now enlightened, and for all others in all places, that having learned the truth, we may be deemed worthy to be found men of godly conversation in our lives, and to keep the commandments, that so we may attain to eternal salvation. When we have finished our prayers, we salute one another with a kiss. After which, there is brought, to that one of the brethren who presides, bread and a cup of wine mixed with water.[1] And he

---

[1] IRENÆUS, in like manner, speaks of the cup of the Eucharist, as consisting of wine mixed with water. He calls it κεκράμενον ποτήριον, (*Adv. Hæres.* Lib. v. c. 2,) and speaks of our Saviour, who in his last supper declared the mixture of the cup to be his own blood: ("*temperamentum calicis* suum sanguinem declaravit:") (Lib. iv. c. 57;) and, in describing the promise of our LORD that he would drink the fruit of the vine new with his disciples in his Father's kingdom, (Matt. xxvi. 29,) he uses the expression, "Hæc enim et Dominus docuit, *mixtionem calicis novam* in regno cum discipulis habiturum se pollicitus." (Lib. v. c. 36.)

Some early heretics, as part of the sect of the Ebionites and of the followers of Tatian, used water only in the administration of the Eucharist; whence they are opposed by EPIPHANIUS (*Hær.* xlvi. Encrat. 4, 16,) who calls them *Encratitæ*; by AUGUSTIN (*De Hæres.* 64,) under the appellation of *Aquarii*; and by THEODORET, (*De Fab. Hæret.* i. 20,) who styles them *Encratitæ* and *Hydroparastatæ*. CLEMENS Alexandrinus (*Stromat.* i. p. 375. Pædagog. ii. 2. p. 177, ed. Potter) mentions the same error. An Epistle of CYPRIAN to Cæcilius (*Ep.* 63, p. 148, ed. Fell) is directed against this practice. His argument is intended to prove, that wine is essential to the sacrament, and supposes that the cup, of which our LORD partook, contained water as well as wine. He imagines that the union of water with the wine indicated a mystical union between the people and CHRIST, and that the absence of either substance dissolves this union. It will be observed, that the object of CYPRIAN in this Epistle, is to show, not that the wine must be mixed with water, but that water alone did not represent sacramentally the blood of CHRIST.

The third council of Carthage, (Can. 24,) decreed that in the Eucharist the wine should be mixed with water. And many other early writers maintain the same opinion.

In the first Common Prayer-book of the Church of England, published by authority of Edward the Sixth, the Minister was directed by the rubric, when he put the wine into the chalice, "to put thereto a little pure and clean water." The same custom existed in the Anglo-Saxon Church. See PALMER's *Antiquity of the English Ritual*, c. iv. sect. 9.

Although, however, this custom is primitive and perhaps apostolical, and although it is probable that the cup which our Saviour consecrated at the last supper did contain water as well as wine, according to the general practice of the Jews, (MAIMONIDES, *Lib. de Solennitate Pasch.* c. 7,) yet it has been long decided by theologians that the

having received them gives praise and glory to the FATHER of all things, through the name of the SON and of the HOLY SPIRIT, and gives thanks in many words for that GOD hath vouchsafed to them these things. And when he hath finished his praises and thanksgiving, all the people who are present express their assent, saying, Amen, which in the Hebrew tongue, implies, So be it. The President having given thanks, and the people having expressed their assent, those whom we call deacons give to each of those who are present a portion of the bread which hath been blessed, and of the wine mixed with water; and carry some away for those who are absent.

86. And this food is called by us the Eucharist, (or Thanksgiving:) of which no one may partake unless he believes that what we teach is true, and is washed in the laver, which is appointed for the forgiveness of sins and unto regeneration, and lives in such a manner as CHRIST commanded. For we receive not these elements as common bread or common drink. But even as JESUS CHRIST our Saviour, being made flesh by the Word of GOD,[m] had both flesh and blood for our salvation, even so we are taught, that the food which is blessed by the prayer of the word which came from him, by the conversion of which (into our bodily substance) our blood and flesh are nourished, is the flesh and blood of that JESUS who was made flesh. For the Apostles, in the Memoirs composed by them, which are called Gospels, have related that JESUS thus commanded them;[n] that having taken bread, and given

---

mixture of water is not essential to the sacrament. Cardinal BONA refers to BERNARD, as speaking of those who considered water to be essential, but, he says, "The judgment of theologians is certain, that the consecration of the elements is valid, even if water be omitted, although he who omits it is guilty of a grievous offence." (BONA, *Rer. Lit.* Lib. ii. c. 9, 3.)

In our present rubric, although the mixture of water with wine is not enjoined, it is not prohibited.

This question is treated by BINGHAM, *Eccl. Ant.* XV. ii. 7; WHEATLEY *on the Common Prayer*, c. vi. sect. 10, 5; PALMER's *Antiquity of the English Ritual*, c. iv. sect. 9, and in a Dissertation by VOSSIUS, *Theses Theologicæ*, p. 494.

[m] See note on Sect. 43, and Bp. KAYE's *Account of Justin Martyr*, ch. iv. p. 86, note 6.

[n] Matt. xxvi. 26. Mark xiv. 22. Luke xxii. 19.

thanks, he said, "Do this in remembrance of me: this is my body:" and that in like manner having taken the cup, and given thanks, he said, "This is my blood;" and that he distributed them to these alone. And this too the evil demons have in imitation commanded to be done in the mysteries of Mithra. For ye either know or may learn, that bread and a cup of water are placed in the rites appointed for the initiated, with certain prayers. After these solemnities are finished, we afterward continually remind one another of them. And such of us as have possessions assist all those who are in want; and we all associate with one another.

87. And over all our offerings, we bless the CREATOR of all things, through his SON JESUS CHRIST, and through the HOLY SPIRIT. And, on the day which is called Sunday, there is an assembly in one place of all who dwell either in towns or in the country; and the Memoirs of the Apostles or the writings of the prophets are read, as long as the time permits. Then, when the reader hath ceased, the President delivers a discourse, in which he reminds and exhorts them to the imitation of all these good things. We then all stand up together, and put forth prayers. Then, as we have already said, when we cease from prayer,° bread is brought, and wine, and water: and the President in like manner offers up prayers and praises with his utmost power: and the people express their assent by saying, Amen. The consecrated elements are then distributed and received by every one; and a portion is sent by the deacons to those who are absent.

88. Each of those also, who have abundance and are willing, according to his choice, gives what he thinks fit: and what is collected is deposited with the President, who succors the fatherless and the widows, and those who are in necessity from disease or any other cause; those also who are in bonds, and the strangers who are sojourning among us; and in a word takes care of all who are in need.[p]

° The previous description was that of the first Communion after baptism: Justin here relates the ordinary celebration of the Eucharist.
[p] Bp. KAYE, in his *Account of Justin Martyr*, p. 91, notices the alterations which had taken place in the mode of celebrating the communion between the time of the Apostles and that of Justin. The

89. We all of us assemble together on Sunday, because it is the first day in which God changed darkness and matter, and made the world. On the same day also Jesus Christ our Saviour rose from the dead. For he was crucified the day before that of Saturn: and on the day after that of Saturn, which is the day of the Sun, he appeared to his apostles and disciples, and taught them what we now submit to your consideration.

90. If now what we have advanced appears to be reasonable and true, honor it accordingly; and if it appears folly, despise it as foolish, but pass not sentence of death against those who have done no evil, as if they were enemies. For we have already forewarned you, that ye shall not escape the future judgment of God, if ye continue in unrighteousness. And we shall exclaim, What God wills, let that come to pass. Although we might demand of you, from the epistle of the most great and illustrious Cæsar Adrian, your father, that which we require, that ye should command right judgment to be made, we have yet preferred that this should not take place because it was so ordained by Adrian, but have made this address and explanation to you, knowing that we demand what is just. And we have subjoined also a copy of the letter of Adrian, that in this too ye may perceive that we speak the truth. The copy is as follows:

THE EPISTLE OF ADRIAN RESPECTING THE CHRISTIANS.

TO MINUCIUS FUNDANUS.

We have received the letter written to me by the most renowned Serenius Granianus whom you succeeded. It seems then to me that the matter must not be left without inquiry; lest those men should be troubled, and a means of evil doing should be open to false accusers. If then the people in the provinces are able to advance so far in their accusations against the Christians, as to answer before the seat of judgment,

---

chief of these was the separation of the time of partaking of the Eucharist from that of their ordinary meal.

let them have recourse to these means alone, and not act by vague accusations or mere clamor. For it is far better, if any one wishes to bring an accusation that you should examine it. If therefore any one accuses them, and proves that they have done any thing against the laws, dispose of the matter according to the severity of the offence. But I require you, if any man bring such a charge falsely, deal with him according to his deserts, and take care that you punish him.

THE EPISTLE OF THE EMPEROR ANTONINUS PIUS TO THE COMMON ASSEMBLY OF ASIA.[*]

The Emperor Cæsar, Titus Ælius Adrianus Antoninus Augustus Pius, Pontifex Maximus, fifteenth time Tribune, thrice Consul, Father of his Country, to the Common Assembly of Asia, sends greeting.

I AM well assured, that the gods themselves will take heed that men of this kind shall not escape: for it is much more their interest to punish, if they can, those who refuse to worship them. Whereas ye trouble them, and accuse the opinions which they hold, as if they were Atheists: and bring many other charges, of which we are able to discover no proof. Nay, it would be in their estimation a great advantage to die for that of which they are accused: and they conquer you, by throwing away their own lives, rather than comply with what ye require them to do.

With respect to earthquakes, which either have happened or do happen, it is not fitting that ye should regard them with despondency, whatever they may be, comparing your own conduct with theirs, and observing how much more confidence they have toward God, than ye. Ye, in fact, at such periods, appear to forget the gods, and neglect your sacred rites. And ye know not the worship which belongs to God; whence

---

[*] EUSEBIUS, *Hist. Eccles.* Lib. iv. c. 13, gives this Epistle, as having been written by Marcus Aurelius Antoninus, although in c. 12, he appears to ascribe it to Antoninus Pius. VALESIUS and SCALIGER think that it was written by Marcus Aurelius. HALLOIX, in his life of Justin, c. 5, and CAVE, in his life of Justin, c. 10, agree in ascribing the letter to Antoninus Pius.

ye envy those who do worship him, and persecute them even unto death. Respecting such men, certain others of the rulers of provinces wrote to my father of blessed memory; to whom also he wrote in reply, that they should in no wise trouble men of that kind, unless they were shown to be making any attempt against the dominion of the Romans. Many too have given information respecting such men to me also, to whom I answered, in conformity with my father's opinion. If then any one shall bring any charge against one of these men, simply as such, let him who is so accused be released, even if he should be proved to be one of this kind of men: and let the accuser himself be subject to punishment.

NOTE

ON

IGNATIUS' EPISTLE TO THE MAGNESIANS.

NOTE C. ON § viii. p. 68.

Λόγος ἀΐδιος, οὐκ ἀπὸ σιγῆς προελθών.

THIS passage has given rise to much discussion: some contending that it has reference to the *Sige*, or "Silence," of VALENTINUS; others that it relates to the erroneous opinions of other heretics, anterior to VALENTINUS: and others, again, that the words refer to no specific heresy, but simply guard against an error which might arise in consequence of JESUS CHRIST being styled the *Word of* GOD.

The sense of the passage seems to be this.—'JESUS CHRIST is the Eternal Word, proceeding from the Father. But this procession must not be confounded with any act of the human faculties. The word, by which the thoughts of man are made known, arises in consequence of a previous mental act; and before man's word goes forth, it is preceded by a state of silence. But, in this respect, the analogy between the procession of the Word from the Father, and the springing forth of the word from the mind of man, entirely fails. The Word of GOD was Eternal, and there was no period preceding the procession of the Word from the Father, corresponding to the silence which exists before the word of man is pronounced.'

IRENÆUS, in exposing the fanciful and impious tenets of the different sects of Gnostics, expresses the same sentiment, on more than one occasion. Thus, *Adv. Hæres.* Lib. ii. cap. 18, he says, "Sed quoniam quidem reprobabilis et impossibilis prima Noos, id est sensus ipsorum, emissio est, manifestè ostendimus. Videamus autem et de reliquis. Ab hoc enim Logon et Zoën fabricatores hujus Pleromatis dicunt emissos, et Logi, id est Verbi, quidem emissionem ab hominum affectione accipientes, et addivinantes adversus DEUM, quasi aliquid magnum adinvenientes in eo quod dicunt à Nu (Νοῷ) esse emissum Logon: quod quidem omnes videlicet sciunt, quoniam in hominibus quidem consequenter dicatur, in eo autem qui sit super omnes DEUS, totus Nus, et totus Logus cùm sit, quemadmodum prædiximus, et nec aliud antiquius, nec posterius, aut aliud alterius habente in se, sed toto æquali et uno perseverante, jam non talis hujus ordinationis sequetur emissio. Quemadmodum qui dicit eum totum visionem, et totum auditum, (in quo enim videt, in ipso et audit; et in quo audit, in ipso et videt) non peccat: sic et qui ait totum illum sensum, et totum verbum, et in quo sensus est, in hoc et verbum esse, et verbum ejus esse hunc Nun (Νοῦν) minus quidem adhuc de Patre omnium sentiet, *decentiora autem magis quàm hi, qui lationem prolativi hominum verbi transferunt in* DEI *eternum Verbum, et prolationis initium donantes, et genesin, quemadmodum et suo verbo.*"

And in a subsequent part of the same chapter;

"Et usque hoc quidem, quemadmodum prædiximus, omnes hominum affectiones, et notiones mentis, et generationes intentionum et emissiones verborum conjicientes verisimiliter, non verisimiliter mentiti sunt adversus DEUM."

In another place (Lib. ii. cap. 47) he approaches still more nearly the sense of this passage of IGNATIUS;

"Hæc autem cæcitas et stultiloquium inde provenit nobis, quod nihil DEO reservetis; sed et ipsius DEI, et Ennϲæ ejus, et Verbi, et Vitæ, et CHRISTI nativitates et prolationes annunciare vultis: et has non aliunde accipientes, sed ex affectione hominum: et non intelligitis quia in homine quidem, qui est compositum animal, capit hujusmodi dicere, sicut prædiximus, (*Lib.* ii. 16,) sensum hominis, et Ennϲæam hominis: et quia ex sensu Ennϲæa, de Ennϲæa autem Enthymesis, de Enthymesi autem Logos: (quem autem Logon? aliud enim est secundum Græcos Logos, quod est principale quod excogitat, aliud organum per quod emittitur Logos:) *et aliquando quidem quiescere et tacere hominem, aliquando autem loqui et operari.* DEUS autem cùm sit totus mens, totus ratio, et totus spiritus operans, et totus lux, et semper idem et similiter existens, sicut et utile est nobis sapere de DEO, et sicut ex Scripturis discimus, non jam hujusmodi affectus et divisiones decenter erga eum subsequentur. Velocitati enim sensûs hominum, proper spiritale ejus, non sufficit lingua deservire, quippe carnalis existens: unde et intus suffugatur verbum nostrum, et profertur non de semel, sicut conceptum est à sensu; sed per partes, secundum quod lingua subministrare prævalet."

It has been conceived that IGNATIUS, in this passage, had a particular reference to the heresy of VALENTINUS, whose notions of the procession of the *Logos* from *Sige* are well known. This appears highly improbable; although VICTORINUS and RUPERTUS say that Valentinus taught his heresy during the life of the Apostle St. John. The latest period fixed for the death of IGNATIUS is A. D. 116: and, according to TERTULLIAN *de Præscriptione Hæreticorum*, cap. 30, Valentinus was living when Eleutherius was Bishop of Rome, which was at least as late as A. D. 185, or seventy years after the death of Ignatius. Unless, therefore, Valentinus lived to be nearly a hundred years old, he could scarcely have begun to disseminate his doctrines before the death of Ignatius. There is, however, no occasion to make the supposition that Ignatius alludes to the peculiar tenets of Valentinus. IRENÆUS, (Lib. i. 5,) TERTULLIAN, (*de Præscriptione Hæret.* cap. 33, 46, 47, *Adversus Valentinianos*, cap. 3, 4,) and other authorities, show that Valentinus, in many of his absurd notions, merely adopted opinions which had been propagated by the Gnostics, Nicolaitans, Simonians, and other heretics. EUSEBIUS (*de Ecclesiasticâ Theologiâ*, Lib. ii. cap. 9,) expressly alludes to Simon Magus, as holding the impious opinion, that there was a time when "GOD and silence alone were." (ἃ δὲ Μάρκελλος ἐτόλμα ὑποτίθεσθαι, πάλαι μὲν λέγων εἶναι τὸν Θεὸν, καί τινα Ἡσυχίαν ἅμα τῷ θεῷ ὑπογράφων ἑαυτῷ κατ' αὐτὸν ἐκεῖνον τῶν ἀθέων αἱρεσιωτῶν ἀρχηγὸν, ὃς τὰ ἄθεα δογματίζων ἀπεφαίνετο λέγων, ἦν Θεος καὶ Σιγή.) And that this passage refers to Simon Magus is plain from EUSEB. *Hist. Eccles.* ii. 13, where he speaks of him in the very same terms: πάσης μὲν οὖν ἀρχηγὸν αἱρέσεως πρῶτον γίνεσθαι τὸν Σίμωνα παρειλήφαμεν.

Bp. PEARSON, in his *Vindiciæ Ignatianæ*, contends that, although it cannot be positively proved that Ignatius was entirely unacquainted with the tenets of Valentinus himself, yet the words in question have no reference to that heretic, but are aimed at the opinions of the Ebionites, received from the older Gnostics.

Bp. BULL, in his *Defensio Fidei Nicænæ*, Sect. iii. cap. 1, examines this passage at length, and arrives at a conclusion somewhat different from that of Bp. PEARSON. He is of opinion, that the heresy opposed by Ignatius is that of the Judaizing Gnostics, of whom Cerinthus was the chief. This conclusion is founded upon a most careful investigation of the whole passage. It is plain, he thinks, from the context, that the heretics whom IGNATIUS opposes are one and the same, throughout the whole of this portion of his Epistle: that, since these heretics maintained that the law of Moses was still binding upon Christians, a tenet never ascribed to Valentinus, they were certainly not Valentinians; and although this error was maintained by the Ebionites, yet that there are other points which evidently refer to some other heretics than they. Thus, the Ebionites had no philosophical notions respecting the procession of the Word from the Father, which Ignatius appears to refute, when he says that "the Word proceeds not from silence." Again, his exhortation, in Sect. 7, that they should come "as unto one JESUS CHRIST, who proceedeth from one Father, and exists in One and is returned to One," is a manifest allusion to the Cerinthian Gnostics, who held that JESUS and CHRIST were two persons; that CHRIST descended and entered into JESUS at his baptism, and before his passion returned into the pleroma: and that the Father of JESUS was the Demiurge, who made the world, but the Father of CHRIST was a higher power. The words in Sect. 8, "For this cause they were persecuted, being inspired by his grace fully to convince the unbelievers that there is One GOD, who hath manifested himself by JESUS CHRIST his Son," refer also to the errors of the Gnostics, who maintained that the world was created either by angels or by a being different and inferior to the supreme GOD, who revealed himself to mankind by CHRIST, his Son. IREN. *Adv. Hæres.* iii. 11. Bp. BULL is therefore of opinion that Ignatius in the words, "not proceeding from silence," intended to oppose some erroneous notions of the same heretics concerning the procession of the Son from the Father; as in Sect. 9, he clearly refers to another error of the Judaizing heretics, who denied the true passion of CHRIST. In Sect. 11, he warns the Magnesians "not to fall into the snares of vain-glory," another apparent allusion to the Gnostics, whose very name was assumed to intimate their superiority in knowledge to other Christians.

He then shows, by the testimony of EPIPHANIUS, PHILASTRIUS, and AUGUSTINE, that the observance of the peculiar rites of Judaism, from prudential motives, was at that period one of the professed tenets of the Cerinthians, although Cerinthus himself did not submit to the rite of circumcision, as he taught others to do. It is thought that St. John alludes to the Cerinthians, when he speaks to the Philadelphians, respecting them of the synagogue of Satan, which say they are Jews, and are not, but do lie. *Rev.* iii. 9; see also *Rev.* ii. 9. And it is remarkable that Ignatius, writing to the same Philadelphians, Sect. 6, says, "If any one preach the Jewish religion to you, hear him not. For it is better to learn the Christian faith from one who is circumcised, than the Jewish from one who is uncircumcised."

Bp. BULL then proves, by the testimony of IRENÆUS, *Adv. Hæres.* iii. 11, that the Nicolaitans, Cerinthians, and other early heretics held tenets of the same absurd kind as those afterward professed by the Valentinians, respecting various orders of Æons, between the supreme GOD and the Creator of the world; and shows that it is highly probable that the very procession of the Word from *Sige*, or "Silence," was one of their notions. GREGORY NAZIANZEN, indeed, *Orat.* 23, enumerates the Cerinthians among those Gnostics who reckoned Bythus and Sige in the number of their Æons.

Upon the whole we may be justified in concluding:

1. That if the words "οὐκ ἀπὸ Σιγῆς προελθών" be an allusion to the opinions of Valentinus, such an allusion cannot be shown to be chronologically impossible; nor would it prove that the Epistle in which it occurs is either interpolated or fictitious.

2. That there is the highest probability that the words refer to the erroneous notions, either of the Cerinthian heretics, or of other Gnostics before Valentinus.

3. That this is a plain testimony of a writer of the Apostolic age to the absolute eternity of JESUS CHRIST, the Word of GOD.

INDEX.

A.

Abraham, example of, 6.
Acts of the Apostles, reference to, by Clement, xxii.
Adam, one of the prophets, 156 n.
Adrian, successors of, 125 n—his paramour, 154—rescript of, 191 s.
Αγεπαν, 92 n.
Agapae, 92 n.
Αγενητος, and αγεννητος, 58 n, 149 n.
Alce, 95, 99, 117.
Altar, need of being within, 58, 75—one, 68, 84.
Altar of GOD, 49.
Αναγωγευς, 60 n.
Anencletus, Bishop of Rome, xv.
Angels, examples of obedience, 20—orders of the, 74—liable to condemnation, 91—good and evil, 129 s—worship of, 131 n.
Anniversaries of martyrs, 118.
Antiquity, no sufficient warrant of truth, 126—of the Christian belief, 148.
Antoninus the philosopher, the emperor, 125, 127.
——— Pius, epistle of, 192 s.
Αποδιυλισμον, 84 n.
Apollonius, 66.
Apostles, peculiar situation of, ix.
Apostolic fathers, value of their writings, ix ss.
——— government of the churches, xxii, 27, 75, 84.
——— succession, 25.
Apostolical constitutions, 172 n, 179 n.
Aquarii, 188 n.
Ascension of CHRIST, prophecies of, 169, 174.
Asiarch, 114 n, 120.
Athanasius, quoted, 58 n.
Atheists, 75, 109 n, 112, 129, 170, 192
Athenagoras quoted, 109 n—apology of, 125 n—quoted, 145 n.
Atonement, 31, 51.
Attalus, 99.
Augustin quoted, 117 n.

B.

Bacchus, a counterfeit of the Messiah, 177.
Baptism, mode of administering, 183 s—called illumination, 184.
Barchochebas, 156.
Barnabas, Epistle of, xiv n, quoted, 165 n.
Bassus, 66.
Bellerophon, a counterfeit of the Messiah, 178.
Bestiarii, 116 n.
Birth, new, 183 s.
Birth-days of martyrs, 118.
Bishops, appointment of, 26, 57, 83—ordination of, 27.
Bishop and presbytery, to be submitted to, 57, 58, 64, 68, 72, 75, 85, 92, 98—union with, necessary, 58—reverence and obedience to, 66 s, 70, 72, 76, 84, 98—source of authority to administer sacraments, 92 s—nothing to be done without him, 92.
Blood of CHRIST, 5, 8, 14, 31, 48, 81, 83, 84—of GOD, 56—charity so called, 75.
Bread of GOD, 58, 81—one to be broken, 64—of, xi, 79.
Britain, introduction of the Gospel into, 40 s.
Burrhus, 56, 87, 94.
Burton, Dr., value of his writings, xi—quoted, xxxiii n, 59 n.

C.

Calling of Christians, 19.
Canons, apostolic, xxi.
Catechumens, formula of dismission of, 172 n.
Catholic, use of the term, 92 n, 111, 116, 120.
Cave quoted, xv, 81 n.
Chains called ornaments, 47, 61, 93.
Charity, 14, 31, 32, 48, 62, 85, 91.
Chastisement, divine, 35.
Chastity, 133.
Chief Priest, 24.
Children, duties to, 14—murder of, 142 n, 152.
CHRIST, blood of, 5, 8, 14, 31, 48, 56, 88—his dignity, 10, 42 ss, 48, 58—manner of his coming, 10, 43—

reverence due him, 14—speaks to us, in the Old Testament, by the HOLY GHOST, 14—our High Priest, 86—and helper, 21 s, 36, 52—his redeeming love, 31, 45—his death for sin, 47, 92—his suffering on the cross to be confessed, 50, 70—one GOD, 63—why born of a virgin, 63 n—our common hope, 65, 70, 72, 87—our eternal life, 66, 90—our Bishop, 67, reality of his birth, life, and death, 75, 88—the bread of GOD, 81—denial of, 90—the name of confounded with χρηστος, 127 n—worshipped, 129, 137—called the apostle of GOD, 136, 185 s—prediction of, 136—appeared to Moses, 185 s.

CHRIST, whence he came, 129—two comings of, 174.

———, belief concerning him, 137, 147, 175.

———, doctrines of, 138 ss.

———, prophecies concerning, 156 ss.

———, person of, assumed by the prophets, 162.

———, all who lived agreeably to reason, partakers of him, 170.

Christian, the name, 78—the mere name made a ground of condemnation, 128, 149—reformation produced in Christians, 137 s, 140, 163—calumnies against the name extended to heretics, 152—ancient philosophers really so, 170.

Christians, primitive, deportment of, xxii, 1 s, 43—a spiritual temple, 60—called *initiated*, 61 n.

Christophori, 55 n.

Chrysostom quoted, 2 n, 33 n, 55 n, 74 n, 112 n, 118 n.

CLEMENT OF ROME, his history, xv—date of his epistle, xvi—value attached to it, xvii—discovery of, xviii—quotations of by early writers, xviii n—contents of, xviii ss—character of, xxv—second epistle of, xxi—spurious writings ascribed to him, xxi—his death, xxi—his supposed resignation of the episcopate, 33—recognitions of, 143 n.

Confectores, 116 n.

Confession of sins, 32.

Constitutions, apostolic, xxi, xxxiii n, 56 n, 69 n, 95 n.

Contention deprecated, 28 s.

Conversion, 183.

Corinth, Church of, divisions in, xxii—character of, 1—antiquity of, 29 n.

Corinthians, first epistle of Paul to, xx, xxii, 29—epistles to, references to, by Clement, xxii.

Crescens, 53.

Crocus, 56, 82.

Cross of CHRIST, the engine used in building GOD's temples, 60.

Cyprian quoted, 27 n, 47 n, 90 n, 118 n.

D.

Damas, bishop of Magnesia, 66.

Daphnus, 95.

Deacons, 189, 190—directions for, 49, 73—conduct of, 66—duties of, 86.

Deaconnesses, 94 n.

Demon, the same as spirit, 89 n.

Demons, evil, the gods of the Heathen, 129, 133—persecutors of Christians, 134, 135, 148—delude the Heathen, 137, 184 s—assist heretics, 152, 181—oppose extension of knowledge, 168—inventors of the heathen fables, 177—limits of their influence, 180.

Demoniacs, 143.

Dionysius of Corinth, xvii.

Docetæ, heresy of the, 75, 88.

Doctrines of the epistle of Clement, xxiv—of the epistle of Polycarp, xxxii—of the epistles of Ignatius, xl ss—of CHRIST, 138 ss.

Dodwell quoted, xv, xvi, 51 n.

Double-mindedness, 7, 15.

Dream of Polycarp, 109 s.

Dreams of the witnesses of Ignatius' martyrdom, 106.

E.

Easter, controversy concerning, xxvi.

Education of children, 14.

Elect, the, 116—of GOD, 1, 29, 72—the number of the elect, 2.

Election, 17.

Emperors, Justin's address to the, 126—apotheosis of, 147.

Encratitæ, 188 n.

Enlargement of heart, 2.

Enoch, example of, 6.

Envy, cause and results of, 3 s.

Ephesus, Church of, its apostolic character, 61.

Επινομη, 27 n.

Epiphanius quoted, 95.

Επιτροπος, 160 n.

Epitropus, 99.

Erebus, 181.

Esther, example of, 34.

Eucharist, offerings in the, 24 n, 28 n, to be often celebrated, 61—one,

INDEX.

84—not to be abstained from, 92—offered by one empowered by a bishop, 92—mode of celebrating, 188 s, 190.
Eusebius quoted, xiv, xv, xvii, xxi, xxiii, xxv, xxxii, xxxviii, xli, 40, 66 n, 89 n, 109 n, 142 n, 171 n.
Eutechicus, 95.
Evadius, bishop of Antioch, xxxiii.
Evarestus, bishop of Rome, xxi—of Smyrna, 120.

F.

Faith, 14, 17, 18, 21, 60, 62, 75, 86, 91.
Fasting, 183.
Fate, 166 s.
Fathers, value of their writings, ix ss, errors of, xii s.
Festivals of martyrs, 118.
Flavia Neapolis, 126 n.
Flesh of CHRIST, faith so called, 75—the Gospel likened to, 84—the Eucharist, 84, 92.
Forbearance, 140.
Foresight, reconcilable with contingency, 168.
Fortunatus, xvi, 37.
Free-will, 134, 153, 167.

G.

Γευητος and γευνητος, 58 n.
Gentiles, who are, 176, calling of, 176.
Germanicus, the Smyrnean martyr, 108 s.
Gibbon quoted, 125 n.
Gnostics, sects of the, 151.
Gnosticism, xxxviii.
GOD, his mercy, 13, 15—his truth, 17—rejoices in his own works, 19 s—his gifts, 20 s—without form, 133—without name, 133 s, 184.
Gods of the Heathen, evil demons, 129—deified men, 133, 150—their examples, 147, 149.
Good-Friday, collect for, 90 n.
Gospel, likened to flesh of CHRIST, 84—our common hope, 85—its records the true ground of faith, 86—dissemination of the, 163.
Gospels, references to, by Clement, xxii, by Polycarp, xxxi, by Ignatius, xl, mention of by Justin, 159, 189.

H.

Hardening of Pharaoh's heart, 32.
Harmony of Christians to the praise of GOD, 57.
Heathen, pollutions of the, 152 s.

Hebrews, epistle to the, xvii, xxiii.
Hell, 145.
Heresy, sin of, 62, 74.
Heretics, early, 86 n—prayer for conversion of, 90.
Hermas, *Shepherd* of, xiv n.
High Priest, 24, 25, 86.
Hippolytus quoted, 39.
Homilies of Clement, xxi.
Hospitality recommended, 7.
Humility, xix, 8, 30—examples of, 11.
Hymns, alternate singing of, xxxiii s.
Hystaspes, 145, 168.

I.

Ιδιωτης, 163, 183 n.
Idol-worship, 133, 146.
IGNATIUS, Epistles of, xxix-xxxvii ss, 53—life and character of, xxxiii s—death of, xxxiv s—*account of the martyrdom of*, xxxvi, 101 ss—his desire of martyrdom, xxxvi.
——, *Epistles* of, their style, xxxviii, their design, xxxviii s, their genuineness, xl ss—editions of, xlii.
Incarnation of the Son, 146, 147 s, 158 ss.
Initiated, the term applied to baptized persons, 61 n.
Irenæus, 120—quoted, xv, xvii, xxv, xxvi, xxviii, xli, 3 n, 8 n, 24 n, 29 n, 31 n, 90 n, 130 n, 143 n, 144 n, 183 n, 188 n.
Irenarch, 110 n.
Isaac, his example, 18 s.

J.

James, Epistle of, allusions to, by Clement, xxiii.
Jerome quoted, 39, 41, 63 n, 79 n, 89 n, 91 n.
Jews, enmity of against the Christians, 155 s.
Judea, devastation of, foretold, 171.
Judith, example of, 34.
Jupiter, sons of, 146 s, 177 ss, example of, 147.
JUSTIN MARTYR, life and writings of, xliii ss—quoted, 8 n, 24 n, 43.
Justification, 19, 86.

K.

Κακοδαιμων, 102 n.
Kaye, Bishop, value of his writings, xi—quoted, 159 n.
Κηυνξ, 108 n.
Kingdom sought for by Christians, 134.

INDEX.

Kiss, a form of salutation among early Christians, 188.
Κληρονομος, 110 n.

L.

Lactantius quoted, 154 n.
Law, Jewish, abrogated, 68 s, 85.
Laws, human, not to be broken, 135.
Layman, use of the term, 25.
Leopards, soldiers called, 79.
Levites, 24.
Life, human emptiness of, 180.
Linus, bishop of Rome, xv.
Lord's day, observance of, 68 n.
Lot, example of, 7.
Lot's wife, the example of, 7.
Love, of Ignatius, crucified, 80 s.
Lucretius quoted, 74 n.
Lustrations, 184.

M.

Magical arts, 137, 142, 150 s, 154, 180.
Marcion, Polycarp's conversation with, xxvii, 50 n—his time and tenets, 151, 180.
Marriage, 154—how to be contracted, 98.
Martyrs, examples of, 4, 51, 108, 112 n, 117.
Martyrdom, desire of, xiii, xxxvi, 77 s, 79 n, 101, 109—an imitation of CHRIST, 56.
Mary, the virginity of, 63 n.
Menander, the poet, quoted, 146—the Gnostic, 151, 180.
Minerva, her birth, a fabulous imitation of the incarnation, 187.
Ministry, succession in the, xvii, xx, 27—of divine appointment, 24 s, 67, 83—orders in, 24—commission of, 25 ss, 58—submission to, 50, 57 s, 67, 73, 85.
Miracles of CHRIST, 148, 154 s, 171.
Miraculous gifts, 103 n.
Mithra, mysteries of, 190.
Moderation, 73, 83.
Montanists, fasts of, 69 n.
Μωμοσκοπεω, 25 n, 49.
Μυσται and αμυσται, 61 n.
Mythology, heathen, 128, 146 ss, 149.

N.

Name, none applicable to GOD, 133 s, 184.
Names not sufficient grounds of judgment, 127 s.
Neapolis, 126 n.
Necessity, fatal, denied, 166 s.

Necromancy, 142 s.
Νεκρομορος, 90 n.
Noah, a preacher of salvation, 5, 6.

O.

Obedience recommended, 6, 20, 57.
Oblation, use of the term, 24 n.
Offerings of the Church, 24.
———, material, not required, 133, 136.
Onesimus, bishop of Ephesus, 56, 58.
Oracles of the Heathen, 143.
Order in the creation, xix. 13—in the Church, xx, 22 ss, 57, 67.
Orders of the ministry necessary to the existence of a Church, 73.
Origen quoted, 27 n, 64 n, 89 n, 152 n.

P.

Pacian quoted, 92 n.
Parabolani, 34 n.
Παρεδροι, 143 n.
Passion of CHRIST, 91, 92—week, 111—predictions of, 157, 160 s, 171 s.
Paul, Epistles of, references to, by Clement, xxii, by Polycarp, xxx s, 48, by Ignatius, xl—martyrdom of, 4, 51—extent of his preaching, 4, 38 ss.
Peace, deep and fruitful, 2.
Peaceableness, 9, 62—of Christians, 134 s.
People, share of, in the appointment of a bishop, 27.
Persecution, not to be sought, 109—folly of, 180.
Perseus, a counterfeit of the Messiah, 178.
Persons, different, assumed by the sacred writers, 161 s.
Peter, Epistles of, allusions to, by Clement, xxiii, by Polycarp, xxxii, by Ignatius, xl—martyrdom of, 4.
Philippi, Church of, 52.
Philo, of Cilicia, 87, 93, 95.
Philosophers, who so called, 131—of different classes, 128, 131, 152—borrow from the sacred writings, 168.
Phœnix, story of the, xx, 16.
Photius, his objection to the Epistle of Clement, xxiv, 42 ss.
Φωτισμος, 184 n.
Plato quoted, 127, 132, 142, 146, 168, 181, 182—indebted to Moses, 181 s.
Πλεονεξια, 52 n.
Pliny the younger quoted, xxxv, 94 n, 112 n.

Poets, heathen, borrow from the sacred writings, 168.
Polybius, bishop of Tralles, 72.
POLYCARP, his history, xxv, 103—death of, xxvii, 109 ss—Epistle of, xxviii, its object, xxix, contents, xxix s—his prayer, 115.
Pontius Pilate, records of, 161, 171.
Prayer, common, 187, 190—enjoined, 68.
Predestination, 55.
Prejudices, not to be retained on account of prescription, 135 s.
Presbyters, directions for their conduct, 50.
Presbytery, 57, 70, 72, 76, 84, 94.
Priests, 24, 28, 30, 86.
Profession, valueless without works, 62—inconsistent, 141.
Prophecy, proof of Christianity from, 155 ss—nature of, 161, 166.
Prophecies, unfulfilled, 174—misunderstood by the devils, 177 s.
Prophets, their faith in CHRIST, 68 s, 84—Jewish, 155—how inspired, 161.
Proserpine, worship of, 187.
Psalms, alternate singing of, xxxiv.
Punishment, future, 145 s, 177, 190—eternal, 113, 132, 135, 142, 169, 175.

Q.

Quintus, a Phrygian, 109.

R.

Rahab, example of, 7.
Reason, CHRIST so called, 170.
Recognitions of Clement, 21.
Regeneration, 183, 189—preached by Noah, 6.
Relative duties, 14, 23.
Relics of martyrs, 106, 117 s.
Repentance, xix, 139, 183—grace of, 5.
Resignation of office, 33.
Resurrection of the body, xix, 15 s, 48, 49, 144 s.
Reward of the blessed, 132, 134.
Rheus Agathopus, 87, 93.
Rites, heathen, inventions of demons, in imitation of those of the true religion, 184 s.
Romans, epistle to the, references to, by Clement, xxii.
Rufus, 51.
Rulers, submission to, 142.

S.

Sabbath, observance of, 68 n, the great, 111, 120.

Saints, adoration of, 117.
Satan, first-born of, 50—ignorant of Mary's virginity, 63 n, his doom, 153.
Scarlet thread of Rahab, 8.
Schism, xix, xxxix, 2, 29, 84.
Scriptures, superiority of to uninspired writings of pious men, xii s—quotations of, by Clement of Rome, xxii s, by Polycarp, xxx ss, by Ignatius, xl ss.
Self-devotion, 32.
Semo Sancus, the Roman god, 150 n.
Septuagint Version, history of, 155.
Serpent-worship, 153.
Sibyl, the, 145, 168.
Silence of CHRIST, 62—of GOD, 64—CHRIST came not forth from, 68—of the Bishop, 58, 83.
Simon Magus, deification of, 150 s, 180.
Smyrna, Bucolus, Bishop of, xxvi—*Epistle of the Church of*, xxvii s, 167 ss—Church of, less ancient than that of Philippi, 52.
Socrates, 129, 170.
———, the historian, quoted, xxxiii.
Sotio, 66.
Soul, Christians compared to the, 44.
Spain, Paul's visit to, 39 ss.
Spikes, instruments of torture, 108 n.
Spirit, the divine nature of CHRIST so called, 159 n—the Holy worshipped, 131, 137, called the word, 159 n, 170.
Star, that revealed CHRIST'S birth, 64.
Stoics, doctrine of the, 145 s.
Sufferings of GOD, 2, 43, 80—of CHRIST, true, 56.
Sunday, observation of, 190 s.
Swearing, forbidden, 140.

T.

Tasso quoted, 74 n.
Tavia, 95.
Temple at Jerusalem, standing when Clement wrote, xvi, 25—one Christian, 68.
Tertullian quoted, xv, 16 n, 29 n, 40, 59 n, 68 n, 69 n, 89 n, 94 n, 118 n, 144 n, 165 n, 171 n, 179 n.
Thanksgiving, a Christian duty, 136 s.
Theodoret quoted, 40, 41.
Theophilus of Antioch quoted, 63 n, 127 n, 145 n.
Theophorus, signification of the name, 55 n, 102.

Trajan's persecution of the Christians, xxxiv s.
Tribute and custom, payment of, 141.
Truth alone to be maintained, 126, 132—the only ground of assent, 148.

U.

Unity, Christian, 57, 67, 70, 75, 83, 84, 85, 96.
Usher, Abp., quoted, xxvi.

V.

Valens, 52.
Venantius Fortunatus quoted, 42.
Verus, the emperor, his genealogy and character, 125 n.
Virgin, conception of the, 158 s.
Virginity, 138 s—of Mary, 63 n.

W.

Wake, Archbishop, his translation of the writings of the apostolical fathers, xiii s, xliv, 56.
Warfare, Christian, 22, 98.
Water, admixture of, with the Eucharistic wine, 188 n.
Widows, 49, 94.
Will of God, the source of blessing, 19, 23, 57—the rule of worship, 25.
Wine of the holy communion, 188.
Women, duties of, 1, 14, 49, 97.
Word, the, 129, 134, 135, 146, 148, 158, 159, 170, 182, 185, 187, 189.
Works, good, recommended, 19 s, 98.
World, destruction of, by fire, 145 s, 182.
Worship, to be orderly performed, 24 s—in one place, 68, 85—the object of the Christian, 129 ss—of false gods, 129, 133—of one God, 140, 190—public, 190.

Z.

Zosimus, 51.

TEXTS.

Rev. ii. 8–10——xxvi.
Eph. iv. 26——xxx.
Phil. i. 23 s——xxxvi.
Gen. iv. 3 ss——3.
2 Cor. xi. 25——4.
Job xiv. 4——11.
James i. 8——15.
Phil. iv. 15——29 n.
Luke xxiv. 39——89 n.
1 Cor. xi. 20 s——92 n.
Rom. xvi. 1——94 n.
Acts xvi. 8, 10——104 n.
—— xix. 31——114 n.
Gen. xlix. 10——156 s.
Isa. xi. 1——158.
—— vii. 14——158.
Ps. ii. 12——165 n.
—— xcvi. 10——165 n.
—— cx. 1–3——169.

CPSIA information can be obtained at www.ICGtesting.com
Printed in the USA
LVOW09*1430010416

481716LV00018B/56/P